D0447712

Finding God
in the Movies

Finding God in the Movies

33 Films of Reel Faith

Catherine M. Barsotti

and

Robert K. Johnston

BakerBooks

a division of Baker Publishing Group
Grand Rapids, Michigan

© 2004 by Catherine M. Barsotti and Robert K. Johnston

Published by Baker Books
a division of Baker Publishing Group
P.O. Box 6287, Grand Rapids, MI 49516-6287
www.bakerbooks.com

Printed in the United States of America

All rights reserved. No part of this publication may be reproduced, stored in a re-
trieval system, or transmitted in any form or by any means—for example, electronic,
photocopy, recording—without the prior written permission of the publisher. The
only exception is brief quotations in printed reviews.

Library of Congress Cataloging-in-Publication Data
Barsotti, Catherine M., 1945–
    Finding God in the movies : 33 films of reel faith / Catherine M. Barsotti
and Robert K. Johnston.
        p.   cm.
    Includes bibliographical references.
    ISBN 10: 0-8010-6481-3 (pbk.)
    ISBN 978-0-8010-6481-4 (pbk.)
    1. Motion pictures—Religious aspects. 2. Motion pictures—Moral and
ethical aspects. I. Johnston, Robert K., 1945– II. Title.
PN1995.5.B34   2004
791.43′682—dc22   2004007276

Unless otherwise indicated, Scripture is taken from the New Revised Standard Version of the Bible, copyright 1989, Division of Christian Education of the National
Council of the Churches of Christ in the United States of America. Used by permission. All rights reserved.

Scripture marked NIV is taken from the HOLY BIBLE, NEW INTERNATIONAL
VERSION®. NIV®. Copyright © 1973, 1978, 1984 by International Bible Society.
Used by permission of Zondervan. All rights reserved.

Scripture marked KJV is taken from the King James Version of the Bible.

Scripture marked RSV is taken from the Revised Standard Version of the Bible,
copyright 1952 [2nd edition, 1971] by the Division of Christian Education of the
National Council of the Churches of Christ in the United States of America. Used
by permission. All rights reserved.

For Rachel, Ruth,
Rebecca, and Faith

in the hope that they will
find God in the midst of life

Natural things
And Spiritual,—who separates those two
In art, in morals, or the social drift,
Tears up the bond of nature and brings death,
Paints futile pictures, writes unreal verse,
Leads vulgar days, deals ignorantly with men,
Is wrong, in short at all points. . . .
Earth's crammed with heaven,
And every common bush afire with God;
But only he who sees, takes off his shoes—
The rest sit round it and pluck blackberries. . . .

Not one day, in the artist's ecstasy,
But every day, feast, fast, or working day,
The spiritual significance burns through
The hieroglyphic of material shows,
Henceforward he would pain the globe with wings,
And reverence fish and fowl, the bull, the tree,
And even his very body as a man.

—Elizabeth Barrett Browning, "Aurora Leigh"

Contents

Reconciliation within Families

Racial Reconciliation

Forgiveness

Community and Friendship

Faith

Faith and Doubt

Living Our Faith

Preface

In contemporary parlance, to be "enthusiastic" is to be excited about something, even passionate. But it is interesting to note "enthusiasm" comes from two Greek words—*en* and *theos*, meaning "in God." We point this out because it is important for readers to understand at the outset our enthusiasm for movies, in both senses of this word. We enjoy watching movies; they are one of our passions. We also have found God to be present in movies; they are *inspirational*. The well-known director Martin Scorcese said, "My whole life has been movies and religion. That's it. Nothing else." This is perhaps overstating the case for us; we love our families, we enjoy the beach, our work is fulfilling, and serving others brings us joy. But we understand something of Scorcese's statement nonetheless.

This book would not have been possible without others who share our enthusiasm, and we would like to thank them for their assistance. Jane Swanson-Nystrom, the managing editor of *The Covenant Companion*, was the first to ask us to write theological reflections on current movies. We have done this on a bimonthly basis for the last eight years. The initial drafts of our "Synopsis and Theological Reflection" that form the core of each movie discussion first appeared in the pages of this periodical. Doug Wysockey-Johnson, executive director of Faith at Work, has also been a strong encourager, using a selection of these same reviews in his journal, *Faith@Work*. During this same time period, we have hosted a movie group that meets regularly to watch and discuss films. The discussion takes place while we eat a meal together in the style of the selected film (yes, even cooking a *Babette's Feast*). These friends have been our dialogue partners and coaches, helping us to understand better what we have seen. We also want to thank our students—those who attend Centro Hispano de Estudios Teològicos and Fuller Theological Seminary as well as the many Young Life staff who have studied with us. Finally, we need to thank the technology support team at Fuller, especially Zachary Abbott. Just as the production of a movie is a corporate act, so our movie dialogue has been a community event.

We have written this book in the hope that our enthusiasm will increase your enthusiasm, initially for film but ultimately for God. Typically, many in the church have bracketed God out of Hollywood's secular entertainment. Isn't it just a mindless escape, at times even faith denying? An understanding of common grace, of the wider work of God's Spirit throughout and within all creatures and creation, would suggest that this is not the case. God is, after all, in the midst of life—all of it. This includes the movies. We hope this book will strengthen your "reel faith."

Finding God in the Movies

An Introduction

Should the church be interested in Hollywood? In her book *God-Talk in America*, Phyllis Tickle makes the provocative claim that more theology is conveyed in and remembered from one hour of television than from all the sermons preached in a given weekend.[1] Perhaps this is an exaggeration, but it speaks to a truth. Solid doses of theology are present in shows such as *The Simpsons*, as any devotee will attest and as Mark Pinsky's recent book, *The Gospel According to the Simpsons*, details so well.[2]

We wish to make a similar claim concerning popular movies. God is present in the movies for those who have eyes to see and ears to hear. Theology is being portrayed in and will be retained from the movies we see each week at the cineplex. Though late to recognize this fact, the church is now awakening to the idea that Hollywood is providing an important resource for its teaching, preaching, youth ministry, and outreach activities. This book is meant to help Christians find God in the movies, to use reel faith to encourage and strengthen real faith.

For some readers, the topic of finding God in the movies will be familiar territory. For others, after you have read this brief introduction to a complex and vibrant topic, you will want to read more. If so, we suggest Rob's book, *Reel Spirituality: Theology and Film in Dialogue*.[3] It is a larger introduction to the subject of theology and film and is being used as a textbook by a number of colleges and seminaries across the country. Nevertheless, we trust this introduction will provide enough information for many purposes, including preparing to lead a film-based discussion group, rounding out one's own view of finding God in the movies, and preaching sermons that either visually or verbally incorporate cinematic sources. Our hope is for this introduction to outline why the church should be taking movies seriously and how we might best uncover a visual story's center of power and meaning.

Big Business

When we ask students how many movies they watch in a month, the typical answer is eight to ten, and responses have ranged as high as fifty-five! People are watching movies in record numbers. In 2002, Americans spent over $9.4 billion on movie tickets, up more than 10 percent from the previous year. Even with higher prices, actual admissions also rose, reaching their highest level in over forty-five years—1.5 billion people. But this is only part of the story. In 2002, DVD sales reached a staggering $8.7 billion, in addition to the $3.4 billion spent on VHS. To give but one example of the lure of DVDs, ticket sales for *Spider Man* in its first weekend at the theaters reached $115 million, while DVD sales on its first weekend range in excess of $190 million.

We can't forget about rentals and cable either. Blockbuster and Hollywood chains are ubiquitous. Home rentals are a weekly ritual for many families, particularly if parents leave the kids with a babysitter. Many who are under thirty consider video, like computers, cell phones, and food, simply a part of normal life. Already in 1998, $8.1 billion was spent on video rentals. Beyond the DVD, a host of television channels such as HBO,

Showtime, and The Movie Channel are part of the viewing habits of still millions more. Moreover, cable seems to know no socioeconomic distinction. Most do not consider it a luxury.

Quite simply, movies are the twenty-first century's primary entertainment. Book sales to adults continue to slump yearly, causing an ongoing crisis in the publishing industry. Audiences at the symphony are increasingly gray-haired, so much so that a number of orchestras are including music written for films in their programming, hoping against hope to lure a younger listener. London's Royal Ballet School reported in 2002 that for the first time in its seventy-six-year history, the institution accepted more boys than girls. They called this the *Billy Elliot* effect, citing the 2000 film in which the eleven-year-old son of a coal miner leaves home to pursue a ballet career. On television, Jay Leno and David Letterman interview a continuing stream of movie stars, *Entertainment Tonight* and *Access Hollywood* have millions more viewers, and the networks' movies of the week attract high Nielsen ratings. Even art museums are not beyond the influence of movies. The Los Angeles County Museum of Art recently had an exhibit of Farrah Fawcett's "art" (in collaboration with sculptor Keith Edmier), and the Pushkin Museum of Fine Arts in Moscow mounted an exhibition in the summer of 2003 of Gina Lollobrigida's sculptures. (Lollobrigida said in publicizing the show that her life in film heavily influenced her work.) Both museums, it seems, were hoping to attract a wider public through their doors based on these movie stars' fame.

Movies and the Church

Hollywood's lure extends into the church as well. Let me give two examples. Ten years ago the several-thousand-member, traditional, evangelical church near our home in Pasadena would not have considered showing a clip from a secular Hollywood film, let alone an R-rated movie, in its morning worship service. They would have said, "We are to convert Hollywood, not be converted by Hollywood." Yet the portrayal of hope and friendship in *Shawshank Redemption* was so powerful that its use (albeit one clip) as part of a Sunday morning sermon proved both compelling and noncontroversial. Likewise, a large, independent church in Phoenix that focuses on ministry to those under forty had a six-week sermon series in the summer of 2003 on the movie *Bruce Almighty*. They realized this was a textbook through which to engage worshippers in dialogue concerning the doctrine of God. Here was a way to bring the Bible into conversation with life.

Movies are increasingly a regular part of the church's Christian education, youth, outreach, and community-building programs. While few worship services used movie clips ten years ago, they are shown today in a wide variety of denominational settings. When they are not, it is technology (or the lack thereof) more often than theology that is the reason. We get calls regularly from churches asking for help in how best to use movies in their worship, education, and outreach. When we speak, there is no more predictable question afterward than, What movies would you suggest we use in our church? Most youth groups can't get along without a DVD player. Adult study groups view and discuss movies nominated for the Academy Awards or other significant films. Movie nights are held for the whole congregation. Neighborhood discussion groups allow Christian believers to reach out to their neighbors in nonthreatening ways. Film clips bring sermons and teaching to life.

While there is in all of this the occasional equivalent to a Farah Fawcett "art" exhibit, such a sellout by the church to the lure of Hollywood—to our entertainment culture—is not the typical scenario despite the rhetoric of some. Like their compatriots in art museums and symphony orchestras, church leaders no doubt hope to balance the gray hair and attract a wider public by bringing the Christian faith into conversation with contemporary culture. But we know (or should know) that just as with the movies, special effects alone wear thin. (We are writing this during the summer of 2003 when one sequel after another has proven a disappointment at the box office because of the attempt to cover lame stories with hypereffects.) A compelling story believably told must be present if the movie's *reel faith* is to strengthen real faith.

The Power of Story

Christians have recognized the power of story ever since the ministry of Jesus himself. The Scriptures Jesus used (the Old Testament) are overwhelmingly narrative—well over 75 percent. The gospel is at its core a story—God acting in history to reveal his love by saving humans. Jesus consistently used parables to communicate truth. Abstract proposition was not his trade. Rather, compelling stories triggered the reason, imagination, and emotion of his listeners as they were invited to deepen their faith and understanding.

The same holds true today for Christian preaching and teaching. What is it that you remember from the last sermon you heard? Chances are it is not the logic of an argument but a story that was told effectively. And it is not just the Christian faith that depends on stories to touch the whole person. Most religious traditions—Judaism, Buddhism, Hinduism, and Islam—use stories to both inform and motivate. Stories give flesh to belief and teach truth. It is the stories of a community that communicate its values, empowering its members to live into their future.

Everyone loves a good story. It's universal. When effective, stories touch us as whole people—our minds, our hearts, even our "guts." By providing us connection with others, they paradoxically remind us of ourselves. Even if they are imaginary tales like the Japanese animation *Spirited Away*, their power is in the ordinary, in their ability to take one life and reveal something about another. We might not be as immature as Will Freeman (note the name!) in *About a Boy*, but if we are honest, his self-centeredness is too much like our own. We might have been spared the physical challenges of *Simon Birch*, but we wish for the clear sense of vocation and purpose that this little person possessed. We might not have been put in prison like Cinque in *Amistad*, but we too long to shout, "Give us . . . us free!"

Like stories more generally, a good movie helps us make sense of the world even as it provides a temporary respite from it. As we watch even the simplest and most commonplace of movies, we are presented with options concerning life. (We aren't thinking here of those storyless movies like *Charlie's Angels: Full Throttle*, which seek to survive at the cineplex on adrenalin rushes alone.) By focusing reality for the viewer, a movie provides us metaphors for understanding life. One of our seminary colleagues, Mark Burrows, has pointed out that in modern Greek cities, the word for mass transportation vehicles—whether buses, trams, or trains—is *metaphorai*. That is to say, one takes a "metaphor" if one wants to go from one place to another. By telling their stories, movies give us a "ride," they fill us with the dreams, hopes, and fears of others, enabling us to move from here to there.

Reel Faith

Stories are *metaphorai*—mass transit vehicles—in a second sense also. Not only do they allow us to enter another's life in order to learn something about our own, but they also use the ordinary experiences of living to usher us into the realm of the spirit. It is not just, or even primarily, the stories of angels and demons that are rightly labeled "spiritual." Rather, God is more typically encountered in the everyday, in the stuff of life. When we truly experience forgiveness, reconciliation, alienation, or friendship at the movies, that is a spiritual experience. Such occurrences are always surprising. They present themselves to the viewer unannounced (we sometimes call them "aha" experiences). We have been drawn into the story because of its humanity; we leave the movie transformed because we have met divinity.

Such experiences are what incarnational theology means for Christians. The invisible realm of the spirit is not to be seen through literal depiction but indirectly, through observing its effect in the lives of others and ourselves. An honest depiction of a creature can reveal the Creator. A truthful telling of the human drama can voice the divine as well. The Catholic novelist Flannery O'Connor, in her classic essay "The Novelist and the Believer," wrote: "The artist penetrates the concrete world in order to find at its depths the image of its source, the image of ultimate reality."[4] Christians have for centuries believed this to be true. This is why we have titled our book, *Finding God in the Movies*. Our world is after all God's world. He has the whole world in his hands, including our stories. If we have but eyes to see and ears to hear, there is a *reel faith* to be encountered at the movies.

Some sociologists have spoken of the movie theater as America's new cathedral. Some of the comparisons are superficial or defective (e.g., popcorn and Coke versus bread and wine, worship music functioning like movie previews, whetting our appetites for what is to follow). And important differences should not be overlooked. Speaking theologically, the chief difference is this: The movie theater's focus, when it gets it right, is *common grace*—God's activity in the wider world. The church, when it gets it right, is concerned with *saving grace*—God's activity in Jesus Christ. The one should not, and cannot, replace the other. However, Christians believe both forms of grace are a gift of the Spirit, so the similarities between churches and theaters need not always be disparaged. Their commonality is found in the unity of the Spirit.

Whether entering a movie theater or a church, one has an expectation that something larger is about to happen. (Here is perhaps why we speak with hushed tones in both settings.) And if it doesn't happen, we feel disappointed as we leave. Just as the medieval cathedral was a place to divert the attention of worshippers from the mundane for an hour or two, so the modern theater provides a similar function. And this diversion is not just trivial. Movies like *Fearless* and *The Apostle* do more than simply entertain; they provide a place for us to pause and meditate on our purpose and place in life. They draw us into common human struggles we all face but too rarely voice. As we watch, if we also experience a moment of transcendence—of awe in the presence of the Eternal—we feel blessed, even as tears roll down our cheeks.

To give two examples, we assigned the movie *Life as a House* to students in one of our classes. The movie tells the story of Sam, an angry teenager who feels abandoned by his divorced, upper-middle-class parents, and George, his father, who has isolated himself from his friends and family. When George is fired from his architectural firm and is diagnosed with terminal cancer, he realizes he wants nothing more than to reach out to his son and reconnect. Having Sam help him rebuild his eyesore of a house becomes a metaphor for the rebuilding of lives that happens concurrently. When students were asked for their reaction to the movie, one man in his late twenties volunteered that he had had an estranged relationship with his father for years. He shared, "I saw Sam and his father, and I wept hard in the arms of my wife." Another woman in her midthirties responded, "I've reached out to my dad."

Later in the course, we had the chance to interview Phil Alden Robinson, the writer and director of the movie *Field of Dreams*. The movie tells the story of Ray Kinsella, an Iowa farmer who hears a voice telling him to build a baseball diamond in the middle of his cornfield. Against all common sense, he proceeds to do just that and as a result is able to connect with his estranged father. The last images of the film are of a game of catch with his father. Robinson discussed the effect the film has had on both sons and fathers. Although he is not a Christian and did not have any explicit theological intention for the movie, he recognized that the movie had spiritually affected scores of people in much the way our students who watched *Life as a House* had responded.

It had encouraged reconciliation. Respectful of the possibility that his film might have had a spiritual influence beyond his intention for it, Robinson spoke humbly and thanked those who shared about what the film had meant to them. God can and does use all of his creation—even the inspired creations of his creatures—to convey his love and grace to us.

Theological Approaches to the Movies

In Rob's earlier book, *Reel Spirituality*, he delineated five approaches to movie watching: avoidance, caution, dialogue, appropriation, and divine encounter.[5] A brief review might be helpful. A few still argue that movies destroy the moral fabric of both church and nation and are thus to be **avoided**. But the presence of a TV in every home, as well as the wonder of movies like *Finding Nemo*, make such blanket condemnation increasingly rare. Even the Southern Baptists lifted their boycott on Disney for two hours so members could watch *The Miracle Maker* on ABC.

More common is the church's warning to be **cautious** with regard to one's film watching. Whether coming from liberals or conservatives, this position purports that movies too often subvert faith and values. (Different values are referenced, of course, depending on the end of the theological spectrum to which one belongs.) There is no question that some movies offer little of value to their viewers. But when Christians go to movies not expecting much, they seldom get much from the experience other than perhaps enjoying some escapist fare. Their caution short-circuits whatever spiritual encounter the movie might otherwise invite.

Recognizing the inherent limitations of coming to a movie with a skeptical eye, moviegoers in the church have often opted instead to **dialogue** theologically with film. They have recognized the importance of first receiving a movie on its own terms before responding from one's own understanding of life and faith. The magazine *Christian Century*, rooted in the mainstream denominations, trumpeted this position as early as the 1960s, but it is also voiced today in the widely read evangelical journal, *Christianity Today*. Many recognize that movies such as *Sister Act*, *Tender Mercies*, and *The Apostle* are religious at their core and invite, if not demand, a response from a Christian perspective. Here is an initial answer to the question of how faithful people might constructively use movies in their life together, an answer that continues to inform the life and witness of the church.

More recently two other voices have emerged from the church. One is rooted in the recognition that Christians can sometimes learn from a film's vision of life. That is, film does not simply provide alternate perspectives that invite dialogue from a Christian perspective. Rather, movies also can expand one's vision, providing new vistas by which to understand truth, beauty, and goodness. In particular, through movies Christians can gain insight into the human spirit. Rob has labeled such an approach **appropriation**. *Life Is Beautiful* can reveal to those who would see what a father's love should be, and *Iron Giant* shows the possibility of choosing nonviolence as an option in life. The other comes mainly from Roman Catholics, who are helping Protestants to understand something of the sacramentality of creation—to recognize that all of life, including the movies, can be an occasion of **divine encounter**. As artist, the filmmaker can disclose God's presence as God chooses to speak through and within his creature's creations. A later chapter, for example, will tell the story of how Cathy heard God speaking to her through the movie *The Year of Living Dangerously*.

In the chapters that follow, readers will note that at times we seek as Christians to *dialogue* with movies, at other times to *appropriate* their portrayal of life, and at still other times to recognize the possibility of a *divine encounter* as the Spirit speaks to us through a film. We also recognize that not all films are suitable for all people, and thus *caution* is sometimes necessary. (Such caution is probably best exercised, however, by choosing which films to watch before going to the theater rather than in coming to a movie with a skeptical or judgmental eye and aborting its charm or truth in the process.) The only approach we would reject out of hand is that of *avoidance*. And we do this not simply for pragmatic reasons (i.e., the difficulty of consistency given the overwhelming presence of the television). We reject any avoidance strategy because of what it says theologically about Christian life and thought.

The task of thinking as a Christian, as we understand it, is always a conversation between our faith and our culture, a dialogue between our stories and God's Story. At its core, theology is interactional—a two-way exchange between Scripture and the Christian community on the one hand and culture and human experience on the other. Because divine truth is culturally embedded and culture is spiritually rooted, any attempt to construct a theology free of culture seems doomed to failure. Rather than shun the culture in which we live, Christians should seek to interact creatively with it. Karl Barth once described the stance of a theologian as having the Bible in one hand and a newspaper in the other. To use the idiom of the movies, we might say that to better understand our faith, we should have a Bible in one hand and a DVD in the other. After all, we hear God in both.

Expressing Christian Faith through Filmmaking

Among Christians in Hollywood, three approaches have surfaced for how to express faith through moviemaking. Some would seek to imitate the Christian music industry and create *faith-based alternatives* that have explicit Christian messages. Their assumption is that surely one can more easily find God in Christian films. Movies such as *The Omega Code* (1999), *Left Behind* (2001), and *Joshua* (2002) have thus been made. Money and creative marketing have been directed to these attempts, but to date such movies, though they have come a long way since Franky Schaeffer or Billy Graham's Worldwide Pictures, nevertheless seem to most viewers too preachy and too poorly made (when compared to industry standards). The one exception perhaps is *Jonah: A VeggieTales Movie* (2002). But even here, this movie's heavy dependence on voice-overs to get its point across, together with its modest budget for an animated feature, work against it in any comparison with a movie like *Iron Giant* (1999), not to mention our current favorite, *Finding Nemo* (2003). Overwhelmingly, the audiences for these movies remain limited to Christians. Ironically, though these movies might be about God, God is not often experienced in or through them. Their messages might help us know something about God, but their stories seldom help us to know God himself.

Other Christians are attempting to help viewers find God through creating what they have called *faith-friendly movies.* These filmmakers are not trying to preach but are seeking to make positive films with Christian values—in particular, movies free of controversial content. A good example is *Extreme Days* (2001), written by our friend Craig Detweiler. But like those movies that seek to provide faith-based alternatives, these faith-friendly movies have perhaps been too narrowly conceived by their Christian producers (though junior high kids love the humor and extreme sports footage of *Extreme Days*). What seems to be the most important criterion for qualifying as a "positive film with Christian values" is the absence of foul language, sex, and violence. But must faith-friendly films be free of all controversial content? Just as the Bible is R-rated at times in order to tell its stories truthfully (e.g., the sexuality of David and Bathsheba or the violence of David and Goliath), so too are the movies. Just because a movie might be inappropriate for an eight-year-old doesn't make it inappropriate for an adult. *Amistad* (1997) has graphic violence and some nudity. The boxing scenes in *The Hurricane* (1999) are brutal. But both movies' stories invite viewers to dig deep and consider anew their faith in the context of the harsh realities of life. Both, in fact, have been the occasion for countless viewers to experience God's presence.

It is our conviction that quality, faith-friendly films can be and are being made by non-Christians too. Moreover, such movies often will have a certain messiness in them, a grittiness consistent with life itself. (It is true that movies can have gratuitous foul language, sex, and violence, but the fact that it is "gratuitous" means that quality has been compromised.) Thus, we are in agreement with a third group of Christians in Hollywood, who argue that what we as Christians should be focusing upon, both in our filmmaking and in our film viewing, is neither explicitly Christian content nor controversy-free material, but *excellence in storytelling*. Such excellence will allow viewers to see reality afresh, perhaps even sacramentally. By helping viewers experience human beings as they were created to be (or as they are kept from being), excellent stories point us to the Divine in whose image we all have been made. As a song from the musical version of *Les Misérables* celebrates, "To love another person is to see the face of God." As Christians, we believe that God has revealed himself most clearly in his Son, Jesus Christ. But God's creatures in their creativity also declare his glory for all who have eyes to see and ears to hear.

The movies we have chosen for this volume present to their viewers excellently told stories that allow us to see humanity with fresh eyes. As such they are faith-friendly and suitable for use in the church (when appropriate notice and venue are given to movies with adult-oriented stories). They provide the possibility of encounters with God and his creation even as they invite dialogue and engagement with our Christian faith. Here are movies that are worth seeing over again, movies that can become our companions.

One can find God at the cineplex whether or not the filmmakers are Christian believers. But this happens only when the movie story is presented compellingly. We were spiritually impacted by *The Straight Story*, *The Year of Living Dangerously*, and *Chocolat*, for example, even though the production teams of these movies had no explicit Christian intention. We also have chosen for this book movies such as *The Rookie*, *Antwone Fisher*, and *Patch Adams*, movies in which the influence of a Christian director is significant. They also spoke to our spirits. Trying to distinguish "Christian" moviemaking from quality movies is a counterproductive task. We have chosen rather to ask, Where have we found God to be present in the movies? And our answer? In good stories that are told with excellence.

Unpacking the Story

Movie stories, when told well, stimulate our imagination and allow us to enter into another time and space. In the process they help us as viewers to translate our beliefs and values into an arena different from our own. Moviegoing can take our faith and put it in dialogue with life. Movies, particularly those that tell good stories, provide occasions for our spiritual growth, for our spirit's encounter with the Spirit.

Some Christian culture watchers believe that when you watch a movie you should always be in a *dual-listening mode*. Even while you are watching, you should be listening for the message of the movie and then comparing and contrasting it with the message of the Word of God. They believe it is relatively unimportant whether you liked the movie or were engaged with it. More important is what you can understand from the movie and how it might be the occasion for some future conversation about the truth that you know. While there is no doubt something to be gained from such an external approach, in our opinion it is deficient because it fails to take the movie seriously as the work of art that it is.

Movies do more than help us critique culture, understand the place of religion in American life, or help us communicate the faith, though they do all three. We need first to watch a movie on its own terms and for its own sake, for film helps us better understand ourselves. As C. S. Lewis wrote concerning the reading of stories, you must first surrender to them in order to receive what the story presents: "Get yourself out of the way.

(There is no good asking first whether the work before you deserves such a surrender for until you have surrendered you cannot possibly find out.)"[6] As we watch a movie, we find our own intentions and desires coming into focus. Movies make claims on us, portraying realities not of our choosing. When we go to get a latte after seeing a movie with friends, we discuss whether the movie grabbed us, what scenes moved us deeply, whether it rang true, and so on. This is as it should be. Movies are to be experienced. But conversation about a movie often stops here, and this is also a mistake. While movies entertain, they also educate. Storytellers have a particular perspective on reality that they are trying to portray for their viewers. They are trying to tap into some truth, portray some beauty, embody some goodness. Here is what the dual-listening culture watchers are trying to get at when they suggest it is important to ask about the beliefs presented in the movie. As moviegoers who love movies and as Christians committed to Christ and his church, we believe both tasks are necessary—enjoyment and discernment. But if our judgments are to have any legitimacy, they must follow, not precede, the enjoyment of experiencing a well-told story. It is a false dichotomy to contrast entertainment and education; they go hand in hand.

Experiencing the Movie's Story

For a movie to transport us into another reality, it must engage us at three levels. Jon Boorstin describes the magic of film watching by using three words starting with *v*—voyeuristic, visceral, and vicarious.[7] This is what our movie entertainment is based on. Watching a good movie will be a *voyeuristic* experience; that is, we are provided entry into a believable world. We are enabled to eavesdrop on others in a different place and time, whether they experience something similar to what we have gone through or take us to places we have not previously gone. Historical accuracy (*The Hurricane* was hurt at the box office by charges that the facts were slightly different) or plausibility (if the story is fictional like *K-PAX*) is crucial. The production designer becomes of necessity a master of details, helping to embody the screenwriter's story. Movies must be true to life, even if they are fantasies such as *Spirited Away* (2002). Movie stories must be made believable; they must make sense to the viewer.

If the first test of a good film is intellectual (Does it make sense?), a second is centered more in the gut (Does it grab me?). A good movie will take its viewers into its grip. Our attention will be captured and held; our stomachs will become tense. We are along for the ride. (Think of *The Matrix*.) Boorstin describes this experience as *visceral*. For example, were you scared as you watched *Signs* or sickened by the human slaughter in *Amistad* or *We Were Soldiers*? Special effects can help achieve these visceral rushes, as can digital sound and strong editing.

Martin Scorcese's *Gangs of New York* gave us a graphic portrayal of working class life in mid-nineteenth-century New York. It was both meticulously rendered (voyeuristic) and frighteningly real (visceral). But without any characters that you cared about, without any *vicarious* attachment, the movie remained stillborn for most moviegoers. Here is the third necessary characteristic of an excellent movie according to Boorstin. Successful movies do not merely transport us somewhere new; they inspire us to become emotionally attached, to become one with the characters. We root for Alvin Straight (*The Straight Story*), we cry with Primo and Secondo (*Big Night*), we celebrate with Jim Morris (*The Rookie*), and we long for the tender mercies of someone like Rosa Lee (*Tender Mercies*). It is the director's role to coach his or her actors so that their performances result in our hearts being touched. The emotional wallop might sneak up on the viewer as in *Smoke Signals*, but if it rings false or is missing, the movie simply fails.

Head, gut, and heart. The best movies will engage the whole person. The movies we have chosen in this volume often do better at one or another of these aspects. But to the degree that one is missing, it detracts from our viewing experience. When they are all present, as in *Life Is Beautiful* or *Spirited Away*, we are riveted to the screen. It is simply magic.

Understanding the Movie's Story

Movies not only entertain, they inform; they not only engage us, they educate us. Thus, while our experience of a movie is primary, our understanding of that experience is also important. Although exceptions to the rule sometimes prevail, the vast majority of movies are first of all stories and only as such invite our critical reflection. As stories, movies portray life; they don't prescribe it. They are more like poetry than proposition. They present; they don't preach. Therefore, it is important when analyzing movies to understand how movie storytelling works.

Limited to more or less two hours of screen time, a movie must quickly focus our attention on a particular emotional theme, on "an irreducible kernel of human nature."[8] Often it is during the opening credits themselves, as the story is being set up, that we are given interpretive clues for how we are to understand what is to follow. Then through its portrayal of a particular story, the movie reveals something fundamental about the human story—something in which we all participate. Perhaps it is the theme of racial reconciliation as in *Remember the Titans* or the need to forgive our fathers as in *Smoke Signals*. The same basic plot can be told in several ways, but the power and meaning of a given movie is communicated through a particular slant, a chosen theme that serves as a unifying thread for the film. We have grouped the movies in this book around thirteen such themes. These themes have theological import and invite our conversation, but they arise first of all from the movies themselves, not from any Christian overlay.

One of our favorite essays on how to respond to stories as Christian believers comes from the field of literature, not filmmaking, but its point is nevertheless applicable. R. W. B. Lewis, in his article "Hold on Hard to the Huckleberries," writes about "an old Boston lady, who once remarked to Emerson about those pious folk of an earlier generation who had to hold on hard to the huckleberry bushes to keep from being translated" to heaven immediately. He used this historical anecdote to craft his thesis: Although a person's Christian beliefs might be fundamental, they are not necessarily the most appropriate starting point for dialogue with a story. He writes, "Absolutely speaking, as between religion and literature [in our case between Christianity and film], religion no doubt comes first; but in the actual study of a particular literary text [or a particular movie], it probably ought to follow, and follow naturally and organically and without strain—for the sake of the religion as well as the literature."[9] We must first seek in our movie watching "to hold on hard to the huckleberries," for the Christian faith is first of all a story to be experienced, not a creed to be defended. The Christian faith must be lived. We do well to have a conversation with a movie's story, not an inquisition.

In a perceptive article in the *New York Times* titled "Spiritual Values Are In, but Please No Sermonizing," religion critic Gustaf Niebuhr reviewed the movies *Braveheart, Dead Man Walking, Babe,* and *The Spitfire Grill.* His point was to contrast the days when Hollywood still made religious epics with the movies of today. Presently, he wrote, spirituality in movies "tends to be subtle, a below-the-radar subtext for those (to borrow a biblical phrase) who have eyes to see or ears to hear."[10] We need, therefore, to learn how to view the story. God will not always be present à la Cecil B. DeMille. Movies might sometimes function as fables, providing metaphors for life. *Chocolat* even goes so far as to say at the beginning that it is "a fable that tells the truth." Movies are all about seeing. As Andreas, the newly licensed theological student in *Italian for Beginners,* says in his sermon, "God is here in compassion, friendship, between us . . . in love, in every moment . . . in the arm you slip around the waist of your beloved." But we must have eyes to see.

To the question, How does one find God in the movies? we respond by saying, unpack the story. Ask yourself, for example, what is more primary in the way the story is shaped? (1) Is it the *plot*, as in the movie *Sister Act*, in which meaning is conveyed through the action that unfolds? (2) Is it the *characters*, as in *Ulee's Gold*, in which what engages us is the nature of this one man (and by extension, all men and women)? (3) Is it the *point of view*, where a story is given value by the perspective of the narrator(s), as in *Smoke Signals*? Or (4) is it the *atmosphere*—those unalterable givens against which the story is told and the characters developed, as in *Simon Birch*, in which Simon just knows "he is a miracle"? Not all movies have a strong plot line. Not to worry; don't therefore spend your energy on the plot. The movie *Titanic*, for example, had a predictable plot (after all, we all knew the ship would sink). Thus, the filmmakers chose to concentrate the viewer's attention on Rose's point of view, on her belief that she had been saved in every possible way through her relationship with Jack. Here, then, should be the point of entry for a theological discussion of that movie. Although all four aspects of a story usually will be present in a movie, not all will be equally emphasized. Concentrate your critical attention on where the filmmakers have centered their attention. By doing this, you will prove a more receptive viewer of the story and perhaps the Story.

How to Use This Book

We intend *Finding God in the Movies* as a resource. Our goal in writing it is to assist Christians in bringing their faith and life together, to link their experience of a story on the screen with their experience of Christ in their churches. Thus, we have chosen to unpack more than thirty films of reel faith in order to facilitate a dialogue around the visual parables of our age. Some of the movies we have chosen will no doubt be familiar to you. Given the VCR and now the DVD player, movies that are judged excellent by the culture (and some that aren't!) are seen by millions of viewers both in the cineplex and in their homes. Others of these visual stories will be new to you. Perhaps you do not live in a major media center and some of the smaller yet also excellent movies got little press in your town. Regardless, we have chosen these movies because their stories have engaged our lives of faith in significant ways, and we write with the expectation that they will engage yours as well.

Format

Each of the movie discussions has a similar format, which we trust will prove easily accessible to you. At the top right of each movie discussion, you will notice a list of themes. We have tried to include all the theological themes and subthemes that seem pertinent to the power of and meaning of the movie's story. The boldfaced theme is the one we consider most central, the italicized type indicates major themes, and the regular type indicates minor themes. Readers can flip through the book for a quick search of themes that seem most appropriate for their circumstances. Another option is to use appendix 2, which lists the movies by topic.

Also at the beginning of each discussion are the basic production notes of a given movie, including date, length, actors, director, screenwriter, rating, and selected DVD features. The ratings of the Motion Picture Association of America ("G," "PG," "PG13," and "R") are notoriously subjective and inconsistent. So in addition to these ratings, we have given brief descriptions of what might prove unsuitable for certain groups. Not all movies are meant to be seen by all age groups. When an R-rated movie is included (for example, *Amistad*), it is because we found the movie to deepen our faith and lives as Christians. Its thematic and visual material, however, are adult in nature and need to be directed accordingly.

The production notes are followed by a synopsis of and theological reflection on the film. Here we help readers into the heart of each movie, looking for what we might learn from the movie that will deepen and extend our faith. Why is it that a Christian should want to engage this particular movie's story? We are convinced that God is present in and through all of life. Where a story helps viewers experience authentically some aspect of truth, beauty, or goodness, there is the energizing presence of God's Spirit. As these visual stories connect us with the human story at its bedrock, they thus become the occasion for us to find God. (Leaders, you might find this section helpful as you preview and select movies for study and discussion.)

Next we have listed a group of biblical texts that raise themes similar to those in a given film; they are listed in order of closest connection to the film. These texts are not meant to be exhaustive, and we hope we have not made them susceptible to misuse by listing one verse after another. With due diligence these texts can be suggestive of themes similar to or complementing those found in the movie. In some cases a text reflects a scene in the movie quite directly; in others the texts are meant to facilitate dialogue. Sometimes the texts reflect an issue that is present in the movie; occasionally they present a biblical alternative. In several chapters, the verses come directly from the movie itself. If the filmmakers thought a biblical citation relevant, we do too. If there is a discernible pattern to the texts, perhaps it is that they center on those parts of Scripture that help us to understand better our God-given humanity (e.g., Genesis, the wisdom literature, the Psalms, Jesus' teachings and parables, and Paul's instruction).

Following the biblical texts are two sets of discussion questions. The first set includes questions of a more general nature, flowing from the whole movie, its overall theme, and its filmmakers' intentions. The second, which we have called "Clip Conversations," includes questions related to particular moments in the movie's storytelling. We have identified these clips by their location in a given chapter of the DVD as well as by the running time of the clip, assuming you set your counter at 0:00 when the studio's logo appears on the screen. This double referencing will help you to locate the clip on either DVD or video. For each clip we have listed the whole chapter of a DVD, even if the particular scene we have targeted for discussion is only a part of the chapter. This is so you can preview the clip's context and tailor its length to your given situation. Together, these questions are meant to take you into the heart of these visual stories and suggest fruitful areas for further discussion.

With each movie discussion we have included "Bonus Material." This section is meant to help readers understand something of both the making and the reception of the movie. We give basic box office numbers, often with the cost of production. We summarize awards information. We provide personal information about how cast or crew members were impacted personally by the making of the movie. If the filmmakers have commented on why the movie was important to them, we will summarize these remarks. At times, we will suggest possible uses for the film in your own context.

It is important to remember in reading the movie discussions that they are meant only as a guide. Some of our questions will not connect. Movies strike different viewers in different ways. A clip might not work for you. Use what is useful. There is more than enough material to lead a vibrant discussion, to use a particular movie to embody a point, or to meditate on film and Scripture as they are allowed to be heard in conversation with each other. Each chapter is intended to give any interested moviegoer a sufficient body of material to enter into a robust dialogue between faith and film.

A Resource and Guide

Finding God in the Movies can be used as a personal resource for your own movie watching. Here are more than thirty movies that we have found both entertaining and educational. Whether fun or provocative, they have challenged and informed us, inviting us into the lives of others who also share God's image. If you use this book as a guide for your rentals at Blockbuster, we suggest you invite a friend or neighbor to watch with you. (Use us as your excuse, if you like. You can say the movie was recommended as being worth viewing.) Movie watching invites conversation and response. To hear a story and have no means of responding to it is to risk aborting its power and significance in your life.

Though individual viewers can benefit from the conversation generated within the pages of this book, the volume is intended primarily as a resource for use by those in group or public settings, particularly those speaking to or leading groups in the church. The book is intended mainly as a guide for those teaching an adult study group, for youth workers leading discussions after viewing movies with students, for those wanting to begin a neighborhood discussion group for Christians and non-Christians alike, or for those wanting help in how to use film clips and Scripture to focus a group's meditation and prayer.

The book is also meant as a resource for church leaders who would like to use film clips and stories in their speaking, teaching, and preaching. Just as many sermons misinterpret a biblical text, using it for unintended purposes, so many in the church who want to connect the Christian faith with wider popular culture often misinterpret film clips and stories and use them to illustrate something other than what a movie is portraying. Some books that churches currently use to interact with movies do not seem to take the movies themselves as seriously as they could, finding in them only pretexts for making theological points arrived at independently. At least this is always a danger. Thus we have tried to engage each movie at the center of the story's power and meaning and to suggest how it might prove useful for those charged with the teaching and preaching ministries of the church.

Each of this book's movie discussions is distinct. Though the discussions have been grouped around similar themes, they need not be read in order. In fact, a reader might pick and choose particular discussions to read while preparing to lead a discussion or preach a sermon that will refer to a particular movie or group of movies.

To help readers determine which movie or movies to use for a given occasion or for a series of group discussions, we have provided two appendixes. The first appendix provides the *biblical texts* used in the book together with the movies that suggested them. These biblical texts range from Genesis to Revelation, with roughly an equivalent number of passages from both the Old and New Testaments. The second appendix provides a list of topics that will help readers identify movies that have particular theological themes or subthemes. This will be helpful to those who are teaching or preaching on a given subject and seek appropriate movie resources. A cursory glance at this appendix will reveal repeated themes in the movies we have selected. Such repetitions can suggest possible points of dialogue between several movies. One might want to compare and contrast the portrayal of forgiveness in the movies *Smoke Signals* and *Antwone Fisher*, for example. Also note that we have written four combination discussions, each of which places two movies in dialogue with each other as well as with biblical texts and theological themes. We have done this because of the insight such dialogue offers. We also aim to help youth groups in picking films for movie marathons or double-feature nights. Each of the movies in these pairings can still be used separately, however, because clips, questions, and bonus material relate to one movie at a time.

The movie groupings in the topical list also will help readers to identify movies for use in a series, whether it be a multiweek adult study group, a monthly family night, a neighborhood film group, a series of sermons, or a youth group series. For a longer series (seven to twelve films), consider the following: Affirming Our Humanity; Beauty, Imagination, and Creativity; Sins by Which We Are Tempted in Our Culture; Community and Friendship; Family (or Reconciliation within Families); Life; Living Our Faith; and Love. For a shorter series (two to five films), consider: Death, The Goodness of Creation, Embracing Our Vocation, Sharing Our Faith, Healing, Images of the Savior, Racial Reconciliation, and Renewing the Church. Appendix 2 will help you select movies that are suitable for such series. We also encourage you to create your own series.

Leading a Movie Group Discussion

Leading a movie group discussion is a subject worthy of a much longer treatment than we can give here, but the following are insights we have found very useful in groups we have led:

1. As the leader, you are not the "expert" but the guide for the discussion.
2. If you are going to see the film together (something we strongly recommend), keep your initial comments very brief. Let the movie introduce itself. Those bonus materials we have provided or other tidbits you uncover might best be used as part of the discussion following the film.
3. After seeing the movie, begin with a question that helps participants express their experience with the film. Ask them to share their response to a scene that was particularly moving to them, or even ask them why they liked or didn't like the movie. There are no right or wrong answers here. If someone starts to analyze the movie in an abstract way, politely ask him or her to respond to his or her own experience with the movie.
4. Always be respectful. Because movies are viewer oriented, what moves one person will leave another cold. We all know this. If someone says something that seems not in keeping with the movie, ask the group if they agree. Let the wisdom of the group carry you forward.
5. Don't be the "answer man or woman." Your background reading and preparation should be directed toward helping the group break open the movie's story and begin a theological dialogue with it. There is no need for closure. Remember that Jesus usually left his parables open ended. The power of story is in its ability to invite ongoing reflection and engagement.

Other Resources and Issues

A host of other resources are available on the more than thirty movies we have selected, and a growing number of excellent books speak to theology and the movies. Following is information on the resources we have found most useful.

Internet Sites

If you have only one "favorites" setting on your web browser with regard to movies, it should be the movie theology site compiled by Gordon Matties at Canadian Mennonite University: www.cmu.ca/library/faithfilm.html.

This site has gathered together resources from all over the Web. It includes, for example, links to forty different websites where Christian reviewers are discussing movies. Some of the best of these are:

- *Christianity Today's* Film Forum, with Jeffrey Overstreet—a digest of his own and other reviewers' comments: www.christianitytoday.com/ctmag/features/columns/filmforum.html
- Damaris Online Resources—study guides to films: www.damaris.org/olr/films.html
- Hollywood Jesus, with David Bruce, who was one of the first to use the Web for dialogue between film and faith. His site is one of the largest and most visual: www.hollywoodjesus.com
- Peter Chattaway's Movie Reviews. He is an excellent Canadian Christian film reviewer: www.canadianchristianity.com/film/

In addition to Christian reviewers, Matties provides links to:

- IMDB—Internet Movie Data Base, the most comprehensive movie reference source that is hyperlinked with thousands of external sites and is updated continuously: http://us.imdb.com/
- Rotten Tomatoes—an archive of movie reviews from newspapers across North America: www.rottentomatoes.com/movies/
- Roger Ebert on Movies—one of our favorite reviewers: www.suntimes.com/index/ebert.html

- ReelViews: James Berardinelli's Movie Reviews—another favorite and the best review of basic plot and story line: http://movie-reviews.colossus.net/

Selected Bibliography

Among a growing list of books on movies for use in the church, we have found the following to be some of the most useful.

Johnston, Robert K. *Reel Spirituality: Theology and Film in Dialogue*. Grand Rapids: Baker, 2000. This is an introduction to Christian thinking about the movies, illustrated with a discussion of several hundred movies.

Malone, Peter, with Rose Pacatte. *Lights Camera . . . Faith! Movie Lectionaries for Cycle A, B, and C*. Boston: Pauline Books & Media, 2001, 2002, 2003. These are helpful, brief discussions of movies by two leading Catholic film critics correlated to the three-year cycle of Scripture readings in the lectionary.

McNulty, Edward. *Films and Faith: Forty Discussion Guides*. Topeka: Viaticum Press, 1999. McNulty, through his magazine *Visual Parables*, was one of the first to publish monthly reviews of movies for use in the church.

Vaux, Sara. *Finding Meaning at the Movies*. Nashville: Abingdon, 1999. Vaux has an excellent appendix on leading a film study group as well as a detailed discussion of copyright issues.

Fields, Doug, and Eddie James. *Videos That Teach 2*. Grand Rapids: Zondervan/Youth Specialties, 1999, 2002. These are books for use by youth leaders written by two well-known youth pastors. The text for each movie is brief and not always helpful, but the clip selections are often provocative.

Copyright Issues

Movies are fully protected by copyright laws, though these laws are often wrongfully ignored. Use of clips in teaching and preaching situations is perhaps a gray area, given the copyright doctrine of fair use. Use of a DVD for informal groups in one's home is permitted, but the showing of movies in a public setting requires a license. An umbrella license to show movies publicly for religious or educational purposes can be easily obtained, however, through the Motion Picture Licensing Corporation (MPLC). For a cost of approximately $100/year, this blanket license covers use of DVDs and videotapes in the same way a CCLI license covers the use of music. For more information, see www.mplc.com.

Affirming
Our Humanity

1. Life Is Beautiful

Italy, 1997
122 Minutes, Feature, Color
Actors: Roberto Benigni, Nicoletta Braschi,
  Giustino Durano, Sergio Bustric,
  Marisa Paredes, Horst Buchholz, Giorgio Cantarini
Director: Roberto Benigni
Screenwriter: Roberto Benigni and Vincenzo Cerami
Rated: PG13 (mature themes, off-screen violence)
DVD Features: theatrical trailer, Academy Award TV commercials,
  "Making Life Beautiful" featurette

Affirming the Human Spirit
*Choosing Life, Family, Humor,
Imagination, Service
Beauty, Celebration,
Sacrificial Love, Trust*

Themes

Synopsis and Theological Reflection

If you buy only one DVD/video this year, buy *Life Is Beautiful.* An Italian movie that was directed and cowritten by its lead actor, Roberto Benigni, it received seven Oscar nominations, including Best Picture, Best Foreign Film, Best Director, Best Actor, Best Score, and Best Screenplay. Throughout its theatrical release, this art-house film attracted a growing audience by word of mouth. (When we first saw the film in December 1997, only a handful of people were in the audience; in February 1998 the theater was full.) *Life Is Beautiful* soon became the all-time leading moneymaker in the United States for any non-English language film (*Crouching Tiger, Hidden Dragon* surpassed it in 2001, as well as *The Passion of the Christ* in 2004). But don't go because it made money; go because it shows you what love and trust within a family should look like. Put quite simply, go to be inspired.

Guido (Roberto Benigni) protects his son, Giosue (Giorgio Cantarini), from anti-Semitic hatred by making a game with him. *Life Is Beautiful* (d. Benigni, 1997). Photo by Sergio Strizzi. Copyright 1998 Miramax Films. All rights reserved.

The movie's story is simple and warm, horrific and yet humorous. Using the languages both of slapstick and romance, Benigni tells the story of a young peasant who comes to the city to work. It is 1939 and anti-Semitism is growing. But Guido, a Jew, is oblivious to the danger. He is in love, and life is beautiful. In one of the funniest courtships to be portrayed in film in recent years, Guido wins Dora (played by Benigni's real-life wife), a schoolteacher with social standing. In fact, he knocks her off her feet (quite literally!). The couple's love is genuine and contagious, and their son Giosue (Joshua) lives in the wonderful embrace of their love.

Then the family is arrested and shipped to a concentration camp. The thought of Giosue suffering in fear is more than his parents can bear. Thus, the second half of the movie shows the extreme lengths to which parents will go in order to protect their children. Guido plays an elaborate game to protect his son from the horrors of the camp. Wanting to be sure Giosue stays in hiding, for example, Guido pretends that all is well while marching with an exaggerated style before his captor. The extent of Guido's love for his boy will bring tears to your eyes, as will the commitment Dora and Guido have for each other. In a scene reminiscent of *Shawshank Redemption*, Guido risks his life to play music for Dora over the camp's loudspeaker. It is magnificent to watch and personally inspiring. Guido will do anything for Dora and Giosue, and the compelling power of his affection is both contagious and reciprocated.

The transition from town to concentration camp is heart stopping. When we saw this movie, the audience was awash with laughter for the first forty-five minutes and starkly quiet the last hour or more. But the contrast works; the joy and innocence of the opening scenes only make the pathos of the second setting more heartfelt. Some have questioned the appropriateness of linking laughter with the unthinkable. Isn't the Holocaust beyond humor? But such a response, however understandable by those who have not yet seen the film, misses both the genre and the intention of the movie. For this film is not just about Italy in 1939 or Germany in 1945. It is instead a celebration of life's possibilities, even in the midst of unspeakable tragedy and pain.

The film begins by saying that it is going to tell a fable, and it does just that. It invites the viewer to see Reality behind and in reality. The humor in *Life Is Beautiful* is inviting. The horror of humankind's inhumanity is chilling. But the love that is shown a boy (one with the biggest eyes you could ever hope to find!) is compelling. How can life be beautiful? How can a waiter's life be redeemed or a Holocaust victim be victorious? Guido's uncle, who is a maitre d', provides the key as he teaches his nephew: "You are to serve, but you aren't a servant. . . . God serves man, but he isn't man's servant." Guido's love expresses itself in service and proves redemptive.

Ultimately the father's love in this film becomes symbolic for us of what a father's (and mother's) love should be; it is analogous to what God the Father's love is. "How great is the love the Father has lavished on us, that we should be called children of God! And that is what we are!" (1 John 3:1 NIV). To be held in your parent's arms and to experience love is transformative (expressed in the words of Giosue as the movie ends, "We won").

In his book *Man's Search for Meaning*, Victor Frankl reflects on those who were able to survive the horror of World War

II concentration camps. It was those who had something to focus on beyond themselves who lived. In our narcissistic and networking contemporary age, self-sacrifice and a focus on the "other" is countercultural. It is also profoundly Christian.

Dialogue Texts

He brought me to the banqueting house, and his intention toward me was love.

Song of Solomon 2:4

You are altogether beautiful, my love; there is no flaw in you. Come with me from Lebanon, my bride. . . . Depart . . . from the dens of lions, from the mountains of leopards. You have ravished my heart, . . . you have ravished my heart with a glance of your eyes. . . . How sweet is your love, . . . how much better is your love than wine.

Song of Solomon 4:7–10

Husbands, love your wives, just as Christ loved the church and gave himself up for her.

Ephesians 5:25

How great is the love the Father has lavished on us, that we should be called children of God! And that is what we are!

1 John 3:1 NIV

Do not be astonished, brothers and sisters, that the world hates you. We know that we have passed from death to life because we love one another. Whoever does not love abides in death.

1 John 3:13–14

Discussion Questions

1. The movie begins with a man wandering through the mist holding a boy while the following voice-over is heard, "This is

a simple story, but not an easy one to tell. Like a fable, there is sorrow, and like a fable, it is full of wonder and happiness." While critics have argued whether *Life Is Beautiful* is merely a Chaplinesque comedy, an offensive mockery, a respectful tribute to Holocaust survivors, or a drama about the human spirit, it has become for many viewers an all-time favorite film. What would you say the film is about? Why? Given the horror of the Holocaust, what is the meaning of the film's title? If you could have changed the title, what would you have called the film? How do the various characters (i.e., the father, the mother, or the five-year-old son) give us their point of view on the story? How are these views similar and different? With whom do you empathize most? Why is the writer/director concerned that you see the story as a fable?

2. In interviews, writer/director/actor Roberto Benigni reported that his film's mixture of humor and Holocaust had stirred up vocal opposition from both Italy's right wing and the left-wing critics at Cannes. Most others found Benigni's risk of marrying comedy and tragedy deeply moving. Perhaps they recognized a common feature of the best humor—it suggests that reality is more than appearances; there is something deeper, more human. Humor points to another world. Do you agree? Why or why not? How does Guido use humor against the reality of the concentration camp? Think of people you have known who, like Guido, act the clown at times. What kind of impact do they have on a group or situation? One viewer wrote on a chat line that *Life Is Beautiful* is neither analytical nor preachy; rather, "viewers are left feeling redeemed and more aware of the love they have in their lives." Would you agree? Why?

3. While comedy is key to the power of *Life Is Beautiful*, Benigni portrays the amazing love and will of the human spirit through other means as well. Think of the characters "Uncle" and "Dora." How do they, in their own ways, portray for the

viewer the dignity and power of our God-given humanity? How does Giosue, in his own way, do the same?

4. As the movie began, so it ends, with a voice-over and the image of a parent with child. As we watch the young Giosue reunite with his mother, shouting of their "victory," the older Giosue says, "This is my story. This is the sacrifice my father made. This was his gift to me." What did you feel as you watched both Dora and Giosue's joyful reunion? Did this story become your story in any way? Why?

Clip Conversations

1. Chapter 5 [11:20–13:30]—"The New Waiter." Guido's uncle is training him to be a waiter, and though humorous at times, it is also quite profound. Why does his uncle use the image of the sunflower when talking of bowing to others? When speaking of service, he says, "You're serving. You're not a servant. Serving is a supreme art. God is the first servant. God serves men, but he's not a servant to men." In your opinion does "Zio" (Uncle) have his theology of serving and of God right? How did Jesus model servanthood? How might you see yourself and others as *servers* not *servants*?

2. Chapters 9 [20:40–25:18] and 15 [47:36–51:13]—"The Superior Race" and "Two Became Three." In the first scene Guido impersonates a school inspector and gives a lecture on "the superior race." In the second scene we see Guido talking to his son about a sign he has seen: "No Jews or dogs allowed." Is he just making light of the situations, or is he turning reality on its head? Why and how? What picture of the real world does he want to give to these students and his son?

3. Chapters 20 [1:05:32–1:09:30] and 25 [1:29:47–1:38:48] —"Learning the Rules" and "For Life." Just enjoy the sheer

creativity of Guido's translation of the camp rules. (Don't miss Giosue's face as he listens.) Also relish the beauty and courage of Guido playing "Belle Nuit" for his wife over the camp loud-speaker while they are separated from each other in the camp. (The piece is from *The Tales of Hoffman*, by Offenback, the opera they went to on their "first date.") Compare Guido's life-giving acts with Dr. Lesser's self-absorption and obsession with riddles. How is Guido's life so much richer than Dr. Lesser's, even though Dr. Lesser is free?

Bonus Material

While not a true story or even based on one, *Life Is Beautiful* is deeply connected to and somewhat inspired by Roberto Benigni's personal life. On the DVD featurette, he says that he poured all his life experience—his thoughts, love, and experiences—into this film. Luigi Benigni, Roberto's father, was a farmer drafted into Mussolini's army. After Italy dropped out of Hitler's coalition, the Nazis captured Luigi in 1943 in Albania. He spent two years in a German labor camp. Years later, when he told his children about his experiences, he told the stories in a humorous way. In a *Salon* interview, Benigni said that his father told the stories as though they were fables, so as not to make the children afraid. "He was protecting us, like I am protecting the son in the movie, because this is the first instinct—to protect the son."

The connections to his personal life continue as Benigni filmed the first half of the film in Arezzo, the town where he grew up. On a trip to Italy in 2000 we stumbled across the town and its memorable square of shops, including his "bookstore," which was actually a photography/stationery shop. The real owner was so kind to us when he heard of our interest in the film that he gave us a personal photo he took of Benigni sitting with little Giorgio Cantarini off set. Lovely—life is beautiful!

Benigni loves riddles and linguistic games, as does his char-acter in the film. As a child he competed successfully in *ot-*

tava rima contests, in which two people debate in the form of eight-line rhymes (watch out rappers and hip-hoppers). He is also known to exchange verbal puzzles with intellects such as Umberto Eco.

One of Benigni's biggest heroes and comedic models is Charlie Chaplin. Like Chaplin, Benigni draws attention to themes through comedy in a way that allows the viewer to empathize rather than become defensive. His performance and even certain scenes in *Life Is Beautiful* echo Chaplin (see DVD featurette for clips of the two actors' similar performances). In honor of Chaplin, the number on Guido's prison uniform is the same number Chaplin's character wore in *The Great Dictator*.

When Benigni approached his wife to take part in the film (she plays Dora), she was hesitant, being fearful of the risk he was taking with the theme and style of the film. Could he really shape a simultaneously hilarious and haunting comedy out of the tragedy of the Holocaust? In what we can only assume was pure Guido style, he won her over, and she is quite proud of how the film can teach us anew. However, Benigni would have to win over other critics also, especially those most profoundly and directly affected by the Holocaust. And for the most part he did. Ben Dworkin, a film reviewer for the *Jewish News*, commended the film. The Anti-Defamation League gave it its Crystal Globe award for illuminating aspects of the human condition and showing that history must not be forgotten. The Jerusalem Film Festival gave the movie its Best Jewish Experience prize. The mayor of Jerusalem also gave Benigni an award for furthering the understanding of Jewish history. Benigni screened the movie at the Simon Wiesenthal Center in Los Angeles and received a standing ovation by viewers. Per Rabbi Marvin Hier, the founder and dean of the center, the film "conquered their hearts." Moreover, their response to the film "meant more to Benigni than that of movie critics."

Life Is Beautiful was nominated for or won numerous awards around the world—Academy Awards nominations as noted above (winning three—Best Actor, Best Foreign

Film, and Best Score), and four Golden Globe nominations (including Best Director and Best Dramatic Picture). Benigni is the first Italian to win an Oscar for Best Actor (two Italian women have won for Best Actress—Anna Magnani in1955 and Sophia Loren in 1966). He is also the first director in fifty years (since Laurence Olivier) to win the Oscar for Best Actor under his own direction. *Life Is Beautiful* is also the first film since *Z* (1969) to be nominated for both Best Picture and Best Foreign Film for the Academy Awards. It also won the Grand Jury Prize at the Cannes Film Festival and swept Italy's David Awards, winning in nine categories. Its budget of $6.5 million, though small in the U.S., was double the average cost for an Italian comedy. Its total box office receipts were over $229 million, with almost $58 million generated by U.S. moviegoers.

Life Is Beautiful, concerned with affirming the human spirit, came to fruition the same year as *Amistad* (movie 2) and speaks to the souls of viewers. This film should be included in every middle school and high school curriculum. Get it for your youth group and have a chat about life!

2. *Amistad*

U.S., 1997
152 Minutes, Feature, Color
Actors: Morgan Freeman, Anthony Hopkins, Djimon Hounsou, Matthew McConaughey, Nigel Hawthorne, Jeremy Northam, Anna Paquin
Director: Steven Spielberg
Screenwriter: David H. Franzoni
Rated: R (violence, mature themes, nudity)
DVD Features: theatrical trailer, "The Making of Amistad," production notes, cast and crew listing

Affirming the Human Spirit
Freedom, Gospel, Inhumanity, Living Our Faith, Sharing Our Faith, Racial Reconciliation
Courage, Hope, Justice, Leadership, Prayer, Repentance

Themes

Cinque (Djimon Hounsou) cries out in the courtroom, "Give us free!" *Amistad* (d. Spielberg, 1997). Photo by Andrew Cooper. Copyright 1997 DreamWorks LLC. All rights reserved.

Synopsis and Theological Reflection

Steven Spielberg is known for such blockbuster movies as *E.T.* and *Jurassic Park*. He has been most honored, however, for *Schindler's List*, his retelling of the story of one man's resistance to the Holocaust. The movie should be seen by all adults and has proven an important contribution to our continuing fight against anti-Semitism.

Now with *Amistad*, Spielberg has again dramatized a historical event of resistance to corporate evil. The film has such symbolic importance for another minority group—African-Americans—that some have questioned Spielberg's right to tell their story. After all, isn't he Jewish? But tell it he does, and the film has moral importance for us all.

The movie dramatizes the story of a group of Africans who rise up against their slave-trading captors on the ship *Amistad* and as a result are brought to trial in a New England court. But that is only one of the stories that this film tells so well. There is the story of slavery, the story of an African who is called Cinque by the Spaniards, the story of Christian abolitionists, the story of two presidents and their own struggles with a nation divided, and even the gospel story. The importance of the historical event may have been the initial reason the movie was made, but the interplay of its various stories is the reason you should see it.

Let's take one story at a time and start where the film opens. In 1839, fifty-three Africans threw off their chains on board the Spanish slave ship *Amistad*, killed most of the crew, and tried to force two of the survivors to sail them home to Africa. Eventually captured by the U.S. Navy because their guides had instead sailed them along the eastern seaboard of the U.S., the Africans and their charismatic leader, Cinque, were forced to go through a series of complicated legal proceedings as their fate became a focal point for the antislavery movement. Former President John Quincy Adams ultimately pleaded the case for their freedom before the U.S. Supreme Court. Yes, Spielberg has certainly brought the skill (and glitz!) of Hollywood to this historical re-creation, and critics may argue minor details (e.g., Morgan Freeman's abolitionist character is fictitious; Adams's speech is not the original words). But the power of this story to name our national sins is evident to all who have eyes to see.

While this *historical story* shows the inhumanity of humankind (as the Africans are treated as mere property) and the degradation of slavery for both slave and slave owner, it is only when the *human story* of Cinque unfolds that the movie becomes powerfully affecting. The screenwriter and director know well the importance of making a story personal. They have President John Quincy Adams, when pressed by the black abolitionist to take the case, ask, "But what is their story, Mr. Joadson?" He realizes that though the trial is at one level about laws and property, it is in reality about people—Africans who have suffered unjustly.

Their story needs to be told. From this point on the abolitionist and young lawyer defending the Africans press Cinque to tell his story. And tell it he does. It is this "story within the story" that proves riveting. We see Cinque's family in Africa. We see his kidnapping and sale into slavery. We see the horrifying voyage to Cuba and the atrocities inflicted on these people. (Note: The violence is too graphic for young children.) We see the dignity, intellect, passion, and grief of a fellow human being. And then we weep for the shame of slavery—our shame and our country's shame. The power of this human story is the power to convict and to call out for repentance.

Yet a third story is present in the movie—the *gospel story*. Some reviewers have questioned this insertion, but the Christian presence in opposing slavery is historically accurate. We see the Christian abolitionists being portrayed at times humorously, at other times cynically, but at still other times kindly. Never has a more beautiful telling of the gospel story been in film as when one of the Africans tells *the* Story to Cinque using only the illustrations from the Bible a Christian abolitionist had given him. He cannot read the English words, but the pictures tell it all and bring hope. From the slaves in Egypt crying out to the God of Salvation, to the baby Jesus' birth, to his teaching and healing, to the cross and then the resurrection, we hear the Good News in all its simplicity and power. Although the African storyteller is fearful that they will be killed, he can point to Christ rising into the heavens and believe that "where we'll go if we die doesn't look so bad." The power of the Story brings hope and freedom.

Like *Schindler's List*, *Amistad* does not simply portray the dehumanization caused by racial bigotry, though it does do that movingly and convincingly. It also reveals human goodness even within evil systems, hope within horror. How is such hope possible? Partly, it rises up from the indomitable human spirit. At his trial, Cinque cries out for us all, "Give us . . . us free!" But Spielberg hints at something more. There is also God's Spirit at work in and through us.

Dialogue Texts

So God created humankind in his image.

Genesis 1:27a

Afterward Moses and Aaron went to Pharaoh and said, "Thus says the LORD, the God of Israel, 'Let my people go, so that they may celebrate a festival to me in the wilderness.'"

Exodus 5:1

For the LORD your God is God of gods . . . who executes justice for the orphan and the widow, and who loves the strangers, providing them food and clothing. You shall also love the stranger, for you were strangers in the land of Egypt.

Deuteronomy 10:17–19

If you see in a province the oppression of the poor and the violation of justice and right, do not be amazed at the matter; for the high official is watched by a higher, and there are yet higher ones over them.

Ecclesiastes 5:8

There is no longer Jew or Greek, there is no longer slave or free, there is no longer male and female; for all of you are one in Christ Jesus.

Galatians 3:28

Discussion Questions

1. Whenever a film is made about a historical event, there are distortions—some events are telescoped, some characters are combined or even left out, and some scenes are fictionally created. Such is the case with *Amistad* (e.g., Congregational churches raised funds and clothing for the Africans as well as provided for their defense in court, and Theodore Joadson [Morgan Freeman] is a composite character, while the famous

abolitionist William Lloyd Garrison was left out). Nonetheless, the film does a great service in bringing the *Amistad* event and trials to the attention of many viewers. This long-buried history comes alive and makes us think about the issues and the people involved. Had you ever read about or studied this event in our country's history? Why or why not? What issues did the film raise for you? Where does your life today fit into this story of slavery, freedom, courage, and the dignity of the human being?

2. In the film there are many occasions for cultural misunderstanding between the whites and the Africans. Which ones can you remember? (Hints: The black coachman entering the territory of different tribes in the prison; Cinque's and Baldwin's use of words—"should" versus "either you do what you say, or you don't"; views on death and burial.) One in particular is perhaps exaggerated by Hollywood's bias. How do the Africans first see Christians in the film? What are their impressions of these people? How did the portrayal of Christians throughout the film make you feel, even when it was true (e.g., a priest giving absolution to slaves and blessing them as they boarded the slave ship)? As Christians, how do we need to confess the sins of the church with regard to slavery?

3. Early on the trial becomes one of property rights rather than human rights. However, Roger Baldwin, the lawyer for the Africans, and the abolitionists disagree on this issue. The abolitionists see human beings; Baldwin and the courts see them as slaves—chattel, property—to be argued over. How does Baldwin change over time through the course of the trials and through his relationship with Cinque? How is he surprised and impressed by Cinque's courage, leadership, and intellectual capabilities (e.g., helping to prepare their defense before the Supreme Court)? How do Baldwin and Cinque view each other as they say goodbye after the Supreme Court hearing?

Clip Conversations

1. Chapter 9 [1:00:10–1:08:50]—"Find Out Who They Are. . . ." After finding out that the judge has been removed and the case must be tried again, Theodore Joadson returns to President Adams. He asks for assistance, advice, anything that might help their case. Adams tells Joadson that in the courtroom the one that tells the best story wins. He then asks him, "What is their story?" He continues, "You have proven that you know what they are; they are Africans. Congratulations. What you don't know and, as far as I can tell, haven't bothered in the least to discover is *who* they are. Right?" What happens because of this conversation? What are some of the things we do or categories we use today that turn people into things rather than maintain their dignity as human beings, created in the image of God?

2. Chapter 13 [1:31:55–1:40:52]—"Give Us . . . Us Free." Cinque has given his testimony of the horrible journey he has made from his home to the courtroom. As he listens to rebuttals and others' testimony, he is overwhelmed with emotion and blurts out his first words in English, "Give us . . . us free." How did various people in the courtroom react—Baldwin, the African sailor, whites, and blacks? How did you feel when you heard him speak these words? This scene also includes Yamba's telling of the gospel story through the pictures in the Bible he was given by the Christians. It is juxtaposed with the judge's entry into a Catholic church to pray for his decision in the courtroom. How did the simple telling of the Good News affect you? What of the judge's faith in the face of the government's pressure and his own desire for a successful career? Did you empathize with him? How would you have responded in this situation?

3. Chapters 20 [2:08:02–2:13:50] and 21 [2:13:50–2:18:45] —"The Supreme Court" and "The Hero." Adams's ten-minute speech about freedom and human values is stunning (though

constructed by the screenwriter and not his actual words). Adams reads from an article by John C. Calhoun, who uses the Bible to argue the case for slavery. How would you debate Calhoun, even using the Genesis account to which he alludes? How does Adams use what he has learned from Cinque in his argument? What does he mean when he says that "who we are is who we were"? How do we as Christians stand on the shoulders of the faithful who have gone before us? How can we continue to learn from these saints and their successes and failures? What can we learn from the Christian abolitionists about living and sharing our faith?

Bonus Material

If you want to read more about this event, there are several nonfictional and fictional accounts of the *Amistad* Africans. In addition, the United Church of Christ reprinted a small book titled *Amistad: The Slave Uprising Aboard the Spanish Schooner*, by Helen Kromer.[11] As was noted above, some of the history was not captured in the film nor even portrayed correctly. Quakers opposed slavery early. Presbyterian Elijah Parish Lovejoy was martyred as an abolitionist. However, it was the Congregationalists who provided the strongest and most widespread support for the abolitionist movement and who were involved in the *Amistad* trials.

Today's Congregationalists—the United Church of Christ (UCC)—were pleased with the event being brought to people's attention, but they were dismayed with some of the distortions. In particular, the portrayal of Lewis Tappan as thinking the Africans would be better as martyrs for the cause is vehemently refuted by the UCC. In addition, the story of social justice did not end with the trials. The return passage for the freed Africans was paid for by funds raised by the churches and the *Amistad* Committee, not by the federal government. Even after the Civil War, this committee became part of the American Missionary

Association, which helped to found schools and colleges for
freed slaves.

As is the custom in Hollywood, each year the Directors Guild
of America nominates five from within its ranks for Outstanding
Director. The five directors are honored at the D.G.A. Theater,
and each one is allowed to show their favorite scene from their
movie. In 1998 Steven Spielberg was nominated for *Amistad*,
and he chose to show the scene in which Yamba tells Cinque
the gospel story from pictures in the Bible.

Amistad was nominated for numerous awards, including four
Academy Awards and four Golden Globes (including Best Director and Best Dramatic Picture). Its total box office receipts were
over $68 million. Though not a picture for small children, this film
should be included in every middle school and high school curriculum. If it isn't, get it for your youth group and spend time talking
with kids about this very important part of our shared history.

3. *No Man's Land*

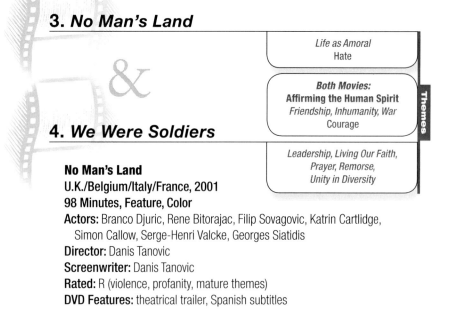

Life as Amoral
Hate

Both Movies:
Affirming the Human Spirit
Friendship, Inhumanity, War
Courage

Themes

4. *We Were Soldiers*

Leadership, Living Our Faith,
Prayer, Remorse,
Unity in Diversity

No Man's Land
U.K./Belgium/Italy/France, 2001
98 Minutes, Feature, Color
Actors: Branco Djuric, Rene Bitorajac, Filip Sovagovic, Katrin Cartlidge,
    Simon Callow, Serge-Henri Valcke, Georges Siatidis
Director: Danis Tanovic
Screenwriter: Danis Tanovic
Rated: R (violence, profanity, mature themes)
DVD Features: theatrical trailer, Spanish subtitles

We Were Soldiers
U.S., 2002
137 Minutes, Feature, Color
Actors: Mel Gibson, Madeleine Stowe, Sam Elliott, Greg Kinnear, Chris
  Klein, Barry Pepper, Ryan Hurst, Don Duong
Director: Randall Wallace
Screenwriter: Randall Wallace
Based on the Book: *We Were Soldiers Once . . . and Young: Ia
  Drang—the Battle That Changed the War in Vietnam,* by Harold G.
  Moore and Joseph L. Galloway
Rated: R (extensive graphic violence, profanity, mature themes)
DVD Features: commentary by director/writer Randall Wallace,
  "Getting it Right" —behind the scenes of *We Were Soldiers,* ten
  deleted scenes with director's commentary

Synopsis and Theological Reflection

Given recent world events, two movies have helped us begin
sorting out our disparate thoughts and feelings about war. One
comes from a Bosnian filmmaker who actually spent months
in the Balkan conflict. The other one comes from a Los Angeles
filmmaker, inspired by the real-life story of Lt. Col. Hal Moore's
experience in the Vietnam War.

No Man's Land

The first, titled *No Man's Land,* won the 2003 Golden Globe
and Academy Award for Best Foreign Film. As the movie begins,
a Bosnian platoon is lost in the night fog trying to find the Serb
front line. When morning dawns they find themselves literally
on top of it. All are slaughtered except for Ciki, who makes it
with his half-dead compatriot (Cera) to a trench in "no man's
land." Two Serbian soldiers are sent out to finish off the possible
survivors. They find Cera, who by now looks dead. For amuse-
ment and spite, one of the soldiers plants an American-made
"bouncing mine" under the corpse. Once his compatriots collect
his body, the mine will pop into the air and blow up everything

Ciki (Branco Djuric) and Nino (Rene Bitorajac) try to calm Cera (Filip Sovagovic),
who is lying on a land mine. *No Man's Land* (d. Tanovic, 2001). Copyright 2001
United Artists. All rights reserved.

in its vicinity. Ciki, hiding in a bunker, kills this soldier and
wounds the other, Nino—a naïve, untrained recruit.

Here the story really begins. We see three men trapped by
history, their emotions (mostly hate), and the absurdity of war
in "no man's land." As Ciki and Nino, once neighbors who dated
the same young woman, argue about whose fault the war is,
Cera awakes from what was only an unconscious state. They
scream for him not to move or they will all die. Both sides soon
become aware of these soldiers' plight. UN troops come charg-
ing in on a white tank, trying to diffuse the situation. Then the
press gets wind of it all, and they become the final partner in
this tragicomedy.

Sadly funny, *No Man's Land* presents the audience with a
grim, realistic view of war, even without the big bloody battle
scenes so typical of Hollywood. This film will stun you, but it
will also make you laugh. There are no heroes in this film (well,
perhaps one, French Sergeant Marchant), mostly victims. You

find yourself not knowing whom you pity (or despise) more: the soldiers trapped in the trench; Colonel Soft, the senior UN official; or Jane Livingston, the anything-to-get-a-story journalist. And you ask yourself, "Does anyone care about the human beings in that trench?"

One person who does care is Danis Tanovic, the screenwriter/director, who had previously filmed for the Bosnian Army archive three hundred hours of frontline footage while under siege in Sarajevo from 1992 through 1994. In *No Man's Land* he combines hauntingly real characters and war's dark humor with his passionate concern for the individuals caught in war's grip. The result is an antiwar film like no other; one that shows the viewer that there is no simple answer to deeply rooted hatred. Here is a message that we should all remember as our government attempts to root out terrorism around the world, but most particularly as we think about the Middle East and Iraq.

We Were Soldiers

From Randall Wallace (screenwriter of *Braveheart* and an engaging Christian) comes a completely different kind of war film, *We Were Soldiers*. Wallace found the book, *We Were Soldiers Once . . . and Young*, by Lt. General Harold G. Moore (Ret.) and Joseph L. Galloway, in a used bookstore and was gripped by its human perspective on the Vietnam War. Basically it is the story of the first major American battle in Vietnam, late in 1965. Moore led the men of the First Battalion of the Seventh Calvary (four hundred troops) into the Ia Drang Valley, known as the "Valley of Death." They were surrounded by two thousand North Vietnamese troops. Moore and his men suffered heavy casualties, even as they killed many more North Vietnamese. It was a painful victory, as expressed in Moore's words to the war reporter, Joe Galloway: "I'll never forgive myself . . . that my men . . . that my men died and I didn't."

Lt. Col. Hal Moore (Mel Gibson) says bedtime prayers with his children. *We Were Soldiers* (d. Wallace, 2002). Copyright 2002 Paramount Pictures. All rights reserved.

The film captures the perspective not only of the charismatic leader, Lt. Col. Hal Moore (a Harvard graduate in international relations, Moore is a family man who is a devout Catholic with an earthy spirituality that will make you smile), but also of his men and their wives and the perspective of the North Vietnamese leaders. The film shows war as horrendous and heartless to all three groups. It is not a political message about the war, it is about men and women trying to survive and, in their efforts, showing the best and the worst of humanity. In the end, they persevered with great courage not for country or cause but for their friends.

The film doesn't glorify the carnage of war, but it does raise up the honor and decency of those who fight. It also refuses to demonize the North Vietnamese. They may be the "enemy," but that doesn't necessarily mean they are evil. Wallace reminds us that everyone in war is a human being.

Our country's leaders continue to face world-altering decisions. As faithful Christians we must not cease praying for them.

But we must, ourselves, also wrestle with the question of war. If, as the preacher of Ecclesiastes states, there is a time for war, we cannot be arrogant in thinking we know exactly how, when, or where. For he also states in that same breath that there is a time for peace (Eccles. 3:8). Moreover, as these movies remind us so eloquently, the "enemy," like us, are created in the image of God (Gen. 1:27).

Dialogue Texts

The nations have sunk in the pit that they made; in the net that they hid has their own foot been caught.

Psalm 9:15

Hatred stirs up strife, but love covers all offenses.

Proverbs 10:12

He shall judge between the nations, and shall arbitrate for many peoples; they shall beat their swords into plowshares, and their spears into pruning hooks; nation shall not lift up sword against nation, neither shall they learn war any more.

Isaiah 2:4

Because you cherished an ancient enmity, and gave over the people of Israel to the power of the sword at the time of their calamity, at the time of their final punishment; therefore, as I live, says the Lord GOD, I will prepare you for blood, and blood shall pursue you; since you did not hate bloodshed, bloodshed shall pursue you.

Ezekiel 35:5–6

Beat your plowshares into swords, and your pruning hooks into spears; let the weakling say, "I am a warrior."

Joel 3:10

But I say to you, Do not resist an evildoer. But if anyone strikes you on the right cheek, turn the other also. . . . You have heard that it was said, "You shall love your neighbor and hate your enemy." But I say to you, Love your enemies and pray for those who persecute you.

Matthew 5:39, 43–44

Bless those who persecute you; bless and do not curse them. . . . Do not repay anyone evil for evil, but take thought for what is noble in the sight of all. If it is possible, so far as it depends on you, live peaceably with all. . . . No, "if your enemies are hungry, feed them; if they are thirsty, give them something to drink. . . ." Do not be overcome by evil, but overcome evil with good.

Romans 12:14, 17–18, 20–21

Discussion Questions

Combo Questions

1. Both *No Man's Land* and *We Were Soldiers* belong to the war movie genre. However, both films, in different ways, turn the type on its head. The first film shows very little fighting and blood but quite graphically shows the absurdity of hatred and war. The second film shows the fighting and blood of battles but also spends time showing the viewer the emotional battles the wives fought back home. *No Man's Land* presents mostly enemies who become victims and few heroes, while *We Were Soldiers* portrays many heroes yet doesn't demonize the enemy. If you had to describe the films, what would you say and why? Then, in what ways are the movies similar or different in how they portray war? What themes do they have in common? How do they portray heroes? How and why is humor used in each film? Which film would you consider the better film and why?

2. From whose perspective do we *primarily* see/experience war in each of the films—politicians, the media, governments and their armies, the soldiers in the field/trenches, or family

members? How are the other perspectives presented? Do you think the struggles of the various participants were portrayed with honesty? Why is it that death often puts perspective on our relationships with loved ones? (Think of the characters of Hal Moore, Jack Geoghegan, or Cera lying on a mine staring at the sky.) What new insights came to you through these films about the people who have to fight in wars?

3. It has been said that American films always need a happy, hopeful, or at least a resolved ending, while films from Europe often are less victorious or even hopeful in their conclusions. Compare the endings of both films. Do the endings fit this generalization? Why do you think that is? How did the endings work in their respective films? Did they have integrity? As a viewer did you feel satisfied, challenged, or cheated? From your perspective, do these films increase understanding about war and its effects? How do these films impact the way you think about the U.S. wars in Afghanistan and Iraq or the longstanding conflict in the Middle East or Northern Ireland?

4. Take a look at the dialogue texts above and put each one into conversation with one or both films. Persons of faith throughout the history of the church have developed different theories of war and the roles Christians might play in such conflicts. What basic theology of war could you begin to articulate by understanding these texts and putting them into conversation with the films?

Clip Conversations

No Man's Land

1. Chapter 5 [27:19–30:17]—"War of Words." Ciki and Nino, enemies trapped in the trench, argue about the war in which they are involved. What strikes you about their respective arguments, experiences, and questions? Why is the question of

who started the war so important to them? Why does it seem almost humorous to the viewer? Why does the writer/director use humor here and throughout the movie? How is the question resolved in this scene and in the next chapter (with the gun in Nino's hands)? By the end of the film, does the question matter to either of these characters or to the other players in this tragicomedy?

2. Chapter 11 [56:30–1:06:02]—"*Global News* Knows." As if the conflict doesn't have enough antagonists, UN officers and soldiers and international reporters enter the fray. How does the director present these "war participants"? (See also chapter 9 [48:50–50:04]—"Nothing I Can Do.") In this scene we hear French Sergeant Marchand explain why he is involved and what he would do if he could. Jane Livingstone, the reporter, challenges his neutrality, to which he responds, "You can't be neutral facing murder. Doing nothing to stop it is taking sides." Would you agree? In your view, what situations justify force? How might Christians respond to situations of injustice and oppression without using force?

3. Chapters 15 [1:22:12–1:31:27] and 16 [1:31:27–1:32:50] —"Pandemonium and Clean-Up" and "Trenches/Credits." Review the events and actors of this penultimate scene. Note how each character deals with what is happening (e.g., the mine expert sits in the trench next to Cera, not able to look him in the face; Ciki explodes with rage toward all those around him, asking the "vultures" [reporters], "Does our misery pay well?"). Finally, as everyone drives off, a photographer asks Jane, "You sure you don't want me to film the trench?" She replies, "No, a trench is a trench; they're all the same." What is the director saying to the viewer about the nature of war? Are all wars the same? Are all victims just casualties? Is Col. Soft right when he says to Marchand, "I know what you're thinking, Sergeant. It wouldn't make any difference, you know. It wouldn't change anything"? As night falls, the viewer is left with a view of Cera

from above. What did you feel when you realized how this film was going to end?

We Were Soldiers

1. Chapter 2 [6:52–12:57]—"Air Cavalry." Can you tell what Hal Moore's philosophy of leadership is from these scenes? How does he demonstrate it here and throughout the movie? (Sometimes it's the little things.) What sorts of things does he say and do to win the respect of his platoon and others? How does he take advantage of teachable moments? How does he mentor young leaders? Take him out of the army context for a moment; what might you learn from his leadership style for your context? (Asking the same questions about Lt. Col. Moore's wife and her leadership and ministry to the other wives is also a valuable exercise.)

2. Chapters 3 [12:57–19:24] and 4 [19:24–24:45]—"Family Prayer" and "A Soldier and a Father." Most war movies don't have much prayer in them. This film has three relatively long portrayals of prayer (see also chapter 13 [1:20:52–1:28:22] —"Words For the Dead"). What did you think about these portrayals? Were you offended or were you drawn into the lives of the characters? Were they included for purely humorous or emotional impact, or were they included to portray something very positive about faith and prayer? How might those outside the church view these scenes? How might you start a conversation about prayer using these scenes? (Note: Lt. Col. Moore is a very devout Catholic. In addition, Mel Gibson and Randall Wallace are persons of faith, from Catholic and Protestant traditions respectively.)

3. Chapter 6 [32:40–41:23]—"We Are All Americans." Hal Moore gives a speech to his battalion before their deployment. What struck you about what he said? How is his speech like a sermon? What biblical images does he use? How is what he said

even more important today as our armed forces span the globe? How are his words relevant to our church and world today?

4. Chapter 18 [1:59:00–3:08:24]—"Aftermath." The battle is over. Fresh soldiers arrive; Moore's battalion can leave. Reporters swarm around Joe Galloway and Lt. Col. Moore. Listen to their questions. How are they similar to or different from the reporters' questions in *No Man's Land*? Both men, numb, escape their questions and find each other. How do Moore's words to Galloway and his tears reflect the kind of leader he is? Compare him to Col. Soft in *No Man's Land*. The Vietnamese commander surveys the battlefield with similar remorse. What message does the movie ultimately give about war and its warriors?

Bonus Material

No Man's Land

Danis Tanovic, the screenwriter and director of *No Man's Land*, was studying film and theater in Sarajevo when the war between Serbia and Bosnia started. He decided to use his camera on the front lines, shooting several documentaries. Though *No Man's Land* is Danis Tanovic's debut feature film, his work as a documentarian is evident throughout the film. He lets us see everything, especially the sky and the land—hills covered with flowers, birds, and insects. Even the background sound is filled with the buzzing of bugs.

Tanovic had only thirty-six days to shoot his film, which turned out to be a minor war in itself. He filmed mostly in Slovenia, where he had ten days of rain. Lightning hit the crew, with three men ending up in the hospital. An assistant drove a truckload of props into a canyon. On one day the assistant costumer had a heart attack and Tanovic's uncle died. Like the pessimist about which the Bosnian soldier jokes in the opening scene of the film, Tanovic thought that things couldn't get any worse. Fortunately, other than the director, the cast and crew were quite seasoned filmmakers, especially the director of photography, Walther Vanden Ende (*Toto the Hero* and *Farinelli*). So the film was shot despite the setbacks. Then Tanovic cut the film in an amazing twelve days. Finally, being an accomplished composer, he also composed the soundtrack, keeping the use of music to a minimum. (He was quoted as saying, "I don't think you need violins to make people cry. If you need that, then you're in deep trouble.")

Minimalism is Tanovic's style in depicting violence as well. His goal was to make an antiwar film, so he wanted to focus on the human aspect, not the killing and destruction. In describing his intention he said, "War is a state of mind, and I wanted the audience to understand that. War is not only grenades and bullets and bombs. When war is finished, war continues in your head for a long time." He also wanted to show that neutrality in such times doesn't exist; everyone is culpable at some point. For an example, he points to the fact that Bosnia doesn't even make mines, yet there are two million of them there. He notes that America does make mines, but none are present in the U.S. His hope is that the film can show just how small our world is by connecting us to the human beings fighting on the other side of the globe and that we as world neighbors can learn how to bring love, not hate, into such conflicts so that neither side is destroyed.

No Man's Land was nominated for forty awards in addition to those mentioned above. It won the Best Screenplay award at the Cannes Film Festival and also took home awards from Italy and Germany as well as from the European Film Academy. Its budget was roughly $2 million, and its worldwide box office receipts were almost $4 million, with $1 million coming from theaters in the U.S. Some critics think that the film did not attract viewers in the U.S. because the film opened just as our country was launching military action in Afghanistan. Regardless of the receipts, the film's 2002 Oscar helped to fuel a new energy in filmmaking in Bosnia. In 2002–2003, three additional films were made, which is more than in the twelve years previous.

We Were Soldiers

It has been argued by some critics that *We Were Soldiers* is a film that is pro-soldier but, in the process, antiwar also. Whether Randall Wallace, the screenwriter and director, or retired Lt. General Hal Moore would agree is debatable. However, if both men are not antiwar pacifists, neither are they hawks looking for battles in which to engage. The following statement by Hal Moore starts the DVD featurette, "Getting It Right": "American soldiers in battle don't fight for what some president says on TV. They don't fight for mom, apple pie, the American flag. . . . They fight for one another."

Here you have the reason that both men worked to make this film. They wanted to show the human face of war. Moore served as a consultant to the film and was present for much of the shooting to ensure that not only technical military aspects were correct but that the stories of real men would be told with dignity. Wallace, not having been a soldier, did as much as he could to get into the skin of soldiers. He went through Ranger School and made his actors go through two weeks of training at Fort Benning. He found veterans to work on the film. He held a chapel event the night before shooting started and invited the real soldiers to share with the cast and crew. He even cast his own son in the role of the French bugler who is shot in the head by a Vietnamese soldier in the opening scene. (Later he said that it was a very hard scene for him, "but I needed it to understand that sons died in Vietnam.")

While most events in the film actually happened, Wallace did create some scenes in order to better tell the story. Often he contacted the people involved or their survivors to get ideas consistent with the person's character. One such scene is the chapel scene between Jack Geoghegan and Hal Moore. Wallace consulted Geoghegan's wife because he wanted to give the viewer some idea of this man's Christian commitment.

Other scenes were filmed exactly as Moore or Galloway reported them. Moore's little daughter actually did ask him what war is the night before he left for Vietnam. He really did walk the perimeter during the night to encourage his men. Major Bruce Crandall really did keep flying the wounded out because the medivac helicopters couldn't get in. (Crandall also served as a technical consultant on the film.) Julie Moore actually had a taxi drive up to her door with a telegram, and from then on she delivered the telegrams to the families personally. Soldiers reported that Moore sat with the dead on the battlefield, weeping and wondering how he could have prevented their deaths.

Before a screening of the film, Wallace talked of how he learned a lot about leadership by observing Moore and talking with those who served under him. "Push the power down" was how Wallace described it, and he tried to use that same philosophy while making the film. He wanted a team working together for the best possible outcome. He also followed Moore's example of respecting the humanity and dignity of the enemy. Wallace said that he wanted to show that "soldiers are human beings—on both sides." Don Dwong, per Wallace, the "Mel Gibson" of Vietnam, was chosen to play the Vietnamese Lt. Colonel. When the film came out, he was briefly put under house arrest by a disgruntled Vietnamese government.

We Were Soldiers was nominated for two minor awards—for sound and stunts. Its budget was $75 million, and its worldwide box office receipts were almost $110 million, with $78 million coming from theaters in the U.S. Though we're sure that Wallace (and Mel Gibson, who also coproduced the film) is not averse to making money or winning awards, that's not why he made the film. As he said at the screening, "If a story doesn't tear at my soul, if it doesn't move me, if I don't love it, how can I shoot it?"

Beauty, Imagination, and Creativity

5. *Spirited Away*

U.S., 2002
Sen to Chihiro no Kamikakushi, Japan,
   2001 (original release)
124 Minutes, Animated, Color
Voices: Daveigh Chase, Suzanne Pleshette,
   Jason Marsden, Susan Egan,
   David Ogden Stiers, Lauren Holly, John Ratzenberger
Director: Hayao Miyazaki
Screenwriter: Hayao Miyazaki
Rated: PG (scary moments, harsh comments, but appropriate for
   children over age seven)
DVD Features: introduction by John Lasseter, "*The Art of Spirited
   Away,*" "*Behind the Microphone,*" select storyboard-to-scene
   comparison, "*The Making of Spirited Away,*" original Japanese trailers

Themes

Beauty, Imagination, Creativity
*Caring for Creation, Loneliness,
Sacrificial Love*
Affirming the Human Spirit,
Courage, Family,
Friendship, Gluttony, Greed,
Identity, Kindness, Pollution,
Sin, Wonder

Synopsis and Theological Reflection

When I (Cathy) was watching TV as an eight-year-old, I
stumbled onto the story of *Alice in Wonderland*—a pretty but
whiney little girl accidentally embarks on a sometimes frightening journey through a fantastical world. This chance encounter
was only the first of many imaginative journeys I have taken to
other worlds throughout my life—*The Arabian Nights, Grimm's
Fairy Tales, The Iliad, The Hobbit, A Wrinkle in Time, The Chronicles
of Narnia,* and even some of the Harry Potter tales, to name a
few. Late in 2002, I again stumbled into another world. Curious about Japanese animation ("anime"), Rob and I went to
see *Spirited Away*—the story of a pretty but whiney little girl
who accidentally embarks on a sometimes frightening journey

Chihiro (voice of Daveigh Chase) comforts No Face. Miyazaki's *Spirited Away* (d. Miyazaki, 2002). Copyright 2002 Nibariki TGNDDTM. All rights reserved.

through a fantastical world. This was an East meets West experience—Studio Ghibli meets Disney/Pixar. But it was so much more that we want to commend this movie for your viewing.

Writing about a film like *Spirited Away* is tricky. Describing plot line, characters, specific scenes, and adventures can only go so far for those who haven't experienced a Hayao Miyazaki film. He is one of Japan's, and arguably the world's, foremost animators. So indulge us if this review feels more like our reminiscence of being swept away by the sheer beauty of a vibrant, colorful world than a critical reflection on a significant movie.

The "Alice" of our tale is a ten-year-old girl named Chihiro. She is moving from the city to the suburbs with her family, and she is not at all happy about the disruption to her life. She complains, sulks, and literally drags her feet when her parents stumble upon an abandoned theme park and decide to explore. While there, she is separated from her parents, who are soon turned into pigs after eating food left for others. But for whom was it intended, she wonders. As night falls she begins to see the answer to her question, as the theme park becomes a bathhouse—a resort of sorts for spirits to rest and rejuvenate. Like Alice tumbling down the rabbit hole, Chihiro finds herself in a strange world with its own rules. It, too, is ruled by a cranky queen, Yubaba. Chihiro must not only summon the courage to fend for herself in this place but also figure out a way to save her parents and return to the human world before she loses her sense of identity.

Basically this story is a *hero myth*. Our heroine is thrown into adventure, overcomes obstacles with the aid of friends, and ends up returning home as a changed person. Important universal lessons of love, courage, kindness, forgiveness, and sacrifice are learned along the way. In fact, all of the central characters have both a light and dark side, so we see their journeys also. Likewise, the viewer is invited to personally consider some of the issues facing the characters: duty, fear, entitlement, selfishness, gluttony, greed, and even treatment of the environment. Animated spirits give shape to these issues in new ways.

This film is the work of human imagination, just like the stories of Homer. In both these works there are elements of a larger worldview to which Christians might take exception, but there is also much to marvel at as creatures of a creative God. Any Christian reader capable of enjoying *The Iliad* the way it was intended to be enjoyed, as a story, can also enjoy or, better, sit in wonder at the imaginative force of the story and the pictures Miyazaki creates for the screen. Some of our favorites are: prickly but lovable six-armed Kamaji looking like a hip revolutionary commanding scurrying little balls of enchanted soot that take on a life of their own; spirits of all shapes, colors, and sizes—our favorite was the Stink spirit; a glittering, ribbon-like dragon floating across the sky; a lamppost that hops along on a gloved hand; and the incredible beauty and color of every background flower, tree, mountain, or sky.

As with any film, not all critics and viewers were as moved by this film as we were. Some Christian reviewers were put off by the movie's pseudoanimistic leanings—seeing gods and spirits in all things—but others, while noting this caution, could still praise the beauty of the film. Other viewers had trouble with the film because it is so different from our Western animation, especially à la Disney. The style is more painterly and invites the viewer to enter into a fine art canvas. Though extremely funny at points due to the quirkiness of the characters, the film is never jokey or cartoonish. While our heroine is on an adventure, action does not drive the film to frenzy. In fact, Miyazaki allows the film to have silences and reflection, which provide rest notes between more exuberant action or even the sometimes grotesque characters.

While the story may be about a ten-year-old girl, it resonates with viewers of all ages (though it probably is too intense for very young children). Roger Ebert called this movie "one of the best films of 2002." That was certainly the feeling at the Berlin Film Festival, where *Spirited Away* became the first animated film in the event's fifty-year history to win the top prize, the Golden Bear. It also won the Oscar for Best Animated Feature. But regardless of the awards, we feel that Miyazaki stands firmly in that wondrous tradition of gifted creators. Perhaps in seeing and experiencing the best of human creativity and imagination, we see and experience glimmers of the divine Animator.

Dialogue Texts

The LORD spoke to Moses: See, I have called by name Bezalel son of Uri son of Hur, of the tribe of Judah: and I have filled him with divine spirit, with ability, intelligence, and knowledge in every kind of craft, to devise artistic designs, to work in gold, silver, and bronze, in cutting stones for setting, and in carving wood, in every kind of craft.

Exodus 31:1–5

When I look at your heavens, the work of your fingers, the moon and the stars that you have established; what are human beings that you are mindful of them, mortals that you care for them? Yet you have made them a little lower than God, and crowned them with glory and honor.

Psalm 8:3–5

When he made firm the skies above, when he established the
fountains of the deep, when he assigned to the sea its limit, so
that the waters might not transgress his command, when he
marked out the foundations of the earth, then I was beside him,
like a master worker; and I was daily his delight, rejoicing before
him always, rejoicing in his inhabited world and delighting in
the human race.

Proverbs 8:28–31

The LORD God took the man and put him in the Garden of Eden
to work it and take care of it.

Genesis 2:15 NIV

Discussion Questions

1. Our heroine, Chihiro, begins her adventure moping in the
backseat of her family's car as they drive to their new home.
Compare her attitude at the beginning of the film to her attitude
at the end. How has she changed? What has she learned along
the way? What events or characters (friendly or not) helped her
to change? What things did you as a viewer learn with regard
to facing change or new/strange twists in your life?

2. Throughout the film the viewer is graphically confronted
with the sins of gluttony and greed (e.g., Chihiro's parents
gobbling food until they turn into pigs; obese, demanding,
self-centered clients; Yubaba's stinginess toward her clients
and staff; workers at the bathhouse groveling for tips). What
do you think the director is saying to Japanese society or
Western cultures about our materialistic quest? Was there
one scene in particular that captured the reality of your own
greed or gluttony?

3. Repeatedly the theme of self-identity—knowing your
name or remembering who you are—is addressed. How does
Chihiro regain her identity and help Haku and her parents do

the same? How does this remembering open the doors for all of these characters to find their real identities and return home? How are things so important to us—remembering, identity, and home—linked together? (Think, for example, of the Exodus story. How were these things linked together for the Israelites?) Did this film speak to you about your own identity and home?

4. Yubaba controls her workers by taking their names and giving them new ones, while her twin sister, Zeniba, reminds Chihiro, "Nothing that happens is ever forgotten, even if you can't remember it." What might the director be pointing to as he gives us twin sisters with such different ways of relating to others? Have you ever felt like your evil twin was getting the better of you?

Clip Conversations

1. Chapter 6 [51:31–1:06:35]—"We Have an Intruder." A stink spirit comes to the bathhouse. Yubaba and her staff cringe and keep their distance as Chihiro is forced to bathe the spirit in the big tub. What did you feel as you watched Chihiro? How has she changed even at this point in the film? How does she push through her own revulsion to help someone so strange to her? But who is this spirit really? What has happened to him to make him ugly? Did Miyazaki's animation help you see pollution in a new way?

2. Chapters 8 [1:16:35–1:24:50] and 9 [1:24:50–1:31:10]—"A Strange Visit to the Nursery" and "The Golden Seal." After finding Haku injured and bleeding, Chihiro musters the courage to enter Yubaba's flat seeking a remedy. She meets Yubaba's baby (who is afraid to leave his nursery for fear of germs) and Zeniba (Yubaba's twin sister). Then she must struggle with a dragon (actually Haku with a spell on him). What newly found traits

does Chihiro demonstrate to these characters? According to Kamaji (and also later Zeniba), what is the basis of her developing characteristics? How does Chihiro's transformation echo St. Paul's words in 1 Corinthians 13?

3. Chapter 10 [1:31:10–1:37:40]—"A Monster Called 'No Face.'" A lonely spirit entices workers with gold and eats everything in sight but still can't fill his emptiness. He confesses his loneliness to Chihiro and admits that he needs her. She feeds him one of the magic balls (that the appreciative river spirit gave her), and he begins to vomit up all of the things with which he's tried to fill himself. Do you think the director might be speaking to a common human condition in his (our) culture? When was the last time you felt like No Face? Later No Face joins Chihiro on her journey to Zeniba's home to save Haku. What might we learn from how Chihiro helped No Face? How might your church minister to those who have experienced such loneliness and emptiness?

Bonus Material

Though unknown to many Americans, Japanese animation has had a long history of producing beautifully imaginative films. Hayao Miyazaki had long been part of that tradition when in 1986 his production company, Studio Ghibli, produced their first feature, *Laputa: Castle in the Sky*. Followed by *My Neighbor Totoro*, *Kiki's Delivery Service*, and *Princess Mononoke*, each of Miyazaki's films has sought to bridge the gap between the animation traditions of Japan (artistry and imagination) and the United States (emotionally gripping stories with clever narration). With the release of *Spirited Away*, many believe he has truly achieved this feat. Two of those fans included Pixar's John Lasseter of the *Toy Story* movies and *Finding Nemo*, and Disney's Kirk Wise, director of *Beauty and the Beast*. Animation stars in their own right, they were recruited to convert the Japanese version of the movie into one for English-speaking audiences.

As with most of Miyazaki's films, *Spirited Away* is filled with experiences and people from his everyday life. Two things gave shape to the story and film: the daughter of a close friend and a song sent to him by a young musician. He had observed the ten-year-old with her father when she visited Miyazaki at his mountain lodge, and he imagined writing a story about and for her. The song "Always With Me" was intended for another of his films, which was never made. He played it continuously while working on *Spirited Away* and decided to include it in the film. In addition, the abandoned theme park turned bathhouse was inspired by the Edo-Tokyo Open Air Architectural Museum in the suburbs of Tokyo, near his studio.

When it comes to the spirits in the film, Miyazaki drew from traditional Japanese myth and his own imagination. Of course, even the more traditional spirits display a Miyazaki riff. If you can have a river spirit, why not a radish spirit? And what happens to a polluted river spirit? Well, he turns into a stink spirit! In fact, Miyazaki's idea for that scene in the film came from working with others to clean out a river near his home. He was so overwhelmed by the amount of discarded junk pulled out by volunteers (including a bicycle), he knew he had to use the image. And some of his close friends argue that the lonely-but-yearning-for-love spirit No Face is actually Miyazaki.

Spirited Away is a lovely, sweet story about a girl developing an inner strength that will follow her throughout her life. However, Miyazaki is as at home with disturbing scenes of creatures throwing up as he is with a tranquil scene of the sea mist settling on the bathhouse. No doubt he intended such juxtaposition—the grotesque and the beautiful, the serious and the comical, the frightening and the enchanting. Together they point to the underlying thread that ties these things together and show us how little distance there is between seemingly incongruent states. Perhaps Miyazaki is a modern-day Qoheleth (the writer of Ecclesiastes) pointing to the fact that all of life—the problematic as well as the playful—is a gift from the Creator.

With the release of the DVD, viewers should take advantage of the bonus material. The Nippon Television special, "The Making of *Spirited Away*," is delightful because the viewer is allowed to see Miyazaki at work. While he is more than sixty years old and his animators are mostly in their twenties and early thirties, there is a wonderful rapport. From acting out the movements he wants for characters to wild facial expressions to cooking for his team to his jokes or admonishments, this visionary artist comes to life. Many compare his antics to those of Walt Disney with his early animators.

Spirited Away was nominated for and won numerous awards throughout the world, including those mentioned above. The film's budget was roughly $16 million (a pittance compared to American animation). After earning $234 million in Japan, the top-grossing film in Japanese history (unseating *Titanic*) premiered at the Toronto Film Festival. It is the first film ever to make more than $200 million before opening in the U.S. Perhaps the Disney dynasty has been replaced by the unassuming Studio Ghibli—something like David and Goliath.

6. *Crouching Tiger, Hidden Dragon*

Themes
Beauty, Imagination, Creativity
Death, Freedom, Leadership
Honor, Humility, Kindness, Love,
Sacrifice, Selfishness, Wisdom,
Women

China, Taiwan, U.S., 2000
(*AKA Wo Hu Zang Long*)
120 Minutes, Feature, Color
Actors: Chow Yun-Fat, Michelle Yeoh,
  Zhang Zi Yi, Chang Cheng, Sihung Lung, Cheng Pei-Pei
Director: Ang Lee
Screenwriter: Tsai Kuo-Jung, Wang Hui-Ling, James Schamus
Rated: PG13 (mild violence, brief sexual scenes, mature themes)
DVD Features: theatrical trailer, photo montage, filmographies,
  commentary by Ang Lee and James Schamus, conversation with
  Michelle Yeoh, "Unleashing Dragons: The Making of Crouching Tiger,
  Hidden Dragon"

Li Mu Bai (Chow Yun-Fat) gives Jen Yu (Zhang Zi Yi) a lesson in discipline. *Crouching Tiger, Hidden Dragon* (d. Lee, 2000). Photo by Chan Kam Chuen. Copyright 2000 Columbia Tristar. All rights reserved.

Synopsis and Theological Reflection

Ang Lee, director of *Crouching Tiger, Hidden Dragon*, said, "It was a tremendous privilege for me to make this movie." This privilege extended to millions of viewers who experienced the beauty, fantasy, and complexity of this movie. Or should we say this *ballet*, this *martial arts competition*, this *love story*, or even this *religious quest*? For *Crouching Tiger, Hidden Dragon* is all of these and more. Like so many viewers, we found the movie mesmerizing. In fact, it was the most successful foreign language film ever (until the opening of the *The Passion of the Christ* in February 2004), crossing the $100 million mark in U.S. sales the week before the Oscar awards.

We sat in Spain on the night of the 2001 Oscars (actually it was nine hours earlier in the U.S.) and wondered what would happen during the awards show. We knew we would have to wait until the next day to read about it in the papers or watch Spanish television report on it. We hoped to hear in *Spanish* that

a film in *Mandarin* had won the award for not only Best For-
eign Film but also Best Picture overall. (As many of you know,
Crouching Tiger, Hidden Dragon went on to win four Academy
Awards—Best Art Direction/Set Design, Best Cinematography,
Best Score, and Best Foreign Language Film. Only the film
Gladiator won more awards that year.) Though *Crouching Tiger*
did not win the Best Picture award, it did prove that an Asian
movie could compete successfully with the best in Hollywood.
Our globe is getting smaller and boundaries are fading. We wish
we could say it was the Christian church that was drawing us
together, but in this case it's the film industry.

The movie's story is based on an early twentieth-century
Chinese pulp novel about warriors who possess strong codes of
loyalty and honor. Li Mu Bai (Chow Yun-Fat) is a famous warrior from the Mt. Wudan School—calm, yet deadly. Despite his
own call to avenge his master's murder, he has decided to retire
to a life of contemplation. He therefore gives his renowned four-
hundred-year-old sword to an honored friend. But no sooner
is it given than it is stolen. Yui Hsui Lien (Michelle Yeoh), a
female "Xia" or wandering warrior, suspects that Jen (Zhang
Zi Yi), the beautiful young daughter of the governor, might be
the culprit. As Mu Bai and Hsui Lien go in search, not admit-
ting even to themselves their love for each other, they discover
that Jen has indeed stolen the sword, for she has given herself
over to tutelage by an evil female criminal. Instead of using her
power for good, Jen has used it selfishly and destructively. The
rest of the movie tells the story of the confrontation between
Hsui Lien and Jen and its tragic consequences.

Seeing this martial arts movie was stunning for two reasons: the
female warriors were portrayed as feminine yet fully the equal of
the male, and the fight scenes were more like ballet than battle.
Strong female characters and the expression of real feelings are
not typical of this pulp genre. It is Ang Lee who developed these
elements in the story. We are given a glimpse into the lives and
feelings of two women, who while competitors, each envy the
life of the other. Hsui Lien, the older, beautiful, gentle, wandering

warrior, longs to settle down with the man she loves (Mu Bai). And Jen, the younger, unhappily betrothed daughter of a wealthy official, wants the freedom she believes comes with being a warrior. They have much to learn from each other (and from Mu Bai). In the process, we too learn about love, honor, and sacrifice.

The movie's martial arts and sword fights, all choreographed by Yuen Wo-Ping (the fight master responsible for the fight scenes in *The Matrix*) include wire-assisted, gravity-defying moves. They are shear visual poetry. (The sword fight among the swaying treetops is destined to become a classic.) And in the background you hear cello passages performed by Yo-Yo Ma.

Here is a movie like no other. How did this ever come together? In an interview director Ang Lee commented:

> My team and I chose the most populist, if not popular, genre in film history—the Hong Kong martial arts film—to tell our story, and we used this pop genre almost as a kind of a research instrument to explore the legacy of classical Chinese culture. We embraced the most mass of art forms and mixed it with the highest—the secret martial arts as passed down over time in the great Taoist schools of training and of thought.

Here is a perspective that we in the church need to consider as we tell our story, the Good News of Jesus Christ. If the genre of Hong Kong martial arts movies can be used and transformed to portray effectively the essence of Taoist thought, can American popular culture similarly be the medium through which to share more effectively our biblical faith? We can take a lesson from Ang Lee and his breathtaking movie: Profound stories with both cultural and religious depth can be winsomely expressed using pop culture's modes of communication.

Dialogue Texts

A desire realized is sweet to the soul, but to turn away from evil is an abomination to fools. . . . The fear of the LORD is instruction in wisdom, and humility goes before honor. . . . Whoever pursues righteousness and kindness will find life and honor.

Proverbs 13:19; 15:33; 21:21

To the Jews who had believed him, Jesus said, "If you hold to my teaching, you are really my disciples. Then you will know the truth, and the truth will set you free."

John 8:31–32 NIV

For freedom Christ has set us free. Stand firm, therefore, and do not submit again to a yoke of slavery.

Galatians 5:1

If I speak in the tongues of mortals and of angels, but do not have love, I am a noisy gong or a clanging cymbal. And if I have prophetic powers, and understand all mysteries and all knowledge, and if I have all faith, so as to remove mountains, but do not have love, I am nothing. If I give away all my possessions, and if I hand over my body so that I may boast, but do not have love, I gain nothing. . . . And now faith, hope, and love abide, these three; and the greatest of these is love.

1 Corinthians 13:1–3, 13

Discussion Questions

1. From accolades of "masterpiece" to "poetry in motion," critics were almost unanimous in their praise of the film *Crouching Tiger, Hidden Dragon*. Some loved it for its action, others for its romance, and others for its spiritual dimension. In fact, many were mesmerized by the fact it was all three of these genres in equally powerful ways, that is, some likened it to the action of *The Matrix* as well as the romance of *Titanic* with a humble warrior hero who meditates. What was your experience of the film as a whole? Have you ever seen a film quite like it? How is it different from the films mentioned above? How is it different from more Western films? With what character did you most connect? Why? To whom or what does the movie title refer?

2. Throughout the film the richness of Eastern culture and philosophy is present. The discipline of Eastern spirituality gives these warriors their power. Yet the main characters seem to question that philosophy and culture (almost rebelling against it in the case of the young Jen). At the beginning of the film Mu Bai describes how his meditation leads him to a place of endless sorrow instead of enlightenment. Hsui Lien later challenges the teaching of Mu Bai's master as she points out that the touch of her hand is real, not an illusion, even though it is of this world. Why do you think the director and screenwriters have their characters question the values by which they live? Are they suggesting alternative ways of viewing the world? How could you put your Christian faith and its beliefs into respectful dialogue with the characters' questions and struggles—these universal questions of life? How might the dialogue texts shed light on the themes the characters are raising?

3. After Mu Bai's death, the heartbroken Hsui Lien sends Jen to Wudan Mountain, saying, "Promise me one thing. Whatever path you take in this life . . . be true to yourself." Jen goes and is reunited with Lo, but only briefly. Ang Lee describes the last scene of the movie as liberation rather than sacrificial love or even despair. He considers Jen as the true hero of the story. Do you agree? Why or why not? You might compare this last scene with the last scene of *Thelma and Louise*. What similarities and differences do you see between these two stories of women, one from the East and the other from the West? What similarities or differences are there between these stories of liberation coming through death and Jesus' message?

Clip Conversations

1. Chapters 4 [8:20–11:45] and 8 [22:03–29:27]—"Jen" and "Flyers." In these two chapters we see the two women protagonists meeting and learning more about each other. Jen, the

governor's daughter who is to be married soon, is fascinated with the freedom of the martial arts "knights" like Hsui Lien. Lien suggests to her that they too must follow rules (like friendship, trust, integrity, honor) to survive. Hsui Lien knows the loneliness of her path and her silent love for Mu Bai. Each is a prisoner of her lifestyle, yearning for what the other has. What do you think the filmmakers are saying to the viewer about the true nature of freedom? How is this question of balancing love, honor, sacrifice, and freedom an ancient but very contemporary one? How have your lifestyle choices made you a prisoner? How does the gospel portray human freedom?

2. Chapter 15 [43:05–46:12]—"Give Yourself Up." Mu Bai intercepts Jen as she is returning the Green Destiny (his sword). They fight, but their styles are so different. Jen is filled with anger and frenetically uses all her strength. Mu Bai is almost emotionless and centered in his effortlessness. At one point in their duel, he tries to teach her in his style (the sword behind his back while he fights her with a stick) and with his words: "No growth without resistance. No action without reaction. No desire without restraint. Now give yourself up and find yourself again." Why does Mu Bai so desire to take Jen on as his disciple? What does he see in her? What are the risks of mentoring her? How does she respond? Why? Is she torn in her response (think of her angry words with Jade Fox following this scene)? How might the interaction of the older warriors with the younger ones be seen as a classic generation gap? Have you ever been in a similar situation? You might also discuss Mu Bai's pithy "proverbs." (For example, how are they similar to or different from some of the Bible's proverbs?)

3. Chapter 27 [1:47:37–1:52:12]—"One Breath Left." Hsui Lien keeps watch as Mu Bai sits dying from the poison dart Jade Fox had meant for Jen. (Remember, this is Chinese pulp fiction with all of the melodrama.) How is this love-death scene similar to and different from more Western films? Listen to the last

words they speak to each other. What strikes you? How does Mu Bai respond to Hsui Lien's classic Eastern philosophy about death and life? What has he learned? What has she learned? How is death the great leveler, putting life into perspective for all of the film's characters?

Bonus Material

Martial arts fantasies, or *wuxia* films, traditionally combine poor acting, slapstick humor, and a silly plot in between elaborate fight scenes. Director Ang Lee fell in love with movies while watching such Hong Kong films as a child growing up in Taiwan. It was his childhood fantasy to make such a film. He made *Crouching Tiger, Hidden Dragon* as a tribute to the form, which as he says in his comments on the DVD, "speaks in the most primitive way to what people wish or dream for." But while his film has no shortage of fights, it also has the scope of an epic and the drama of a Greek tragedy.

We might also say that the making of the film had both scope and drama. After receiving permission from the Chinese government to film at the Beijing Film Studio and various other locations, Lee started shooting in the Gobi Desert. He was immediately beset by problems ranging from his crew getting lost in the desert, to sandstorms and temperatures over one hundred, to a freak rainstorm, which ruined the production schedule.

His challenges didn't just stop with locations and crew. Three of his four lead actors of an all-Asian cast did not speak Mandarin, which Lee insisted on using instead of Cantonese to achieve a more classic, lyrical feel. Chow Yun-Fat (Hong Kong), a famous actor internationally, had to do twenty-eight takes the first day just because of his difficulty with the language. Michelle Yeoh injured her knee in one of the first fight scenes and had to have surgery and spend one month in rehab in the U.S. Even master fight choreographer Yuen Wo-Ping of *Matrix* fame was put to the test. Lee's vision for the fantastic fights on rooftops and atop the branches of bamboo trees required weeks of exhausting and dangerous wire and harness work.

Thus, the filming required an immense effort from all involved. Zhang Zi Yi (Jen) went to Lee's boot camp for several months to study calligraphy and martial arts. Likewise Chow Yun-Fat trained for months with a martial arts coach. Both Yeoh and Yun-Fat had to study Mandarin and often memorized their lines phonetically. The Hong Kong crew, with two teams, was forced to shoot around the clock for almost six months. Lee himself spent almost nine months in China working on the film. Filming was followed by seven weeks of editing (including meticulous digital wire removal). Composer Tan Dun was only given two weeks to compose the score before recording was done with Yo-Yo Ma and Coco Lee in Shanghai. While all made sacrifices and experienced some of the most difficult work challenges in their careers, they all said it was worth it to have worked with Ang Lee.

Crouching Tiger, Hidden Dragon was nominated for and won numerous awards around the world. Some of those include: ten Academy Awards nominations, winning the four noted above; fourteen British Academy Awards nominations, winning three; and three Golden Globe nominations, winning two. The film's budget of $15 million was rather small for an action film, but its box office total was not. Worldwide the film grossed $209 million at theaters, with $128 million in the U.S. While we found the Mandarin version with subtitles to contribute to the film's power, with its video/DVD release, viewers who don't like reading subtitles can watch a fairly well-done English-dubbed version. This might be good for young viewers or older people who might skip the movie because of the subtitles.

"Crouching tiger, hidden dragon" is a quote from Chinese mythology. It refers to hiding your strength from others. While the characters in the film illustrate this in various ways, it is the film itself that is truly a "crouching tiger, hidden dragon," for what may be first thought of as pulp fiction is seen to have hidden meaning and value—at least for those who have eyes to see.

Choosing Life

7. Big Night

Themes

Choosing Life
Clash of Cultures, Life as Sacramental, Materialism, Reconciliation within Families, The Lord's Supper Celebration, Creativity, Food, Integrity

U.S., 1996
107 Minutes, Feature, Color
Actors: Stanley Tucci, Tony Shalhoub,
Minnie Driver, Ian Holm,
Isabella Rossellini, Mark Anthony,
Allision Janney, Campbell Scott
Directors: Campbell Scott and Stanley Tucci
Screenwriters: Stanley Tucci and Joseph Tropiano
Rated: R (profanity, brief sexual scenes, mature themes)
DVD Features: theatrical trailer, wide-screen anamorphic format,
Spanish subtitles

Synopsis and Theological Reflection

What do *Eat, Drink, Man, Woman*; *Babette's Feast*; *Like Water for Chocolate*; and *Big Night* have in common? In one word: food. Over the last decade moviegoers have been treated to a small but significant number of movies that revolve around sumptuous meals.

Babette's Feast, the Scandinavian entrée, shows the healing possibilities of a shared meal. The extravagant spread is almost sacramental, both for those in the film and for us, the viewers. *Eat, Drink, Man, Woman* portrays a Chinese father whose ongoing point of contact with his adult daughters is a ritual—an extravagant meal he prepares for them weekly. Food and family are closely intertwined. *Like Water for Chocolate* is Latin in its flavors, and its kitchen recipes become the focal point of this rhapsody on life.

Primo (Tony Shalhoub) and Secondo (Stanley Tucci) are two Italian immigrant brothers attempting to save their failing restaurant business and attain the American dream. *Big Night* (d. Scott and Tucci, 1996). Photo by John Clifford. Copyright 1996 Rysher Entertainment. All rights reserved.

Big Night, the latest addition to this international, visual feast, is located on the Jersey shore, but the heart and soul of the film is Italian. In his first feature film, Stanley Tucci has not only cowritten and codirected but even costars as one of the two brothers who struggle to keep open an Italian restaurant that serves risotto and timpani.

Primo, a master chef with an artist's soul, refuses to compromise his menu: "If you give the people time, they will learn." Secondo, his younger brother, is the businessman. When Primo refuses to mix starches for a gauche customer who wants meatballs and spaghetti with her risotto, Secondo says, "This is what the customer asked for. Make it." How much should one compromise for the sake of money? Is anything okay in order to climb the ladder of success in America?

When Pascal, the opportunistic owner of a neighboring Italian restaurant that packs in the patrons with philistine fare and schmaltzy music, suggests that the brothers put on a dinner for the musician Louis Prima in order to get some free publicity and new clientele, the plot is established. The film shows us the preparation for the Big Night and then the elegant, six-course dinner that is served to the brothers' neighborhood friends—the flower clerk, the barber, the car salesman, and so on—when Prima fails to show up. It is almost beyond imagination.

Pascal is also present for the meal, blaspheming this Last Supper because he wants the money that would come in if Primo were his cook. The tensions that arise between the brothers and with their friends cause momentary anger and heartache. But as Primo tells Ann, his shy friend who sells him flowers, "To eat good food is to be close to God. To have the knowledge of God is the bread of angels. I'm not sure what it means, but . . ."

Viewers also will sense this mystery. On a surface level, the film portrays the dangers of a pragmatic, crass materialism. The simple story posits instead the value of integrity, not only toward food but with family, friends, and coworkers as well. But beneath this surface story line is another possibility. For *Big Night* presents its food as a metaphor for the sanctity, the sacredness of life—all life. The appetite, which arises in the viewer, is more than simply the desire to find the best Italian restaurant nearby (though the movie will do this!). There is also the deep desire to be rooted in something that can truly sustain.

Do not go to this film expecting the pace or special effects of an action adventure. This meal is to be eaten leisurely, to be savored and enjoyed. But there is much for the palate if one chooses to partake. We left the theater recalling one of our favorite aphorisms: "It's a sin to eat bad ice cream." So too, pasta!

Dialogue Texts

God saw everything that he had made, and indeed, it was very good.

Genesis 1:31

Go, eat your bread with enjoyment, and drink your wine with a merry heart; for God has long ago approved what you do.

Ecclesiastes 9:7

The mouth of the righteous is a fountain of life, but the mouth of the wicked conceals violence.

Proverbs 10:11

The righteous have enough to satisfy their appetite, but the belly of the wicked is empty.

Proverbs 13:25

Discussion Questions

1. *Big Night* is aptly named, as the directors devoted nearly half the filming schedule and half of the film's running time to the elaborate preparation and presentation of the feast. This slow and methodical depiction was intended to let the viewer enter into the experience of the two brothers and their community. How was the experience for you? What role has food played in your family? Have you ever had, or could you imagine having, an almost transcendent experience through food and community? How do the ordinary things of life become an occasion for experiencing the goodness of creation?

2. Primo, the older brother and chef, is an old world purist. For him, cooking is a gift, an art, and a way of life. He's angry that he is being asked to cater to the tastes of ignorant Americans. Secondo, the younger brother and manager, is happy to give people what they want because he wants the business to succeed. He is chasing the American dream. What can these two brothers learn from each other? With which brother do you most resonate? How have old world values and the American dream collided or cooperated in your life? How can the church help newcomers to this country make this journey? How might this experience of conflicting values be

present within your church? How might we help the members of different generations or new believers navigate through the waters of conflicting values?

3. Using the dialogue texts above from Proverbs, how would you talk about the owners of the two restaurants in the movie? How do you deal with situations in which the wicked (the Philistines) prosper and the righteous (the authentic) suffer? What do you think or do when good people in your life suffer and bad people have nothing but success? Is it fair that Pascal succeeds while Primo and Secondo fail and suffer? At which restaurant would you rather eat? Why?

Clip Conversations

1. Chapter 8 [22:52–32:38]—"At Pascal's." One night after closing their Paradise Restaurant, Secondo walks across the street to Pascal's Italian Grotto. Here the music and the food are poor imitations of the real Italian fare, but people flock to the restaurant. In Pascal's office, Secondo and Pascal have a conversation about doing business in America. Notice the filming as the characters speak. How does it nuance what they are saying? Think about the advice that Pascal gives Secondo: "Work hard . . . climb the ladder . . . land of opportunity." "Give people what they want, then later you can give them what you want." "Bite your teeth into the a—— of life and drag it to you." How are these messages helpful or hurtful?

2. Chapter 25 [1:09:50–1:11:41]—"Kitchen of Love." Primo is in the kitchen with Ann, showing her his simple love for cooking and good food. He talks of the food of his homeland, which is "so good you have to kill yourself." To prove his point he gives her a taste of what he is cooking, to which she swoons, "Oh my God" (three times). "Oh my God is right," Primo agrees. "Now you know that to eat good food is to be close to God."

What does he mean? Have you ever had that experience with food (or some other part of creation)?

3. Chapter 28 [1:16:30–1:25:20]—"Dinner Is Served." The meal is finally served—all six courses. What strikes you about the food/meal itself? What strikes you about the reactions of the participants? How do the characters change during the meal? For everyone, including Primo and Secondo, it's a night to remember. What did they each learn?

4. Chapter 32 [1:40:32–1:45:55]—"Breakfast." Reviewer James Berardinelli said of *Big Night*, "The two brothers rediscover something they've known all along: that food, like love, is an unspoken, universal means of communication." We see this in the scene of the next morning, which is an amazing, unbroken five-minute take. The two brothers share an omelet in silent affection. How does the act of cooking and sharing an omelet become an act of reconciliation? How does the Lord's Supper function similarly, or differently, for the Christian community?

Bonus Material

Big Night won the Waldo Salt Screenwriting Award and was nominated for the Grand Jury Prize at the Sundance Film Festival when it premiered in 1996. It went on to win the Grand Special Prize at the Deauville Film Festival. It was especially honored among independent filmmakers by being nominated for Best First Screenplay, which it won, and Best First Feature at the Independent Spirit Awards. In addition, the New York Film Critics Circle honored Stanley Tucci and Campbell Scott with their prize for Best New Director. Its total box office receipts were $12.6 million. In some ways these awards and numbers show us that *Big Night* is truly the Paradise Restaurant of movies, not Pascal's Italian Grotto.

8. *Fearless*

Choosing Life
Arguing with God, Death, Isolation
Hope, Images of the Savior,
Life as a Gift, Materialism,
The Mystery of Life, Parenting,
The Randomness of Life, Salvation

U.S., 1993
121 Minutes, Feature, Color
Actors: Jeff Bridges, Isabella Rossellini,
   Rosie Perez, John Turturro,
   Benicio del Toro, Tom Hulce
Director: Peter Weir
Screenwriter: Rafael Yglesias
Rated: R (accident scene, mature themes, brief profanity)
DVD Features: full-screen format

Synopsis and Theological Reflection

On 12 November 2001, American Airlines flight #587 crashed shortly after taking off from JFK Airport in New York City. Students in Rob's theology and film class met that evening to discuss the preassigned movie, *Fearless*. It is a lyrical and introspective film by Peter Weir that first screened in 1993. Though the movie garnered critical acclaim, it died at the box office. Now students found it a riveting experience. What made the difference this time around? *Fearless* is a movie about a plane disaster. What a difference a day makes.

Most disaster movies build their suspense throughout the film, with the crash happening near the end. But not Weir's movie. Instead, it *begins* with scenes of the crash and of Max Klein (Jeff Bridges), one of the few to survive the catastrophe. As the cameras roll, we are looking at idyllic cornfields that have been changed forever by the terrible crash. (Those who have seen Weir's movie *Witness* will recall the fields of grain that similarly suggested an innocence being transgressed.) What follows as the film unfolds is a moving meditation on the meaning of life by someone who has been forced to face the inexplicable and irrational reality of death. All of us could identify with it.

Max's secure and successful life as architect and father has been shattered forever. Fame, money, and wisdom no longer seem

Dazed but alive, passenger Max Klein (Jeff Bridges) walks away from an airplane crash. *Fearless* (d. Weir, 1993). Photo by Merrick Morton. Copyright 1993 Warner Bros. All rights reserved.

significant to him. Although Max has rescued two children from the plane, he shuns becoming a media celebrity. An ambulance-chasing attorney wants to help him make millions, but to no avail. A trauma psychiatrist wants to help him readjust, but he is ineffective. It is almost as if they were Job's friends; none are able to offer helpful advice. These counselors cannot enter Max's grief-dominated world; it has become a different universe.

For a time Max assumes an air of invincibility, tempting fate (or is it God?). He eats strawberries that previously would have caused him to choke in an allergic reaction. He walks across a busy intersection and later balances high on the ledge of a building. Looking up to heaven, he desperately mocks God, "You can't do it! You want to kill me but you can't." Viewers hear the pathos of this modern-day Job as he addresses the heavens, but we see something more as well. For as Max screams, we find ourselves watching him from a camera suspended high above him. Like God himself, we find ourselves looking down on Max, aching patiently for him.

There is a subplot to the simple story as Max finds comfort in reaching out to help Carla (Rosie Perez), another of the crash survivors. From the opening camera shots that focus on Max's side, which has been pierced in the crash, to Max taking children in his arms and later reaching down to make some mud out of the dirt he has spit on, viewers are encouraged to look at Max as a savior figure. But the spiritual core of the film is not in Max's Christ-like, sacrificial acts. The movie is, instead, about Max's own salvation, something he cannot win for himself.

In the final climactic moment as Max discovers the wonder of life, particularly given the irrationality and amorality of death, director Weir chooses as the background music a haunting piece by the contemporary Polish composer, Henryk Gorecki. Symphony No. 3 was composed in 1976 for a performance at St. Magnus Church near Auschwitz. It is known as the "symphony of sorrowful songs." But as in other of Gorecki's compositions, there is heard through the pain a note of hope. As one conductor put it, in this symphony we hear "a hope born of sorrow but not itself sorrowful." Such a summary describes *Fearless* as well.

Student discussion of Weir's movie that evening centered on the film, but never far removed were our own reactions to the plane crashes of the last months, to the inexplicable horror we continue to witness, even to our own primal fears of dying in a plane crash. But life's randomness did not have the last word, for neither Weir's movie nor our biblical faith would permit such fatalism. Instead, students encountered a hope blossoming out of the very depth of our pain—we might even say as a result of our pain. We might lack answers to all that happens—injustice, amorality, suffering, and death. The Old Testament sages, like Max, recognized that, but with Max they could nevertheless embrace the taste, love, and beauty of life. Life has a transcendent mystery that invites our wonder.

Fearless will not give its viewers the roller coaster ride so typical of disaster genre films. It offers something far more significant. We as viewers are drawn by the portrayal of this airline crash and its aftermath to consider introspectively our own spiritual beliefs concerning life and death, death and life. Like Max, we are encouraged to choose life.

Dialogue Texts

For whoever finds me finds life and obtains favor from the LORD; but those who miss me injure themselves; all who hate me love death.

Proverbs 8:35–36

But whoever is joined with all the living has hope, for a living dog is better than a dead lion.

Ecclesiastes 9:4

Go, eat your bread with enjoyment, and drink your wine with a merry heart; for God has long ago approved what you do. Let your garments always be white; do not let oil be lacking on your head. Enjoy life with the wife whom you love, all the days of your vain life that are given you under the sun, because that is your portion in life and in your toil at which you toil under the sun.

Ecclesiastes 9:7–9

Therefore I tell you, do not worry about your life, what you will eat or what you will drink, or about your body, what you will wear. Is not life more than food, and the body more than clothing? . . . And can any of you by worrying add a single hour to your span of life? . . . So do not worry about tomorrow, for tomorrow will bring worries of its own. Today's trouble is enough for today.

Matthew 6:25, 27, 34

Discussion Questions

1. Director Peter Weir likes to use a classic film type and subvert it or cross it with elements of other genres. *Fearless*, for example, is a disaster movie. But in order to emphasize that the real suspense

is internal and not external to his character, the disaster happens at the beginning of the film, not the end. How did this reversal of the typical disaster film plot affect you as a viewer? How does walking away from an airplane disaster impact Max Klein? How does the disaster play out in his subsequent life?

2. Another characteristic of Weir's films is the clash between two cultures, not in order to provide political insight but to reveal a greater depth of meaning lurking behind and under these surface confrontations. Weir's main characters are typically newcomers from an outside world who encounter a new culture and struggle to understand it. In *Fearless*, the alien culture turns out to be Max's own after surviving a near-death experience in a plane crash. In what ways does Max have to learn about and experience his world anew after the crash? What is most difficult for him? What guides are provided to help him? Are they helpful? Why or why not? Have you ever had a similar entry (or reentry) experience?

3. Weir's characters, when faced with a universe they can't control (the chief obstacle being death itself), begin to ask, "What then must we do?" (These are words of a character in one of his other films. See the discussion of *The Year of Living Dangerously*.) They become aware that life has layers of meaning of which they were previously unaware, and they begin to explore the uncanny or the mysterious. They realize that they must get beneath the surface, for life is precious and valued. In *Fearless*, how does Max fit with Weir's focus? How was the crash "the best thing that ever happened to him" (Max's words)? Have you had such an experience that helped you see past the *reel* to the *real*?

Clip Conversations

1. Chapters 7 [23:20–26:50] and 8 [26:50–32:30]—"Byron Feels Safe; Max Acts Unsafe" and "I'm Not Afraid." We see

Max acting as if he thinks he's invincible. He even shouts to the heavens, "You can't do it! You want to kill me but you can't." But then, in a flashback, we see his experience in the last moments before the plane crash. Why is he fearless at this point? Who is he talking to in the plane and on the bridge?

2. Chapters 9 [32:30–38:32] and 10 [38:32–41:48]—"The Good Samaritan Calls" and "No Reason to Love." Carla, a fellow survivor, is devastated by the death of her baby. The psychologist assigned to the survivors thinks that Max and Carla might help each other. They talk about death. What do you think about their conversation? How are Max and Carla thinking differently about what happened and about death? How would you talk to them about death? What biblical resources might you use?

3. Chapter 18 [1:06:19–1:10:08]—"Let Me Be a Part of It." Max and his wife, Laura, talk about his life before and after the crash. It is as though they are living in two different universes now. Why? What has Max experienced that Laura can't understand? What does Laura know that Max can't experience?

4. Chapter 26 [1:42:34–1:44:38]—"Drawing Near to the Divine." While Max is in the hospital after his latest "invincible" feat, Laura sneaks into his studio and finds pictures he has drawn or collected. One says, "The soul comes to the end of its long journey, and naked and alone, draws near to the divine." What are Max, Carla, and Laura, like all of humankind, struggling with as they live their lives? Of what truth do the Scriptures remind us?

Bonus Material

Fearless is a film that gets the viewer to think while still telling a gripping story. The issues it raises are not easy to grapple with, nor are there pat solutions or firm answers given in the

film. During the course of the film we are made to reflect on
the nature and fragility of life, given death. We are also led to
consider the relationship between God and humankind. This
might be a helpful film to discuss with friends and colleagues,
Christian or not.

In addition to the comments above about Weir's style and
content, it should be mentioned that he is often inspired by
music to make his movies. "Storytelling is my trade, my craft.
But music is my inspiration; and my goal, my metaphor, to affect
people like music. The images should float over you like music,
and the experience should be beyond words."

Weir's most powerful use of music to provide a point of view
that evokes a sense of wonder is in *Fearless*. The playing of such
popular music as U2's "Where the Streets Have No Name" re-
inforces Max's dislocation. It is not until the sequence at the
end of the movie, though, when a flashback is shown of the
inside of the plane during the crash that a sense of transcendence is achieved. The mystery of death and life is conveyed
in part through the use of blue light and slow motion. But it is
the music, Henryk Gorecki's Symphony No. 3, that transports
the viewer. Gorecki chose for the text of his first movement a
fifteenth-century Polish lament of Mary, the mother of Jesus:
"My son, my chosen and beloved, share your wounds with your
mother. . . . Although you are already leaving me, my cherished
hope." The symphony's text continues with a prayer that was
found inscribed on the wall of a cell in the Gestapo's headquar-
ters in Zakopane. And it concludes with a Polish mother's folk
song lamenting the loss of her child who "lies in his grave and I
do not know where though I keep asking people everywhere."
It is this last movement that Weir has chosen to use in the film.
But the cumulative power of the three movements is simply
overpowering in the context of the story. Who will bear our
sorrows? Here, too, is the wonder of *Fearless*. The music and the
image have joined to portray a hope beyond sorrow. As Laura
pleads with Max not to die, he opens his eyes. "I'm alive," he
gasps. Life begins anew from out of the ashes.

Fearless was nominated for Best Supporting Actress (Rosie Perez) for the Academy Awards and the Golden Globe Awards. At the Berlin International Film Festival she won the Silver Bear Special Mention for Outstanding Performance for her role in the film. While not a blockbuster—its total box office receipts were only $8.4 million—*Fearless* was given high praise by movie critics. Regardless of either fact, the film should provide for lots of postmovie conversations, because it is not a film that you walk away from and immediately forget.

Embracing
Our Vocation

9. *The Rookie*

U.S., 2002

127 Minutes, Feature, Color

Actors: Dennis Quaid, Rachel Griffiths, Brian Cox, Jay Hernandez, Beth Grant, Angus T. Jones

Director: John Lee Hancock

Screenwriter: Mike Rich

Rated: G (nothing offensive—excellent for children)

DVD Features: commentary by John Lee Hancock and Dennis Quaid, deleted scenes introduced by director, "The Inspirational Story of Jim Morris," "Spring Training: Tips from the Pros"—Mark Ellis, baseball technical advisor for the film, gives tips on baseball techniques, Spanish subtitles

Embracing Our Vocation
Children, Dreams/Hopes,
Reconciliation within Families
Parenting, Play, Promise Keeping,
Second Chances, Service

Themes

Synopsis and Theological Reflection

Baseball is struggling. Once the national pastime, it now is played by 14 percent fewer teens than just ten years ago. This is the result of a combination of greed, which has forced ticket prices too high; arrogance and amorality, which have made too many professional baseball players reverse role models; and redirection of teenage adrenaline to snowboarding, skateboarding, and in-line skating (up 538 percent in ten years). The popularity of baseball, which was once of mythic proportion, has been shrinking almost as fast as tech stocks did at the turn of the millennium.

Nevertheless, a good baseball story is still capable of capturing our nation's attention. We all rooted for our favorite during the home-run race between Mark McGuire and Sammy Sosa,

Coach Jim Morris (Dennis Quaid) and his Big Lake High School players stand for the national anthem. *The Rookie* (d. Hancock, 2002). Photo by Deana Newcomb. Copyright 2002 Disney Enterprises. All rights reserved.

which obliterated the mystique of Babe Ruth. The World Series battle in 2001 between the underdog Arizona Diamondbacks with their star pitchers and the legendary New York Yankees with their come-from-behind magic was riveting.

It is not just live-action baseball that can be compelling. *Field of Dreams* and *The Natural* are two baseball movies that have attracted large numbers of fans, as has perhaps the best baseball movie that has yet been made, Ron Shelton's *Bull Durham*. These stories are fictional, but they have provided metaphors for life that continue to be compelling.

Add to this list *The Rookie*. Based on a true story, it offers viewers a model for playing the game of life. If we did not know that truth is sometimes stranger than fiction, our jadedness might not allow us to let this story work its charm on us. After all, we know the futility of following your dream, whatever the odds. We all know that a small, rural high school with a ragtag team can't win a championship. And a thirty-five-year-old pitcher with an arm injury can't come back fifteen years after his initial tryouts to pitch in the big leagues. But we root for them none-theless, and as we watch, our tears are genuine!

Most viewers walking into the theater know the movie's outcome ahead of time. Yet we still find ourselves cheering for Jim Morris, the high school science teacher and baseball coach. When he challenges his losing team not to give up on its dream, they respond that that is what he has done. So a wager is struck: If they win the district championship, their coach will try out again for the majors, fifteen years after his first attempt. They do and he does, and Morris goes on to pitch for the Tampa Bay Devil Rays—at age thirty-five the second oldest rookie to enter the big leagues. It matters not that Morris pitches only fifteen innings of relief in his short stint before returning to teaching. That he got to the stadium in Arlington, Texas, is more than enough.

The fact that the story actually happened makes us believe this unbelievable tale. But what makes us more willing to appropriate its story as a parable about life in general is its combination of be-lievable characters, honest script, and good direction. Dennis Quaid plays his role as Jim Morris without a trace of sentimentality. He has what one reviewer called "a rugged, effortless decency." Though he is an exemplary teacher, father, and baseball coach, he has a melancholy about him, knowing what might have been. As he throws his baseballs into a backstop at night using the lights of his truck to see, we ache for him, knowing he had hoped for more.

Brian Cox plays Morris's rigid, insensitive father and helps give the story a grittiness and ambiguity that makes it real. The Australian Rachel Griffiths, who plays his beleaguered wife, pro-vides Morris a convincing reality check as he eventually chases what seems like an impossible dream. She loves him but also has honest doubts, knowing she must raise their two children with little money in the rural dust of West Texas.

Are dreams of the big leagues only for children? We wonder along with Jim and Lorri Morris if it's worth it, particularly as he toils in the minor leagues with players half his age, hoping for his chance. But without spoiling the ending (though we all know how it must end), we can say this much: We should not, we need not, let our childhood dreams die. Even given the inevitable disappointments and failures life brings, hope can transform life. What Morris taught his high school players he himself must learn. In the process so do we.

Director John Lee Hancock, a faithful Catholic, has created a lyrical baseball movie that is also true to the game of life. The baseball episodes are fun to watch and suspenseful even though we know what the ending will be. They remind us of the importance of play both in and for itself and as a metaphor from which to learn about life. This Disney movie is a treat for young and old alike.

Dialogue Texts

The LORD spoke to Moses: . . . I have filled him [Bezalel] with divine spirit, with ability, intelligence, and knowledge in every kind of craft, to devise artistic designs, to work in gold, silver, and bronze, in cutting stones for setting, and in carving wood, in every kind of craft. . . . I have given skill to all the skillful, so that they may make all that I have commanded you.

Exodus 31:1–6

Hope deferred makes the heart sick, but a desire fulfilled is a tree of life.

Proverbs 13:12

For surely I know the plans I have for you, says the LORD, plans for your welfare and not for harm, to give you a future with hope.

Jeremiah 29:11

Like good stewards of the manifold grace of God, serve one another with whatever gift each of you has received.

1 Peter 4:10

Discussion Questions

1. The movie starts with the telling of an old Texas story about two nuns, baseball, oil, and St. Rita, the patron saint of

impossible dreams. (A true story—the Santa Rita well was the well that started the oil boom in Texas. The original derrick sits on the campus of the University of Texas in Austin.) How is the director setting the stage for what is to come in the film? What stories in the film connect to this original story? How was the story an encouragement to the young (and older) Jimmy Morris? What impossible dreams do you have?

2. As Jimmy pitches against the radar gun, the song "Stuff That Works" by Guy Clark and Rodney Crowell is heard. The singer (Guy Clark) tells what his life is made of in the chorus:

> Stuff that works. Stuff that holds up.
> The kind of stuff you don't hang on the wall.
> Stuff that's real. Stuff you feel.
> The kind of stuff you reach for when you fall.

How is Jimmy's life a reflection of the song? What things are important to him? What things would you include if you were singing the song? How do the song and the scene set up the tension between what his life is and what he still dreams about (especially in the context of the previous scene—see Clip Conversations, "The Deal")? Have you ever experienced that tension? If so, in what way? How has the director let the viewer in on something that Jimmy doesn't know yet?

3. Hunter, Jimmy Morris's eight-year-old son, adores his father, loves baseball, and is the team's batboy. When he smiles, laughs, or dances, the viewer just has to also. What role does he play in the film and in his father's life with the joy he exudes? How does his relationship with his dad contrast with the relationship Jimmy had as a child and has as an adult with his father?

Clip Conversations

1. Chapter 4 [28:00–35:13]—"The Deal." After a terrible loss, Coach Morris gives the team a talk about having dreams. He

says, "You don't have dreams, you don't have anything." They in turn challenge him to have a dream—of pitching in the big leagues. They strike a deal. How is this a turning point in the two stories—the team's and Coach Morris's? Besides having a dream, what sorts of things helped make the difference for each of them? How can the church be an encourager of dreams?

2. Chapter 9 [1:12:12–1:23:45]—"Family Concerns." After throwing 98 mph pitches at a tryout, Jimmy Morris has won a spot with the minor league team of the Tampa Bay Devil Rays. However, playing the Southern League for the summer will mean big sacrifices for his family. In the torment of the decision, he even asks his estranged father for advice. His father says, "Your grandfather once told me it was okay to think about what you want to do until it was time to start doing what you were meant to do." How is his father's advice ironic, given Jimmy's gift? But how is it similar to his wife's initial feelings about the chance to pitch again? What, or rather who, changes her mind? Are dreams just for eight-year-old boys? Who has encouraged you in your dreams? (Cf. Prov. 12:11.)

3. Chapter 15 [1:58:22–2:02:22]—"Thanks for Coming." After his first game in the major leagues, Jimmy finds his father standing outside the clubhouse. They talk, sharing words never heard before between them—words of understanding. As his father turns to go, Jimmy calls him back, gives him the game ball, and says, "Thanks for coming." What can we learn about reconciliation from this film? What allowed each of these men to let go and embrace each other?

Bonus Material

Director John Lee Hancock, as well as others, was taken by the real-life story of Jimmy Morris because it was several stories in one. It wasn't just a story about winning in a game but also of winning in life. It was the story of the Regan County High School Owls' winning season and the story of Jimmy Morris fulfilling a dream. In fact, almost all of the scenes portrayed in the film actually happened, with the exception of Jimmy throwing against the roadway radar gun (completely made up by the writer) and that he struck Royce Clayton out with three pitches (it was actually four) as depicted in the movie (but Royce Clayton did actually play himself in the movie).

Jimmy Morris "had a ball in my hand since I could crawl" and was an all-around athlete. He also played football in high school (according to Morris, all you did in West Texas was "go to church and play football") but was drafted by the Brewers to pitch. One of the producers of the film, Mike Ciardi, was actually his roommate one season on the minor league team. However, Morris had little success due to injuries and four operations. He went back to college in his twenties, where he became the punter for the football team. His senior year he was an All-American. After college he returned to his high school to be a science teacher and eventually coach a struggling baseball team. Several years in a row the team won only one game the entire season, that is until that incredible season of 1999.

The team's winning season forced Morris to try out with the Tampa Bay Devil Rays (and he did go with all three kids in tow). His first pitch was 94 mph and the second 96 mph. He then threw twelve straight pitches at 98 mph. When the pitching scout, scratching his head in disbelief, told the scouting director about it over the phone, the director shouted back, "I don't care if he's fifty. If he can throw like that, I want him!" And the rest is history.

Both Hancock and Dennis Quaid are Texas natives and wanted to make a Texas story—"where Texas is a character in the film." Though Hancock came with some baseball background (his dad was a coach), Quaid did not. So prior to filming, Quaid took instruction from Los Angeles Dodgers pitching coach Jim Gott for three months. He also pitched side-by-side with Morris and studied Morris's game films. Morris was on the set a lot, which Quaid liked. Morris and professionals in baseball say Quaid was stunning in picking up the form of a pitcher. Doubles were not needed for the pitching scenes.

The climactic scene of Morris running out onto the field of his first major league game was actually filmed during the seventh inning stretch of a Rangers-Indians game. The pitching scenes were filmed after the game, but fifteen thousand of the forty thousand people who attended the game stuck around to be extras in the film.

The Rookie won the Las Vegas Film Critics Award for Best Family Film and was nominated in the same category by the Broadcast Film Critics Association and the Young Artist Awards. Its total box office receipts were $75 million with video sales having reached over $21 million by the end of 2002. It just goes to show that people are hungry for a good story. (And if you want more interesting stories about Jimmy Morris or the making of the film, check out the Bonus Materials of the DVD.)

10. *Billy Elliot*

U.K., 2000
111 Minutes, Feature, Color
Actors: Julie Walters, Jamie Bell,
    Jamie Driven, Gary Lewis, Jean Heywood
Director: Stephen Daldry
Screenwriter: Lee Hall
Rated: R (profanity, violence)
DVD Features: theatrical trailer, production notes, cast and filmmakers,
    "Billy Elliot: Breaking Free" featurette

Embracing Our Vocation
Creativity, Freedom,
Reconciliation within Families,
Poverty
Children, Clash of Cultures,
Courage, Joy, Love,
Parenting, Social Justice,
Wonder

Themes

Synopsis and Theological Reflection

Can you remember when you were a kid and jumping on your bed was the most wonderful experience in the world? Those were

Ballet lesson over, Billy Elliot (Jamie Bell) can't stop dancing. *Billy Elliot* (d. Stephen Daldry, 2000). Photo by Giles Keyte. Copyright 2000 Universal Studios. All rights reserved.

the brief moments when in child-like abandon you were free to be fully yourself, to let both body and spirit soar (that is until your parents heard you and ordered you to stop). In his book *Dangerous Wonder*, well-known youth-ministry specialist Mike Yaconelli shared about his bed-jumping days and wondered why and where they'd gone. He rightly saw a connection with our inability as adults to "wonder," to marvel at the goodness of life from the Creator himself. We've forgotten how to jump; we've silenced "the voice of wonder and amazement, the voice of God, which has always been speaking to us, even before we were born."

As the movie *Billy Elliot* opens we see Billy jumping, rather leaping like a modern dancer, on his bed. Not a care in the world, he seems made for movement, even when his world comes crashing in and we wonder just how many dancing days this poor child has left. You can expect howling laughter, a bit of emotional tear jerking, and a lot of inspiration from this English comedy. This movie is tough—tough language, tough breaks, tough striking miners, and a tough family situation. But it's also gentle and sweet as you watch a young boy experience freedom, love, and transcendence, of which bed-jumping is but a parable.

The story unfolds in a British coal-mining town where a working-class boy, Billy Elliot (Jamie Bell), is forced by his father to take boxing lessons. He is, however, anything but a "Rocky." Moreover, life at home is anything but *Ozzie and Harriet*. His father (Gary Lewis) and older brother Tony (Jamie Draven) are striking miners. His mum has died young, and they are all still barely coping emotionally. His doddering grandmother (Jean Heywood) lives most of the time in her own little world, wandering away from home when not watched. No wonder that Billy has grown up quickly, given the adults he has to navigate.

One day, while supposedly practicing his boxing, he sees at the other end of the town's community center ballet lessons being taught by a chain-smoking disciplinarian (Julie Walters). His eyes light up. Soon he is awkwardly joining her class—the only boy in a crowd of tutus. But as one critic has observed, even before he takes a liking to ballet, Billy feels the music in his life, running and jumping when everyone else is marking time. Some of the best scenes in the movie are the ones without words, only movement, ones in which Billy is jumping on his bed or tearing down the streets of his hometown, often with the classic rock/pop music of T. Rex in the background.

As one can imagine, Billy's father is less than thrilled when he finds out just how his son has been spending his time and the family's scarce money. In fact, father and older brother want to box Billy for his "poof" (read "homosexual") tendencies. But Billy is neither a stereotype nor a homosexual. He is a child in love with music and movement—a child wanting to fly. And through him, the adults in the story (not to mention the viewers) actually soar with him.

While there are moments in the movie that are hard to believe if looked at as a documentary, the film is meant more as fable and fantasy. It definitely falls into the triumph-over-trouble genre. Inevitably, familial love goes to battle with ignorance and stereotypes, and family wins. We weep as we see the healing that takes place as the love of father and son transcends all union rules and homophobic worries. And we weep at the portrayal of joy, pure joy, as we watch Billy Elliot living into how the Creator fashioned him. But we also weep because we too long to soar—to be all that the Creator imagined us to be.

Dialogue Texts

So God created humankind in his image, in the image of God he created them; male and female he created them.

Genesis 1:27

You have turned my mourning into dancing; you have taken off my sackcloth and clothed me with joy, so that my soul may praise you and not be silent. O LORD my God, I will give thanks to you forever.

Psalm 30:11–12

Train a child in the way he should go, and when he is old he will not turn from it.

Proverbs 22:6 NIV

Discussion Questions

1. Many reviewers talked about the film *Billy Elliot* as being about family relationships and about a boy finding the courage

to pursue his dreams. Both of these are true, but as theologians we might say that ultimately Billy's dream is to be who he was created to be—a beautiful, passionate dancer. In dancing Billy experiences internal fulfillment and freedom. From what sorts of things is he free during those moments of dancing into his creation? How do the other characters experience freedom in the film? As you watched the film, what did you learn about your own interior freedom? Are you living into your created self?

2. Family relationships are crucial in the film, especially between Billy and his dad. Father-son relationships fill the pages of books, including the Bible, and have been recurring film themes. What strikes you most about the relationship Billy has with his father? How does it change during the film, or does it? What lesson is there in this film for you as a father, son, or family member?

3. *Billy Elliot* also deals with poverty and social justice. The director helps the viewer experience the struggles of coal miners to obtain fair wages and benefits. How did you feel seeing the violent clashes of strikers, scabs, and police? Think about the scene in which Billy's dad finally crosses the picket line because he needs money for his family. What did you feel for him, for the other strikers? What did you feel when the strike was settled? Where was the church in such scenes? Where should the church be in such situations? (Note: The 1984 coal miner strike was the worst strike in postwar England. Prime Minister Thatcher and the miners locked horns, and the result was the effective end of coal mining in England. With its end came the end of numerous communities and economic hardship for many.)

4. Discuss the last scene. What emotions did you feel as Billy's dad and brother enter the theater, as you see Tony for the first time, and as you see Billy soar across the stage?

Clip Conversations

1. Chapter 7 [38:05–47:55]—"Private Lessons." Mrs. Wilkinson and Billy meet in the gym to begin choreographing his audition dance. They sit down on the dusty boxing ring floor. Billy has brought some personal items to show her in the hope of inspiring his dance: a football shirt, a tape, and an envelope. He explains that his mum wrote a letter for him before she died. As Mrs. Wilkinson reads the letter, Billy, who knows his mother's words by heart, joins in. It is a moment of profound sadness and yet love, for Billy's mum wrote, "Please know that I was always with you through everything. I always will be. I'm proud to have known you, and I'm proud you were mine. Always be yourself. I'll love you forever. Mum." Billy looks wistful and rests his head on the ropes. Minutes later he is dancing joyfully with Mrs. Wilkinson. What did you learn about Billy and Mrs. Wilkinson in this scene? What did you learn about yourself?

2. Chapter 11 [1:03:45–1:07:18]—"Christmas." Picture the scene: It's Christmas and the snow is falling heavily. It's a postcard scene. However, when you have no fuel to heat your house, Christmas snow is a curse, not a blessing. In the social club, the miners gather in a show of solidarity to wish each other Merry Christmas. But Billy's dad is not there. He's in his backyard with a sledgehammer, painfully destroying his wife's old piano. Billy, from the background, asks his dad if he thinks she'll mind. "Shut it, Billy. She's dead," he replies coldly. We cut to Christmas dinner where the family is balancing their meager dishes on their laps. The fire is blazing, but the flames seem only to remind all of the absence of Billy's mum. His dad breaks the silence by saying, "Merry Christmas." "Merry Christmas," they reply. And then, in the silence, Billy's dad begins to sob as the fire crackles. What did you learn about Billy's dad in this scene? What did you learn about the pain this family is experiencing?

3. Chapter 12 [1:07:18–1:11:20]—"A Dance of Defiance." Billy's father and friend are walking back home, past the gym. They notice a light on and see Billy dancing with his best friend, Michael, who is dressed comically in a tutu. They are having fun, lost in dancing. Billy's dad walks into the gym. The shock is tangible for everyone, and Michael wriggles out of his tutu. Billy stares at his dad, but neither of them talks. So Billy decides to let his feet do the talking. He starts to dance, aggressively at first and in his dad's face. It's as though he is saying, "This is me. I am your son. Take me or leave me, but this is who I am." Then he fills the room with movement—strong, beautiful, powerful dance. He ends his dance with a flourish, triumphantly, right in front of his father. Silence. Michael tentatively claps. Billy's father leaves without a word. What do you think Billy learned about himself in this scene? What did his father learn that night in the gym? How did it change them both forever?

Bonus Material

Billy Elliot deals with the theme of triumph over adversity and was itself such a triumph. Many thought that a film about a ballet-dancing boy set in a coal-mining town during a strike would be a disaster. Stephen Daldry had been a successful theater director, but this was his first feature film. He soon learned about the dynamics of making a film when he started to scout locations (i.e., there were very few mines left in England to use in the film) and when he began auditioning actors for the film.

The director and producers were looking for a young boy (eleven to thirteen years of age) from the northeast of England (to get the accent correct) who could dance, act, and have the focus to work on a feature-length film. There were moments when they thought they would never find the right boy. The star, thirteen-year-old Jamie Bell, was plucked from over two thousand kids who tried out for the part. Encouraged by his mom, Jamie started dancing at age six, but he had never told his friends and classmates. When his mom heard about the auditions, she encouraged Jamie to try out. When word leaked out that he'd gotten the part of a dancer in a movie, many of his classmates couldn't believe it. Some even kidded him about being a dancer rather than playing football (read "soccer") with them.

When selected, Jamie was scared but was excited to do his best. He spent three weeks in dance rehearsals with Peter Darling, the film's choreographer. Darling recognized immediately that Jamie—like Billy Elliot—had an incredible gift and determination. Choreographer, actors, and crew watched this young man blossom before their eyes. At the premier, Jamie confessed to still being afraid to see himself dance.

The film was originally titled *The Dancer* and was a great hit at the Cannes Film Festival. However, the name was changed to the name of the lead character, *Billy Elliot*, because it was felt it would do better at the box office. It went on to critical acclaim and box office success.

Billy Elliot was nominated for twenty-five awards in all—three Academy Awards (including Best Director), thirteen British Academy Awards, one French Academy Award, two Golden Globes, two National Board of Review Awards, three Screen Actors Guild Awards, and one Writers Guild of America Award for Best Original Screenplay. It won five awards, including the British awards for Best British Film and Best Actor (Jamie Bell). The National Board of Review also picked it as the number five film of the year and gave Bell the Best Young Actor award. Its worldwide box office receipts were $71 million.

11. *The Apostle*

U.S., 1997
148 Minutes, Feature, Color
Actors: Robert Duvall, Farrah Fawcett,
Miranda Richardson, John Beasely,
June Carter-Cash, Walt Goggins,
Billy Joe Shaver, Billy Bob Thornton
Director: Robert Duvall
Screenwriter: Robert Duvall
Rated: PG13 (brief profanity, brief violence, mature themes)
DVD Features: theatrical trailer, production notes, cast and filmmakers,
commentary with director, MCA Records soundtrack presentation,
"*The Journey of The Apostle,*" Spanish subtitles

Themes

Embracing Our Vocation
Arguing with God, Baptism, Prayer,
Renewing the Church,
Repentance, Sharing Our Faith
Role of Clergy, Salvation,
Sanctification,
Transformation, Worship

Synopsis and Theological Reflection

Graham Greene's novel *The Power and the Glory* tells the story of a "whiskey priest" in northern Mexico who continues to administer the sacrament despite his flawed life. There is no one else to represent Christ to the town's people. Through it all, you realize where the real power and glory in ministry lies—with God and his church, not with ourselves. Viewers will encounter this same, profound truth as they watch Robert Duvall's *The Apostle*, as complex a portrayal of a minister as has come to the screen in a long time.

Like many of Duvall's characters (one thinks of Mac in *Tender Mercies* [see the discussion later in this book] or Boss in *Open Range*), Euliss "Sonny" Dewey is stereotypically masculine. He is also both sinner and saint, solitary while charismatic, hard to domesticate, yet deeply caring. Above all, he is someone struggling to live into his own salvation. Different than Mac or Boss, however, Sonny is a Pentecostal minister working to accomplish the salvation of others. Thus the story interweaves two ministries—one to Sonny's congregations and the other to himself.

Sonny (Robert Duvall) knows he is called to preach. *The Apostle* (d. Duvall, 1997). Photo by Van Redin. Copyright 1997 October Films. All rights reserved.

As the film begins, we see Sonny stop at a highway accident and invite a dying young man to accept Jesus as his Savior so he can go to heaven. Later, after cracking open the skull of his estranged wife's boyfriend with a baseball bat and fleeing town, we see this preacher go to the river and baptize himself "the apostle E. F." in order to start life again. E. F. is a self-described "Holy Ghost, Jesus-filled, preachin' machine." But it's hard to doubt either his faith or his gifts. He might use the huckster's craft at times, but his motives are genuine. There is an earthiness to his life, but Sonny has been called to preach the gospel. And preach he does.

There are several memorable scenes in the film:

A Hispanic woman translates for Sonny at a tent meeting, using his body language as well as his words.

Sonny goes up to the attic and cries out to God after losing both his church and his wife. "I'm confused, mad. . . . Give me peace. . . . I know that I'm a sinner, a womanizer, but I'm your servant. What should I do, Jesus?"

Sonny confesses to his church that he shouldn't have beaten up a racist heckler. "I know that you're supposed to turn the other cheek, but I ain't goin' to let anyone steal my church."

Sonny lays his Bible under the bulldozer and dares the heckler who has returned to come ahead and bulldoze his church building if he thinks he can get away with blasphemy against God.

Written, directed, produced, acted, and funded by Duvall himself, *The Apostle* was thirty-five years in the making. Ever since he wandered into a small Pentecostal church in Hughes, Arkansas, in 1962, Duvall had wanted to do a movie on a southern preacher. Encouraged by his writer-friend Horton Foote to do it himself, over a decade ago Duvall started studying in earnest the style of southern preachers, particularly black Pentecostals. (Duvall calls it "the true American art form.") Duvall says on one Sunday he heard six different sermons! And his homework has paid off. The worship that is portrayed is genuine, as is the power of personality. The belief is real, as is the gift for sales.

During the final twenty minutes of the film, we see E. F preaching his last service as the police wait for him at the door of his church. There is a wonderful mixture of folk in the church, black and white, old and young. When E. F. tells his people that it's "a one-way road to heaven" where Jesus is calling us and then begins singing, "Softly and tenderly Jesus is calling," a young mechanic comes forward wanting to be saved. The moment is real and the tears heartfelt. It is not just the mechanic who is being given a new life, however. Sonny is also living into his baptism. He has confessed his past to his copastor and has turned from his womanizing, and now he is even willing to give up his church. E. F. is at peace. As the credits roll, we see Sonny on a prison work crew cutting weeds at the side of the highway. As he works freely and joyously, he is again that

"Holy Ghost, Jesus-filled preachin' machine," leading his fellow prisoners in praising Jesus!

Appearing on the David Letterman show after release of the film, Duvall was asked, "Is Sonny doing this because he is good at it or because he has accepted Jesus Christ as his Lord and Savior?" Duvall responded, "What do you think?" and Letterman said, "Probably, he's good at it." "No," Duvall corrected, "it's both. That's why I put in the first scene (at the car wreck)." Reinforcing the fact that he hadn't gotten it, Letterman proceeded to show a clip of the film in which E. F. is trying to talk his way into the house of a hoped-for girlfriend for a tryst. But though the film shows Sonny as a *sinner*, it is ultimately more about him as an *apostle*. God's power and glory shines through him—even through the whiskey. Perhaps it takes "eyes to see."

Dialogue Texts

Nathan said to David, "You are the man! Thus says the LORD, the God of Israel: I anointed you king over Israel, and I rescued you from the hand of Saul; I gave you your master's house, and your master's wives into your bosom, and gave you the house of Israel and of Judah; and if that had been too little, I would have added as much more. Why have you despised the word of the LORD, to do what is evil in his sight? You have struck down Uriah the Hittite with the sword, and have taken his wife to be your wife.

2 Samuel 12:7–9

In those days John the Baptist appeared in the wilderness of Judea, proclaiming, "Repent, for the kingdom of heaven has come near." This is the one of whom the prophet Isaiah spoke when he said, "The voice of one crying out in the wilderness: 'Prepare the way of the Lord, make his paths straight.'"

Matthew 3:1–3

For I am not ashamed of the gospel; it is the power of God for salvation to everyone who has faith, to the Jew first and also to the Greek. For in it the righteousness of God is revealed through faith for faith; as it is written, "The one who is righteous will live by faith."

Romans 1:16–17

Am I not free? Am I not an apostle? Have I not seen Jesus our Lord? Are you not my work in the Lord? If I am not an apostle to others, at least I am to you; for you are the seal of my apostleship in the Lord.

1 Corinthians 9:1–2

For I am the least of the apostles, unfit to be called an apostle.

1 Corinthians 15:9

You were taught to put away your former way of life, your old self, corrupt and deluded by its lusts, and to be renewed in the spirit of your minds, and to clothe yourselves with the new self, created according to the likeness of God in true righteousness and holiness.

Ephesians 4:22–24

Discussion Questions

1. During the opening credits, we see Sonny as a small child in a black holiness church. (Rev. Hickman, an actual blind holiness preacher, fasted for twenty-four hours before doing the scene. Though Duvall cut the scene early, Rev. Hickman and the parishioners carried on a forty-five-minute service.) This scene is followed by Sonny, as an adult, at the scene of a car crash. Duvall says this scene came from the true story of a friend whose mother was a preacher. Duvall insisted on these opening scenes to show Sonny as a sincere man on a mission. How did they strike you—as Duvall hoped or as David Letterman experienced them? What were you thinking while Sonny and his mother prayed for the crash victims or when the injured woman moved

her hand? How did this scene challenge or confirm your ideas about prayer and miracles?

2. After his baptism, the Apostle E. F. sets off again as "a soldier in the army of the Lord" (the song playing in the background). What sorts of things does he do and say now that he's trying to follow the Lord? When he comes upon a Catholic priest giving the annual blessing of the bayou boats he says, "Glory . . . Glory . . . You do it your way, I do it mine, but we get it done, don't we?" Do you think that it is a realistic comment from a holiness preacher? How might this statement even indicate a change in his life?

3. The Apostle arrives in Bayou Bouttè. How does he connect with people? He and Reverend Blackwell discuss God's guidance of E. F. in bringing him to the Reverend as well as to the town and to planting a church. How would you describe their theology of how God leads his people? Per Rev. Blackwell, what checks and balances are there in discerning God's leading? What would you have said to E. F. about how God leads individuals?

4. E. F. has two confrontations with the troublemaker, played by Billy Bob Thornton. Compare his first encounter with his second one (chapters 27 [1:32:48–1:35:50] and 30 [1:39:14–1:47:18]—"Not Like Other Preachers" and "Nobody Moves That Book"). Duvall says that both scenes are based on true stories from preachers he knows (J. Charles Jessup and Paul Baggett). What do they show about the Apostle's commitment to God and his church? Did you find the troublemaker's conversion believable, unbelievable, corny, honest, moving, over-the-top . . . ?

5. As the movie ends we see Sonny. Where is he and what is he still doing? What do you think the director is telling us about Sonny and his journey?

Clip Conversations

1. Chapter 8 [25:30–27:40]—"Yelling At the Lord." Sonny's wife has told him that she wants a divorce. His church elders have told him that the church has been taken from him. In this scene we see Sonny shouting his lament to God. The psalmists did the same thing. What do they and Sonny include in their laments—complaint, beseeching God to work as he has in the past, confession, profession of faith or trust, etc.? Have you ever yelled at God? What did you experience through your lament?

2. Chapters 13 [40:50–43:30] and 14 [43:30–45:00]—"Heal This Broken Heart" and "The Apostle." Sonny is on his journey and he's camping out in a pup tent. He prays (with the prayers being a voice-over in his wife's voice), fasts, reads Scripture, remembers his life and call, and weeps in contrition and sadness. We then see him baptizing himself as an apostle of the Lord. What do you notice about this baptism? What does the director want us to think about Sonny's past life and future life? Do you believe these scenes show Sonny's sincere desire to change?

3. Chapter 25 [1:21:05–1:27:10]—"Small, but Powerful." Sonny, Rev. Blackwell, and a small group of followers start the church. What strikes you about that first service? What sorts of things do they do to impact the community? How does the church grow?

4. Chapters 32 [1:50:35–2:07:35] and 33 [2:07:35–2:09:35] —"The Last Meeting" and "I'll Fly Away." The Apostle E. F. preaches his last sermon as the police wait to take him away. What strikes you about this service? During the altar call Sammy comes forward. What did you feel as you watched his conversion being portrayed? (Duvall shares on the DVD that this actor had actually received the Lord as a young person but then became disillusioned with religion. Duvall says that he never saw an

actor so overcome with emotion. He believes that Walt Goggins was reborn/resaved that day. Duvall also admits that there were several times that he was also overcome with emotion. What happened went far beyond the script he wrote.)

Bonus Material

As the actors and crew reflected on their experience in making *The Apostle* (see DVD), many commented on the profound effect the film had on their own lives. Rob Carliner, the producer, says it was a "passionate and personal experience for everyone." Others called it a deeply spiritual experience. Some examples are noted above, but an additional special moment happened in the filming of the tag-team preaching scene (in which the preachers are all real preachers). One of the crew drivers was touched by the preaching. After the scene was finished, the preachers gathered around the man and laid hands on him. He was saved that day.

What happened through and to the professional actors and crew was dynamic, but the nonprofessional actors also brought the story to life. Duvall, inspired by the documentary-style filmmaking of Ken Loach, decided to use many actual holiness preachers and churchgoers. One such person was Rick Dial, who played Elmo, the radio station owner. He is actually the manager of a furniture store who sings in his local church choir. He in fact had to have the shooting schedule fit around the summer furniture sale he was having at the store. Also Sister Johnson with the twin boys and Sister Delilah are loyal holiness church members who had never been in a movie. The bayou man who was so gracious and gentle to Sonny in his time of repentance and rebaptism is Reverend Cole, a preacher from Dallas, Texas. When Duvall asked him to play the part, he responded that he didn't even go to movies.

Since this movie was so completely connected with Robert Duvall (screenwriter, director, lead actor, and executive producer), it behooves the viewer to understand what the film meant to him. On the DVD you can hear much of his testimony about the film. Here we just want to highlight some of his comments. Though the film was very difficult to get off the ground, Duvall says that once it started, "It was like it was really meant to be." He felt it was important to "get it right" about people in the south who have faith, and he wanted to show the "strange coexistence of black and white in the holiness churches." He also shares that at several points in the film he was overcome with emotion (e.g., when he apologizes to the congregation about his fighting with the troublemaker and during his last sermon). Speaking of the film and its meaning in his own life, Duvall said on the DVD, "It was the greatest experience of my work life. . . . It will really never be behind me. . . . It was the most important time of my life. . . . Between the cradle and the grave, you try to contribute something. This is something that I've felt that . . . I've contributed to humanity. The very thing that I had hoped for . . . is that it has been accepted by the hip secular film community and others, and by all the religious community." (In fact both Howard Stern and Pat Robertson endorsed the movie when it came out!)

The Apostle won eight awards for Best Actor from film critics across the country and received nominations in this category from both the Academy and the Screen Actors Guild in the U.S. The film's budget was roughly $5 million, which Duvall put up himself. After its premier at the Toronto Film Festival, he sold the film to October Films. Its total box office receipts were just over $20 million. Viewers and critics alike recognized what a landmark film The Apostle is because of its portrayal of religion and the spiritual quest, its direction of actors and nonactors, and the performance by Robert Duvall, who some call "American cinema's greatest living actor." We'll leave it to God to know whether Duvall counts himself in the body of Christ, but we look forward to hearing him sing hymns like "I Love to Tell the Story" in heaven.

Reconciliation
within Families

12. The Straight Story

U.S./France, 1999
111 Minutes, Feature, Color
Actors: Richard Farnsworth, Sissy Spacek,
Harry Dean Stanton
Director: David Lynch
Writers: John F. Roach and Mary Sweeney
Rated: G (nothing offensive)
DVD Features: theatrical trailer

Reconciliation within Families
*Beauty of Creation, Balance in Life,
Perseverance, Wisdom*
Affirming the Human Spirit,
Humor, Role of Clergy

Themes

Synopsis and Theological Reflection

This Disney movie is G-rated but not particularly of interest to children. Its pace is too slow, its dialogue sparse, and its action almost nonexistent. Kids will get fidgety, but you won't. The film is lyrical and humane, filled with yearning, wisdom, and hope. Here is a movie for parents to take grandparents to see and then to reflect on afterwards over a cup of coffee.

The movie is fablelike, yet it is based on a real-life story. Alvin Straight, a fiercely independent seventy-three-year-old in failing health, makes a three-hundred-and-seventy-mile trip across Iowa to seek reconciliation with his brother who has suffered a stroke. What makes this journey unique is the fact that given his bad hips, failing eyesight, and limited budget, Alvin can only get there by driving his John Deere lawn mower!

Straight's family was initially concerned that their father would be turned into a laughingstock by the movie, particularly when they learned that David Lynch would direct the film. But they had no need to fear. A painter who has turned to film in

Alvin Straight (Richard Farnsworth) drives his '66 John Deere from Iowa to Wisconsin to see his brother. *The Straight Story* (d. Lynch, 1999). Copyright 1999 Disney Enterprises. All rights reserved.

order to get motion into his images, Lynch has created a visual masterpiece. Seen chiefly through the eyes of Alvin, the photographic images of the rural Midwest are stunning. Dubbed the master of the weird for being the director of *Eraserhead*, *Blue Velvet*, and the TV series *Twin Peaks*, Lynch has chosen a different direction here, creating an elegant, if quirky, portrayal of what it is to be truly human. He has returned in style and theme to his Oscar-nominated *The Elephant Man*, the true story of how the real humanity of a badly deformed young man is discovered.

Crucial to the movie's success is the actor Richard Farnsworth who plays Alvin Straight. Seventy-nine years old himself at the time of the filming, Farnsworth was a movie stuntman for most of his adult life before becoming an actor. Time and again (after all, a power lawn mower can only go about four miles an hour), the camera lingers on Farnsworth's face, particularly his eyes, and then on what Farnsworth sees. As it does so, we see straight into the very soul of Alvin (or is it into our own souls?). The effect is iconic.

A few years back our local art museum had an exhibit on how photographs of the human face can capture the real self. But as a reviewer wrote, "When it comes to the mysterious matter of portrait photography and the human soul, it's neither the artist's nor the sitter's soul that can be accessed with any reliability . . . only

the soul of the audience is present and accounted for." This critic
is right. As we look at Farnsworth's character, it is ourselves that
we see. Alvin helps us get in touch with our own humanity.

The Straight Story is at one and the same time comic and wistful, offbeat and yet ordinary. It allows viewers to reflect on the
importance of perseverance, of family, and of a wisdom that
comes through life.

Alvin Straight succeeds in his journey for he simply won't
give up—not when his hip gives out, not when his friends try
to dissuade him, not even when the lawn mower breaks down.
When someone who befriends him along the way offers to drive
him to his brother, Alvin even refuses this offer. "You're a kind
man talking to a stubborn man," he says. "I still want to finish
this the way I started." He must seek to end his estrangement
with his ailing brother himself. And when his brother asks him,
"Did you ride that thing all the way out here to see me?" we
sense the wisdom of his decision.

Behind Alvin's journey is his recognition of the importance
of family. On his six-week journey, Alvin encounters a pregnant teenager who is running away from home out of fear that
her family will reject her. He tells her that he used to play a
game with his kids where he gave each a stick and told them
to break it. They easily could. Then he would bundle all the
sticks together and have them try to break them again. They
couldn't. Alvin then tells the girl, "That bundle—that's family."
Alvin's own daughter is living with him because she is a "little
slow." Wonderfully played by Sissy Spacek, Rose has had her
own children taken away by authorities because they claimed
Rose couldn't take care of them properly, and Alvin and Rose
live daily with the pain of their absence. This estrangement is
beyond their control, but Alvin can attempt reconciliation with
his brother, Lyle, after a decade of anger and silence. So Alvin
boards his lawn mower. With every mile, we sense Alvin's
growth toward wholeness and peace.

Finally, Alvin gives to those he encounters a wisdom tem-
pered by the pain and disappointment of his life. He sarcastically

tells some young bicyclists who are belittling him, "The worst part of being old is remembering when you were young." But it is precisely such experiences that allow Alvin to see life more clearly. Throughout the movie, the viewer looks at what Alvin sees—the landscape, the line on the road, the sunrise, and the faces of those he meets. And as we see what Alvin sees, we see our own lives. Alvin's gift to us is the gift of his simple humanity. Here's the straight story.

Dialogue Texts

Behold, how good and pleasant it is when brothers dwell in unity!

Psalm 133:1 RSV

But Esau ran to meet [Jacob], and embraced him, and fell on his neck and kissed him, and they wept. . . . Jacob said, "No, please; if I find favor with you, then accept my present from my hand; for truly to see your face is like seeing the face of God—since you have received me with such favor."

Genesis 33: 4, 10 (the reconciliation of Jacob and Esau, Genesis 32–33)

Then Joseph could no longer control himself. . . . And he wept. . . . Joseph said to his brothers, "I am Joseph. Is my father still alive?" . . . Then he fell upon his brother Benjamin's neck and wept, while Benjamin wept upon his neck. . . . Israel said, "Enough! My son Joseph is still alive. I must go and see him before I die."

Genesis 45:1–3, 14, 28 (the story of Joseph, Genesis 37–50)

So when you are offering your gift at the altar, if you remember that your brother or sister has something against you, leave your gift there before the altar and go; first be reconciled to your brother or sister, and then come and offer your gift.

Matthew 5:23–24

Discussion Questions

1. David Lynch was a painter before he was a filmmaker. His way of storytelling is to paint canvases of meaning for the viewer rather than just use words to explain his point. Think about the opening minutes of the film: the night sky full of stars, the grain harvester kicking up dust, the neighbor lady methodically sunning herself in her yard, and Alvin's buddy coming to search for him. How do these "canvases" prepare you for what is to come? What does the director want us to know about these people and their corner of the world? What are some pictures/scenes in the movie that spoke to you as powerfully as the dialogue?

2. Another brilliant touch to the film is the director's and actor's collaboration in letting us see the world through Alvin's eyes. (Richard Farnsworth's face is a work of art itself. As one reviewer put it, he can "express more emotion with his face than in reciting pages of dialogue.") Whether it's the expanse of creation—clouds, cornfields—or the wonder of human inge-nuity—bridges, trucks, roads that stretch forever—we *see* what Alvin sees. Why do you think the director presented the story in this way? Can you think of a scene in the film in which Alvin's eyes opened up new ways of seeing for you?

3. While Lynch is mostly known for his visual creations, he also loves jamming with musician colleagues (he likes to play the guitar upside down!) and overseeing musical scores with longtime collaborator Angelo Badalamenti. The composer's score is simple and moving with a country edge, using strings, classical guitar, and synthesizer. Music reviewers have suggested that the music conveys the film's sense of regret and tender eccentricity, which has a way of reaching the viewer's heart. Do you agree? Compare the road/travel music with that which is played when Alvin meets people along the way. How do the styles change, and how does this impact the viewer?

Clip Conversations

Note that the director, David Lynch, refused to divide his movie into chapters for the DVD, saying a movie cannot be divided up like a book. The titles for the clips we have chosen are therefore our own.

1. "A Runaway Teenager" [38:25–49:14]. Alvin's first encounter on his road trip is with a pregnant teenager running away from her family who she says hate her. Alvin shares the story of his daughter, Rose, and her longing for her children who were taken from her because she's a "little slow" and thought to be unable to care for them properly. He then tells the young teenager about a game he used to play with his children (see Synopsis above). The next morning the teenager is gone, but a bundle of sticks remains. How did Alvin's conversation speak to you and your family situation? As a viewer, what did you experience when you saw the bundle? What had more impact for you—hearing the story Alvin told (words) or seeing what the teenager did with the story (symbol)? How could this "parable of the bundle of sticks" apply to your church? How can we help people hear and see such good news?

2. "Another Dead Deer" [56:40–59:50]. Not all of Alvin's encounters are as deep or serious. Later in the journey a car zooms past him only to brake suddenly. Alvin's face reflects the screeching of the brakes and the thud we hear. As he approaches, he asks the driver, a woman, if he can help. She laments, "No one can help me. I've prayed to St. Francis, St. Christopher . . . I've still killed thirteen deer in seven weeks on this road. And I have to travel this road every day forty miles back and forth to work." She looks over the empty plains and wonders, "Where do they come from?" After looking at the dead deer she shouts, "And I love deer." She jumps into her crumpled car and continues on. Alvin eyes the dead animal. In the next scene he is roasting venison over an open fire in someone's garden,

surrounded by decorative deer statues. (If you haven't laughed yet in this scene, please do so now!) Through humor we see the absurdity of life. Compare the speed at which the woman is traveling down the road with the speed at which Alvin is traveling. With Alvin's bad eyes and bad hips, how many deer will he kill? Is this a metaphor for life? At what speed are they each traveling through life? Whose life is more in need of pace—and peace? At what speed are you traveling?

3. "Last Night on the Road" and "Reaching Lyle's Place" [1:31:20–1:37:00 and 1:44:45–1:47:55]. Alvin camps out in a Catholic church's cemetery very close to his final destination, his brother's home. The priest brings him dinner and joins him for conversation. As they talk, the priest realizes that he visited Alvin's brother in the hospital. Lyle had told the priest a lot of things but never mentioned having a brother. Alvin responds, "Neither one of us has had a brother in a long time. . . . It's a story as old as the Bible, as Cain and Abel . . . anger, vanity, mixed with liquor. I want to make peace." To which the priest affirms, "Well, sir, I say amen to that." The next morning Alvin makes it to his brother's home. When his brother sees the lawn mower he asks, "Did you ride that thing all the way out here to see me?" Alvin answers, "I did, Lyle." No more is said as they sit together, brothers reconciled. What did Alvin's act of reconciliation create in his brother? What does it say to us about the cost of reconciliation? How can your community foster such acts of reconciliation?

Bonus Material

David Lynch decided to make *The Straight Story* because "It's got great elements. It's got an old guy who is a real individual, who does something for a beautiful reason, against all odds. He's somebody I think people would like to see on the screen and experience the journey with him." According to Sissy Spacek, actor and friend of Lynch, the cast and crew of the film became totally devoted to the director, who was patient, humble, and tenderhearted. He once shortened his bio to read simply, "Eagle Scout, Missoula, Montana."

Lynch shot *The Straight Story* on location. He made a point of filming it along the same route, from Iowa to Wisconsin, that the real-life Straight took in 1994. Thus, the cast and crew got to meet a lot of the people who helped Straight on his journey. Wherever they went people had a good word to say about the old man on the lawn mower. Lynch wanted viewers to see the beauty of the American heartland and the beauty of riding a lawn mower (i.e., the beauty experienced going at the speed of a lawn mower). It has been called "a four-mile-an-hour road picture."

Though Lynch was the director, the film was actually a community project of his friends and family. Coscreenwriter, coeditor, and coproducer Mary Sweeney is Lynch's companion and business partner. John Roach, a childhood friend of Sweeney, wrote the screenplay with her. Sissy Spacek is married to Jack Fisk, the production designer and college friend of Lynch. In keeping with the film's story, eighty-one-year-old cinematographer Freddie Francis, who worked with the director on *The Elephant Man*, worked on the film.

Probably most importantly, David Lynch knew that Richard Farnsworth was born to play the part of Alvin Straight. Farnsworth began his movie career in 1938 as an extra. From there he became a stuntman and was a stunt double for such actors as Montgomery Clift, Henry Fonda, and Kirk Douglas. He then tried his hand at acting in a Roy Rogers movie with disastrous results. It was many years later that he tried it again, and with drastically different results. In 1978 he was nominated for an Oscar for his role in *Comes a Horseman*, and in 1983 he was acclaimed for his role in *The Grey Fox*.

At age seventy-nine and walking with canes when he took on the part, Farnsworth really knew some of Straight's experiences. In fact, Lynch commented that because of his hips, Farnsworth was in a lot of pain during the shoot. But Farnsworth kept on and won the admiration of all the cast and crew. Sissy Spacek, playing Straight's daughter, found it quite easy to bond with Farnsworth since he was such a funny, humble, and tender man. He received a standing ovation at the Cannes Film Festival for his role as Alvin Straight.

The Straight Story was nominated for the Academy Award for Best Actor. It also was nominated for two Golden Globes—Best Actor (drama) and Best Original Score. It also won the European Film Academy Award for Best Non-European Film and two New York Film Critics Awards—Best Actor and Best Cinematography. Finally, it was chosen the number five film of the year by the National Board of Review. The film cost $8.5 million to make and had box office receipts of $10.1 million in the U.S. and abroad. Again, viewers and critics saw that great movies could be made with small budgets. And with video and DVD distribution, many more have experienced the film's beauty (though only the big screen can really do justice to it).

13. *Ulee's Gold*

Reconciliation within Families
Death, Friendship, Healing, Lament, Redemption
Beauty of Creation, Brokenness, Children, Compassion, Isolation, Loneliness, Love, Parenting, Suffering, Work

Themes

U.S., 1997
111 Minutes, Feature, Color
Actors: Peter Fonda, Patricia Richardson, Jessica Biel, J. Kenneth Campbell, Christine Dunford, Steven Flynn, Dewey Weber, Tom Wood, Vanessa Zima
Director: Victor Nunez
Writer: Victor Nunez
Rated: R (profanity, brief violence, mature themes)
DVD Features: theatrical trailer, production notes, collectible making-of booklet

Ulee (Peter Fonda) and his granddaughter Penny (Vanessa Zima) work the bees. *Ulee's Gold* (d. Nunez, 1997). Photo by John Bramley. Copyright 1997 Orion Pictures Corporation. All rights reserved.

Synopsis and Theological Reflection

In 1997, Peter Fonda commented on Hollywood's reticence to back low budget movies. He had in mind the film *Ulee's Gold*, in which he starred that year (as well as his 1959 antihero classic, *Easy Rider*). Fonda criticized the big studios for their commitment to hype over storytelling. Bemoaning the 1997 flicks that were marketed with product tie-ins and TV commercials (think of *The Lost World* or *Independence Day*), he said, "Unfortunately in Hollywood, the idea has been, the deal is more important than the product. But I've heard for years there are three things that should make a good film—a good story, a good story, and a good story."

Ulee's Gold is a good story! Written, photographed, directed, and produced by Victor Nunez, an independent filmmaker, it is an adult tale of redemption. (Note: Nunez has included strong language appropriate to some of the characters but not appropriate for children.) The plot is simple, in some ways all too familiar, like many fables. A Florida beekeeper withdraws into his work after experiencing the multiple traumas of Vietnam, his wife's death, a jailed son who is a failure as a father, and a daughter-in-law who abandons her two girls for drugs. But given his commitment to his work and his family, and given the developing friendship of a neighbor woman (Connie Hope), Ulee brings home the gold—literally and figuratively. Despite circumstances, Ulee is able to harvest the Tupelo honey (honey's golden finest) and rescue his daughter-in-law, Helen, returning her to her daughters and their family to his son.

That we are to understand the film as a fable about family loyalty and love is underscored by the names of the central characters. Like Homer's *Odyssey*, Ulysses (Ulee's given name) is married to Penelope and must leave to fight battles and rescue Helen. Despite his travails, he remains faithful to those who love him. The parallels are not fully developed, but the suggestion is present.

More effective than these mythic allusions in helping us understand the moral of the story, however, is the simple parable that Ulee's granddaughter Penny tells her mother. Wanting to give a gift to her mother, who is going through detox against her will, young Penny draws her a picture about beekeeping, something she has just learned from Ulee. She sits by the side of her mother's bed and explains the drawing: "Sometimes the bees get confused and run away, but they don't really want to. They are glad when someone helps them back into their home. But you have to stay calm." Here is the film in a nutshell, whether it be Helen's escape into drugs or Ulee's withdrawal into his bees. Both need the calm hand of someone who will help them come home.

This film is quiet, evocative, and peaceful. We listen through much of it to the haunting music of piano and strings. The camera lingers on the characters and lets us reflect on their feelings. Silences speak as eloquently as dialogue. We are allowed to eavesdrop on Ulee as he works extracting the honey and as he slowly breaks out of his isolation with the help of Connie and his two granddaughters.

However, what *Ulee's Gold* will be remembered for is not the plot or setting but the characterization. Put simply, this is Peter Fonda's film. As Fonda plays him, Ulee is a hero in spite of himself. Through most of the story, Ulee lacks the love that one might hope to find in a father. He takes care of his granddaughters mostly out of obligation. Like Helen, he too has run away from caring, but his escape has been the solitude of his bees. As Ulee painfully works for his family's external redemption, however, he discovers his own internal healing. And so do we.

Some might say that *Ulee's Gold* actually presents the story of *two* fathers and sons—Ulee and his son, Jimmy, and Peter and his father, Henry Fonda. For as we watch Ulee deal in an almost expressionless, stoic way with the rebellion of a son, we see on the screen something of Peter's father. Peter has commented that his father actually used to keep bees, but the associations in this film run much deeper. Like many of Henry's characters (and unlike our summer action heroes), Peter's Ulee has a certain mystery. The lone hero, he is almost iconographic. More like Jimmy, Ulee's son, through much of his career Peter has most often portrayed (and been portrayed as) the rebel. But in *Ulee's Gold*, the rebel has matured and come home. The son has become the father.

Dialogue Texts

The fathers have eaten sour grapes, and the children's teeth are set on edge.

Jeremiah 31:29 NIV

The LORD is merciful and gracious, slow to anger and abounding in steadfast love. . . . As a father has compassion for his children, so the LORD has compassion for those who fear him.

Psalm 103:8, 13

For thus says the Lord GOD: I myself will search for my sheep, and will seek them out. As shepherds seek out their flocks when they are among their scattered sheep, so I will seek out my sheep. I will rescue them from all the places to which they have been scattered on a day of clouds and thick darkness.

Ezekiel 34:11–12

A few days later the younger son gathered all he had and traveled to a distant country, and there he squandered his property in dissolute living. . . . "We had to celebrate and rejoice, because this brother of yours was dead and has come to life; he was lost and has been found."

Luke 15:13, 32

Discussion Questions

1. Victor Nunez, who wrote and directed *Ulee's Gold*, also does most of the camera work in his films. His films are slow moving with signature close-ups—focusing on a part of a person's body, whether in silence or while the dialogue continues. Some of the strongest moments in his films don't contain a word. The viewer's mind is forced to create the scene using the few simple visual clues given. Thus, the viewer becomes involved in the story by first observing, then by entering into the creative process with the director, and finally by identifying with the lives of the characters. How does your church or Christian community communicate the Story to the "viewers" around it? How might Nunez's approach to storytelling instruct us as we seek to communicate the Good News?

2. Nunez is known for his character-driven stories that are morality fables (stories that try to find or simply defend reasons to live right). Critics often say that his films deal with values that transcend religious or political bent—fairness, decency, and compassion. How do Jesus' stories and characters (e.g., the Good Samaritan parable) compare with Nunez's? How

can we continue in this rich storytelling tradition as we seek to bring our story and God's Story together? How can your church help those who don't know God's Story hear, see, and experience it?

3. Most viewers agree *Ulee's Gold* deals with redemption—of a family and of a man. This redemption is shown in a slow, almost meditative way, to which viewers are invited to journey over an extended period of time. Trace Ulee's movement from a physical and emotional recluse, starting with the sheriff's plea to Ulee at the beginning of the film, "You can't stay cut off forever," to Ulee inviting Connie Hope in for a cup of tea at the end of the movie. How does Ulee's journey, slow and bumpy, honestly portray the times you've felt alone but in need of others? How can the church help people along this journey?

4. Ulee's youngest granddaughter, Penny, picks up a photograph of Ulee's Vietnam unit. She stares intently and then asks, "They're all dead, every last one, except you?" "That's right," Ulee responds. "Had they been bad . . . did they deserve to die?" Penny asks. "No, no, Penny, they did *not*." "Why, then?" "Those were good guys. . . . Your grandpa was tricky, lucky. . . . That's why I made it out. But I shouldn't be talking to a little kid about . . ." "But it's so sad, Ulee," Penny responds. "You like sad?" Ulee asks her. "No, but sometimes, inside, it makes you quiet," she whispers. What truth does Penny understand that her grandfather hasn't yet? How else does Nunez have Penny teach the adults in her midst?

Clip Conversations

1. Chapter 6 [11:40–14:50]—"Heart-to-Heart." Ulee and Penny talk about the photograph taken in Vietnam (see discussion question 4 above). With whom do you most resonate, Penny or Ulee? How is Penny as wise as Job? How can you learn to let

sad things show you God's presence (see Eccles. 7:2)? Have you ever had such an experience? If you feel comfortable, share the experience in the group setting.

2. Chapter 21 [51:00–53:15]—"The Poison Persists." Helen, Ulee's daughter-in-law, is fighting her way through detox and against everyone around her. Her anger is especially directed toward Ulee. He fights back, accusing her of taking off and abandoning her children. She hisses back, "Your heart took off a long time ago." Both of these individuals are dealing with enormous past hurts. Even voicing them is the first step on the journey to wholeness for each. How have past hurts kept you stuck in unhealthy patterns? In the Psalms, voicing your hurt and frustration is called a lament. The psalmists were great at lamenting. See Psalms 13, 22, or 73 for a sample. How do the psalmists usually end their laments? The process of lamenting brings the psalmist where?

3. Chapter 22 [53:15–1:00:10]—"Tea and Sympathy." Connie Hope, the nurse renting their cottage across the street, has been helping Ulee and the girls deal with Helen's withdrawal symptoms. Connie has heard the biting words between Ulee and Helen (as noted above). Inviting Connie for tea, Ulee begins to share his story of disappointments, suffering, and death. She too shares her story. How has Connie created space for Ulee to begin the process of healing? As you think about your past wounds, what things have helped you experience healing and restoration? Was there someone to help you voice your hurt? How can your small group be a place of safety where people can share their hurts as they journey to shalom?

4. Chapter 25 [1:05:10–1:07:55]—"A Picture for Mom." Penny has been spending time with Ulee working with the bees. Helen has been painfully recovering. One day Penny comes home from school with a picture for her mother. It's a picture of Ulee leading wayward bees back to their hive. Penny

explains the picture to her mom saying, "Sometimes the bees get confused and run away, but they don't really want to. They are glad when someone helps them back into their home. But you have to stay calm and don't panic when they sting, 'cause they don't mean nothing by it." Who in your life needs calm, gentle leading back home—you, a friend, a family member? How might this parable be one that Jesus would have told? Can you think of one of his parables that has a similar theme or feel?

Bonus Material

The subject of bees is most likely an unattractive one to the average person. Not so for at least two of the central forces behind the movie *Ulee's Gold*. Victor Nunez once saw an old photo of a man and a child gathering honey in the Tupelo swamps of Florida and never forgot it. Born in Tallahassee, Nunez returned to the Apalachicola River swamps (one of the few places in the world where Tupelo honey is produced commercially) to create a story about a beekeeper. In the town of Wewahitchka, Florida, he bought some Tupelo honey from Ben Lanier, a third-generation beekeeper. Ben became his guide into the world of bees, and Nunez was off and running. Peter Fonda likewise had some experience of beekeeping because his father, Henry Fonda, worked several hives while Peter was growing up. He heard about Nunez's screenplay and called him saying, "I've got to play this part. I know this character!" And what he didn't know about handling bees, Ben Lanier taught him.

The bees and their production went on to much acclaim. Nunez presented Robert Redford with a jar of Tupelo honey when *Ulee's Gold* was shown as the centerpiece premier at the Sundance Film Festival. Not only that, but did you notice that the bees themselves are credited at the end of the film?

Ulee's Gold is a "hybrid/indie" film, since it was backed by a large studio (Orion Pictures) yet directed by an independent filmmaker. Victor Nunez has been writing, directing, shooting, and editing his own projects for twenty years. But *Ulee's Gold* pushed his film involvement to a new level—he got stung by some of his crew! Yes, he was stung twice, once on the stomach and once on the tip of his finger. But that didn't stop him, as he had only two months of spring (because Tupelo honey is harvested only in April and May) to shoot the film.

Nunez made the film for the modest budget of $2.7 million dollars. Its U.S. box office receipts were $9.2 million, with another $500,000 in international receipts. The film was nominated for two awards—Best Actor for the Academy and Best Actor in a Dramatic Picture for the Golden Globes. Fonda took home the Golden Globe but not the Oscar. Many felt the movie should have received more awards or at least received more press. But 1997 was the year of *Titanic*, so this bit of treasure got lost in the big splash of an ocean liner. Nevertheless, as *Rolling Stone's* Peter Travers put it, "This is no bakery-grade honey. *Ulee's Gold* is Tupelo prime!"

14. *Fly Away Home*

Themes

Reconciliation within Families
*Caring for Creation, Courage,
Parenting, Perseverance,
Second Chances*
Creativity, Grief, Home, Love,
Promise Keeping, Sanctity of Life

U.S., 1996
106 Minutes, Feature, Color
Actors: Jeff Daniels, Anna Paquin,
   Dana Delany, Terry Kinney,
   Holter Ford Graham, Jeremy Ratchford
Director: Carroll Ballard
Screenwriters: Robert Rodat and Vince McKewin
Rated: PG (nothing offensive—excellent for children)
DVD Features: theatrical trailer; commentary by director,
   cinematographer, and composer; exclusive featurette: "Operation
   Migration: Birds of a Feather"; documentary: "The Ultra Geese"; link
   to Operation Migration website; Spanish subtitles and dubbing

Amy Alden (Anna Paquin) feeding her geese. *Fly Away Home* (d. Ballard, 1996). Photo by Takashi Seida. Copyright 1996 Columbia Pictures. All rights reserved.

Synopsis and Theological Reflection

C. S. Lewis, in writing about children's stories, commented that any story worth reading as a child should be worth rereading as an adult. Unfortunately, anyone with children knows that such a standard is not too often realized. But *Fly Away Home* is one of those wonderful exceptions—a children's movie the whole family will enjoy. Here is a film to watch together and then discuss over a meal.

Fly Away Home is about parenting. Amy, a thirteen-year-old New Zealander played by Oscar winner Anna Paquin, loses her mother in a car crash as the film opens (the scene is not gruesome) and must go to live with her father on a small farm in Ontario, Canada. Thomas Alden, an eccentric artist and inventor who creates strange metal sculptures and constantly tinkers with the latest glider or ultralight plane, largely ignores his daughter out of guilt for the divorce and because of his preoccupation as an artist. For her part, Amy disengages from life at her new home out of pain and confusion. Does he care? Can I trust him?

Amy's isolation and her father's bewilderment begin to change only when Amy finds sixteen goose eggs, their mother the victim of a land developer's bulldozer. Amy rescues the eggs and helps them hatch in a drawer of her mother's old scarves. These goslings literally become her new family. The chicks imprint on Amy, following their "mother" anywhere and everywhere.

As the new "family" develops, so too a bond begins to form between father and daughter. Thomas realizes the geese are important to Amy and tries to help them escape the overzealous clutches of a ranger. We follow father and daughter as they first teach the young geese to fly and then to migrate south for the winter, their only hope of survival. The unwavering trust of the geese in Amy becomes mirrored in the growing trust between Amy and Thomas.

Father and daughter soar in their ultralight planes with the geese in formation behind their "mother." And the movie soars too. There is a serene quality to the photography as we glide with the geese over fields, lakes, and cities. Even a contrived deadline set by evil real estate developers in North Carolina cannot derail the movie. The message of "garden over machine" is too simplistic for real life, but in this fable, it works. You will cheer for Amy and her geese.

The movie is based *very* loosely on the experiments of artist-writer-naturalist Bill Lishman. During the mid-1980s he showed that newly hatched geese would imprint to humans and follow them in flight as they guided geese southward using small planes. But this film is not meant to be realistic biography; it is a fable meant to inspire and evoke.

Stunningly photographed by Caleb Deschanel and lyrically directed by Carroll Ballard, *Fly Away Home* was made by the same team who created the children's classic, *The Black Stallion* (1979). The film includes a beautiful score with a haunting ballad sung by Mary Chapin Carpenter ("Fair thee well my own true love, farewell for awhile, I'm going away . . .").

There are some magical moments in this film, as when Amy and a gosling just hatched look each other in the eye, or when Amy and her father emerge unexpectedly from the fog to find themselves among the skyscrapers of Baltimore. But equally awe-inspiring is the growth of a new love between father and daughter. When Amy asks her dad why he never came to see her, Thomas answers, "New Zealand's really far away." Only for Amy to reply, "That's a really lame excuse, Dad." And Thomas is finally able to say, "I was afraid, Amy. Angry. I'm really sorry." Not only have the geese found their way to a new home in North Carolina, Amy (and Thomas) have come home too.

There are several themes in this film worth discussing with family or friends: the sanctity of life, all life; perseverance pays off; human inventiveness is a wonderful thing; it is important to keep promises. But first and foremost, the film portrays the rebirth of a family—families can have second chances too.

Dialogue Texts

By the streams the birds of the air have their habitation; they sing among the branches. From your lofty abode you water the mountains; the earth is satisfied with the fruit of your work. You cause the grass to grow for the cattle, and plants for people to use, to bring forth food from the earth, and wine to gladden the human heart, oil to make the face shine, and bread to strengthen the human heart. The trees of the LORD are watered abundantly, the cedars of Lebanon that he planted. In them the birds build their nests; the stork has its home in the fir trees.

Psalm 104:12–17

The wolf shall live with the lamb, the leopard shall lie down with the kid, the calf and the lion and the fatling together, and a little child shall lead them.

Isaiah 11:6

Those with good sense are slow to anger, and it is their glory to
overlook an offense.

Proverbs 19:11

Then the father said to him, "Son, you are always with me, and
all that is mine is yours. But we had to celebrate and rejoice,
because this brother of yours was dead and has come to life; he
was lost and has been found."

Luke 15:31–32

And, fathers, do not provoke your children to anger, but bring
them up in the discipline and instruction of the Lord.

Ephesians 6:4

Discussion Questions

1. Through the artistry of the director, cinematographer, and
composer, *Fly Away Home* teaches us not only about family but
also about the environment. What scene was most beautiful and
inspiring to you with regard to the geese? How did the music
help you enter into their world? How did the film further your
wonder or love for God's creation?

2. At the heart of creation is the human family. But like
the first family, life is *not* Edenic for the Alden family. Both
Amy and her dad have big hurts and unanswered questions
to deal with. Amy asks, "Why did all this have to happen?"
(losing her mom, leaving her home in New Zealand, living
with an eccentric dad she hasn't seen since she was three
years old). Thomas Alden is also struggling to know how to
relate to Amy. How do you see their relationship at the start
of the film? How would you have felt in Amy's or Thomas's
shoes? What events or characters in the film help to initiate
change in their ability to feel again and to reach out to each
other?

3. How does the larger community of family, friends, well-wishers along the route, conservationists, and media play a role in Amy accomplishing her goal? What motivations do they have for getting involved? Where were the churches? Or why didn't the director include any church communities?

Clip Conversations

1. Chapter 17 [54:10–58:15]—"Amy Takes Flight." Seeing that her dad's idea of having the geese follow him in his ultralight to migrate south is just not working, Amy tries flying herself, if even for a few feet and a few moments. When she comes to a crash stop, Thomas Alden runs to Amy, thinking that she is hurt or worse. "You're crying," Amy says and hugs him. How has their relationship changed by this point? How does this event crystallize their love for each other?

2. Chapter 24 [1:22:35–1:30:15]—"Media Coverage Begins." As news spreads of Amy's journey with the geese, folks along the way look out for her and help her. One night bunked down in a little old lady's house, Amy and her dad talk about the past. What strikes you about this conversation? How has their relationship changed to allow for such vulnerable sharing and confession?

3. Chapter 26 [1:31:20–1:37:25]—"Father Goose Down." Having crash-landed his ultralight, Thomas Alden tells Amy she must continue the last thirty miles by herself. She resists, saying, "I can't find my way without you." But he reminds her of the courage and presence of her mother to carry her through to the end. "She's all around you, and she won't let you down," he encourages her. How has remembering a loved one encouraged you in hard times or in completing a goal?

4. Chapters 27 [1:37:25–1:40:15] and 28 [1:40:15–1:43:15] —"10,000 Miles" and "Mission Accomplished." As Amy makes

the last leg of the journey, a song plays. It is the same song with which the movie started, "10,000 Miles." How has Amy's journey been more than the six hundred miles from Canada to North Carolina with sixteen geese? As she came over the sand dunes onto the marshlands with her family of geese, what feelings did you have? What journey did you make during this film?

Bonus Material

Fly Away Home was inspired by the real-life story of Bill Lishman. He is a Canadian artist, turned scientist, who loves to fly ultralight aircraft. Along with his colleagues, Joe Duff and Dr. William Sladen, he has been devoted to saving endangered species of birds. His migration experiments of flying geese south became "Operation Migration" and were the basis for the trip Amy takes in the film. In 1993, *20/20* aired a segment on Lishman that drew the attention of numerous studios and screenwriters. In 1994, Columbia Pictures bought the rights to Lishman's life story. In 1995, filming began on *Father Goose*, the working title, which came from Lishman's nickname. Lishman's work was packaged in the fictional story of a father and daughter and retitled *Fly Away Home* when it was released in 1996.

The first scenes shot were the actual hatching of the goslings. In all, sixty geese were prepared for the film. Bill Lishman helped to imprint the geese to Anna Paquin by having his own daughter play tapes of Paquin's voice repeating the words "goose, goose, goose" while they were still in the incubator and when they began to walk around. When Paquin arrived on location, the goslings quickly accepted her as their "mother." Some were also imprinted to follow the aircraft.

The cinematography of Caleb Deschanel is one of the movie's highlights. The view of what is clearly real geese winging along at close range was breathtaking, as well as a challenge. A special plane with extra-long wings was designed to fly slowly enough to film the geese (goose speed is 32 mph, which is stalling speed for most aircraft). In addition, it had to be able to handle the weight of camera equipment.

Bits of Bill Lishman's day-to-day life are included in the film. For example, the refrigerator and shower portrayed in the film are actually his inventions and in his house. In addition, Bill's daughter is in the film as one of Amy's classmates. Finally, every time there is a shot of Amy's dad taking off in his ultralight (not the hang glider), it is actually Bill Lishman flying the aircraft. He and Jeff Daniels are of similar build and both have beards, so Lishman was able to be his flying double.

Both the Academy Awards and the American Society of Cinematographers nominated Caleb Deschanel for an award for *Fly Away Home*. The movie's total box office receipts were over $32 million. As a family film, you can't beat *Fly Away Home*, which the Broadcast Film Critics Association recognized in giving it an award. With its human drama, adventure, technical details about flying, and cute and funny animals, it has something for every personality and generation.

Racial
Reconciliation

15. *Save the Last Dance*

&

16. *Remember the Titans*

Creativity, Dreams/Hopes, Grief, Guilt

Themes

Both Movies:
Racial Reconciliation
Community, Friendship, Interracial Relationships, Racism, Stereotypes
Courage

Leadership, Unity in Diversity

Save the Last Dance
U.S., 2001

112 Minutes, Feature, Color

Actors: Julia Stiles, Sean Patrick Thomas, Kerry Washington, Fredro Starr, Terry Kinney, Bianca Lawson, Vince Green, Garland Whitt

Director: Thomas Carter

Screenwriter: Duane Adler and Cheryl Edwards

Rated: PG13 (brief violence and profanity, sexual situations, mature themes)

DVD Features: theatrical trailer, commentary by director, "The Making of Save the Last Dance," four deleted scenes, cast and crew interviews, and K-Ci & JO JO music video, "Crazy"

Remember the Titans
U.S., 2000

113 Minutes, Feature, Color

Actors: Denzel Washington, Will Patton, Donald Faison, Wood Harris, Ryan Hurst

Director: Boaz Yakin

Screenwriter: Gregory Allen Howard

Rated: PG (mature themes, mild violence)

DVD Features: theatrical trailer, commentary by real coaches Herman Boone and Bill Yoast, commentary by filmmakers, six deleted scenes,

two featurettes—"Beating the Odds" and "Denzel Becomes Boone,"
ABC Special, "Remember the Titans: An Inspirational Journey Behind
the Scenes," hosted by Lynn Swann

Synopsis and Theological Reflection

In January 2001, *Save the Last Dance* was a surprise box office hit. With no stars to grace the marquee and a price tag of
only $13 million, the film made over $90 million in U.S. box
office receipts alone. The movie is a Romeo and Juliet story
with an edge, told with dance as its primary metaphor. One
reviewer described it as "ballet meets hip-hop." Sara is a white,
high school ballerina from a small town that Norman Rock-
well might have painted. She has Julliard ambitions—that is
until her mom is killed in a car crash and she has to move in
with her estranged father on the South Side of Chicago. Sullen and disillusioned, she is brought back to life (and dance)
by a smart, self-assured African-American classmate, Derek,
who is himself pursuing his dream of getting into Georgetown
and becoming a pediatrician. It is Derek who teaches Sara
hip-hop, helps her overcome her false guilt over her mother's
death, and coaches her in her free-form, balletic dance for the
climactic audition. The story is predictable, but the emotion
and ambition are real. And by the end we want both of these
young heroes to succeed.

Some older-generation viewers might find the movie un-
comfortable because it portrays a white girl dating an African-
American. ("We didn't do that in our day.") However, by their
overwhelming attendance, teenage viewers have voted in favor
of being color-blind. It's simply not an issue to them. Or possibly, the issue for them is acceptance rather than intolerance.
If there is a tension for the filmmakers, it is elsewhere, in the
rightful jealousy of the black high school girls who resent having such a promising "catch" taken away from them by one
of the few white girls in their school. But ultimately, for both

Derek (Sean Patrick Thomas) teaches Sara (Julia Stiles) hip-hop. *Save the Last Dance* (d. Carter, 2001). Photo by Michael Tackett. Copyright 2000 Paramount Pictures. All rights reserved.

black and white, love prevails. In this movie, relationships are more important than the boxes we often create for them.

The same theme is to be found in the popular movie *Remember the Titans*, which played some months earlier. Here again is family entertainment with a message. Based on a true story but told more as inspirational drama than documentary, the movie recreates the story of the integration of T. C.

Coach Boone (Denzel Washington) and Coach Yoast (Will Patton) confer with players during a game. *Remember the Titans* (d. Yakin, 2000). Copyright 2000 Disney Enterprises and Jerry Bruckheimer, Inc. All rights reserved.

Williams High School in Alexandria, Virginia, in 1971. The all-white high school, state champions in football, is merged with a nearby black school. A black coach, Herman Boone (played wonderfully by Denzel Washington), is brought in from the south to coach the integrated team. Part of the resulting drama has to do with whether the Titans's much-loved white coach, Bill Yoast (Will Patton), who has been demoted to assistant coach in the changeover, and Boone, with his bottled-up rage over bigotry, can model a better way. Will the segregation that has characterized much of the town's adult population be allowed to continue? We think that we know what the answer will be (at least in this movie), but we still care how the players and coaches live into it. We clap and cry along with them.

Just as *Save the Last Dance* avoids sinking to the level of cliché while following a predictable trajectory, so *Remember the Titans* dances around multiple sports clichés without being reduced to caricature. And just as with *Save the Last Dance, Remember the Titans* shows us a better way through the wisdom of the teenagers it portrays. While the adults are scheming to maintain old structures or are reticent to engage the new, it's the students who want to win and thus come together to create a color-blind team. Black defensive star Julius Campbell becomes the friend of and co-captain with the white team captain, Gerry Bertier. Even when personal tragedy strikes, their friendship prevails and the team proves victorious.

Both of these teen movies are at their best when we are allowed to enter the high school world on its own terms and observe its chatter, its values, and its dreams. Neither is great cinema, nor were they created to be. Instead, they were filmed to be engaging entertainment with a moral. We know we are being manipulated, but whether through dance or football, we are inspired nonetheless. There is not meant to be much complexity here. Rather we are given fables rooted in reality that show us all a better way to live. We need not continue with our cautious patterns of polite segregation. In fact, tolerance needs to be not merely tolerated but embraced.

Both *Remember the Titans* and *Save the Last Dance* recognize that for those under twenty, intolerance is perhaps the number one sin. "Different strokes for different folks" is their proverb of choice. Whatever helps one to fulfill his dream or to live out her choices should be affirmed, even celebrated. Such a life philosophy can have its limitations, but there is a lesson here for all of us. We in the church too often organize our lives around models of exclusivity. We want our church to become multiracial, multicultural, and gender inclusive, yet our churches continue to be the most segregated institutions in our land. Rather than help all people to dance again, we make the steps too complicated, limiting ourselves to only the "right" dancers. In the process the church's celebration of the Good News becomes anything but a joyous reunion of the whole family of God.

Yet we want better. Could these teen movies help us by their example? Do you recall the words of Isaiah? "The wolf shall live with the lamb, the leopard shall lie down with the kid, the calf and the lion and the fatling together, and a little child shall lead them" (Isa. 11:6). Perhaps part of that eschatological prophecy concerning inclusiveness can be understood to have begun already with our youth.

Dialogue Texts

There is no longer Jew or Greek, there is no longer slave or free, there is no longer male and female; for all of you are one in Christ Jesus.

Galatians 3:28

Train children in the right way, and when old, they will not stray.

Proverbs 22:6

Remember your leaders, those who spoke the word of God to you; consider the outcome of their way of life, and imitate their faith.

Hebrews 13:7

The wolf shall live with the lamb, the leopard shall lie down with the kid, the calf and the lion and the fatling together, and a little child shall lead them.

Isaiah 11:6

Discussion Questions

Combo Questions

1. Some critics have focused on *Remember the Titans* as a sports epic of losers becoming winners. Others have critiqued it for not being more hard-hitting in its portrayal of racism in the U.S. And the two real-life coaches have commented about their desire at the time to develop leaders and prepare kids to "relate in a diverse society." If you had to describe the theme of the film, what would you say and why? Now ask yourself the same question about *Save the Last Dance*. Then, in what ways were the movies similar or different in how they tackled issues of racism, power, or interracial friendships/relationships?

2. A big difference between the films is their respective settings—time period (1971 and 2000), geographical location (suburban and urban), and music (sixties pop music and hiphop). What challenges are specific to their settings? How do these differences and challenges play into how the characters deal with similar issues? Did you perceive any stereotypes (fair or unfair) portrayed about such settings? What stereotypes of yours were challenged (or reinforced) by these movies?

Save the Last Dance

1. While many film critics panned *Save the Last Dance* for its formulaic, predictable story line, it surprised them all by its success at the box office. Movie chat sites received numerous positive reviews from teens across the country. Why do you think teens were attracted to the film? Was it content (the issues), form (the hip-hop scene), or both (check out the attitude and words of the hip-hop in the movie)? Why do you think adults were not as drawn to or impressed by the film?

2. U.S. society, from small town to large city, continues to struggle with racism. Many wonder, "Where are the Christians? Where is the church?" Our track record isn't great, and critics like to point out that currently Sunday morning is the most segregated hour in America. The filmmakers seem to be making a point along this line also. Think about Sara's friend at her old school praying for her first audition for Julliard (opening scenes) and then her phone call with Sara after she's moved to Chicago and is attending her new school (chapter 7 [42:36–47:05]—"Lesson Number One"). How is this young Christian portrayed? Is she a sympathetic character? Why or why not? Did she make you feel good about calling yourself a Christian? What can we "Christ ones" learn from her about how Christians are perceived by others regarding racism? How is Sara a better model for understanding those contexts and people who are different from us?

Remember the Titans

1. Coach Boone knew that he had to create a new community—a community of understanding and trust. Review the steps he took to create such a community (e.g., take the team away to camp, pair up black and white players as roommates, force them to learn about each other). What can we learn from Coach Boone as we seek to build new communities within churches and across neighborhoods?

2. Different players dealt with the racial tensions in the local community and on the team in various ways (e.g., Lewis Lastik, humor; Ronnie "Sunshine" Bass, his laid-back playfulness; Jerry "The Rev" Harris, faith; Darryl "Blue" Stanton, song; Ray Budds, anger). Even coaches Bill Yoast and Herman Boone had different ways of dealing with prejudice. With which characters did you most sympathize? How did these characters develop or change their way of thinking and acting? What can we learn from these characters?

Clip Conversations

Save the Last Dance

1. Chapter 8 [47:05–52:30]—"Malakai Threat." After unknowingly walking into one of Malakai's "business deals" gone bad, Sara is scared and confused. How can Derek and Malakai be such good friends when they are so different? Derek tries to explain, but Sara challenges his explanation. When Derek then inquires about Sara's parents, she's the one to become defensive. They obviously have different ideas about and experiences of friendships/relationships. What can/does Sara learn from Derek and vice versa? How have your personal experiences affected how you view relationships? How can we honor our roots while not getting bound up by them? How do we move forward into new relationships with people who are different from us?

2. Chapters 13 [1:13:20–1:20:35] and 14 [1:20:35–1:30:15]—
"Madness and Mayhem" and "Two Different Worlds." In these two
chapters, all of our characters are struggling with the boundaries
of friendships/relationships, including such things as loyalty, guilt,
peer pressure, self-esteem, pride, racism, and fear of abandonment.
Discuss Derek and Malakai's conversation in the diner about relationships with women (white or black) and their own relationship.
What seems to be going on, and what issues are at stake for each of
them? Then discuss Chenille and Sara's conversation in the clinic
about Sara's relationship with Derek. Again, what's at stake for
each of them? Do you feel like there are two or more worlds you
live in or around? Finally, Derek and Sara have to deal with what
others are saying. What's going on internally for each of them?
How did these scenes make you feel? What might you learn from
your own reaction to these reel interactions?

Remember the Titans

1. Chapter 10 [30:50–34:00]—"Lesson from the Dead." Coach
Boone gets the team up at 3:00 AM for a night run to the cemetery at Gettysburg, where Boone tells them, "Fifty thousand
men died right here on this field, fighting the same fight that
we're still fighting amongst ourselves today. . . . Listen to their
souls. . . . You listen. Take a lesson from the dead." Listen to
the whole speech. Watch how players and coaches react. How
would you have reacted if you'd been on the team? Watch the
following scene and discuss whether you think this experience
of Gettysburg helped the team understand its own need for
reconciliation and unity. Share with each other some of those
experiences that have moved you into acts of reconciliation.
How can the church model and nurture such experiences? (In
actuality Coach Boone took the team to the cemetery one late
afternoon. There a man in his eighties who had given Gettysburg
tours for sixty years gave them a tour and told them much of
what was in Boone's speech. Coach Boone exhorted the team
to take a lesson from what the man had said.)

2. Chapter 15 [46:32–49:24]—"Rule Like Titans." Boone's locker-room speech before the first game is filled with confidence and determination. They are one team who has dealt with race and "are stronger for it." (Remember he's just tossed his cookies himself, and the real-life coach said he vomited before every game.) Could the team be one not just at camp but in the real world? Compare this to the experiences of Christians at camp and what happens when they return to the real world. How can we be a community that lives out our unity in everyday life and not just on special occasions (e.g., Promise Keepers events or special multiracial church services)?

3. Chapter 25 [1:26:17–1:32:37]—"Fallen Titan." After the second-to-last game, Gerry Bertier is involved in a car accident, which paralyzes him from the waist down. He refuses to see anyone until he can see Julius Campbell. (In fact, Bertier was in an accident after the state championship and was paralyzed from the chest down. And Julius was the first person he asked for, even before his parents.) When Julius enters the room, a nurse tells him only family can enter. Gerry says, "Alice, are you blind, don't you see the family resemblance? That's my brother." Watch the whole scene and ask yourself how two men could have become so close when they started so far apart. How did their developing relationship speak to you? As disciples of Christ, how can we live into reconciling relationships?

Bonus Material

Save the Last Dance

As noted above, *Save the Last Dance*, while a hit among some viewers, was not critically acclaimed. This MTV movie, released by Paramount, was thought of as a teenybopper flick. (It did win three Teen Choice Awards as well as the MTV Movie Award for the Best Kiss.) It is interesting to note that while somewhat gritty in its style (but nothing compared to *8 Mile*), the sugarcoated ending of "love conquers all" was actually a well-received note of hope for many younger viewers. Often characterized as cynics, today's generation seems to be able to hold their cynicism and hope in close proximity (compare *Punch Drunk Love* and *Moulin Rouge*). Older viewers have more trouble doing this and often do not give the film a chance to draw them in.

In preparation for the dance numbers in the film, Stiles spent over a month in dance training, both ballet and hip-hop. In addition, Stiles and Thomas spent eight hours each weekend in dance studios and hip-hop clubs.

Hip-hop culture is perhaps the dominant pop culture in the U.S., if not the world. It behooves us as adult Christians to expose ourselves to ways of understanding this phenomenon that is so attractive to youth. Getting the soundtrack from this movie and studying the words and themes of the songs might shed some light on ministry to today's youth.

While hardly a masterpiece of filmmaking, this movie has much to say to all generations. We think it's a perfect movie to facilitate some intergenerational dialogue. For parents, the film provides a window into teen life, especially hip-hop culture, as well as contemporary attitudes toward racial politics and interracial relationships. For teens, the film is a perfect vehicle for discussing some of the issues they are living with these days (and studying the words of the songs would also be beneficial). In conversation together the generations might actually learn something from each other's viewing and discussion of the film.

Remember the Titans

Screenwriter Gregory Allan Howard overheard the story of the 1971 Titans football team in a barbershop in Alexandria. He was so intrigued that he started interviewing the coaches and players from the team who were still in town. He said that it was amazing to hear about the team and what it accomplished athletically (e.g., Gerry Bertier was probably the greatest high school player in Virginia at the time). But even more compelling was the way the team portrayed leadership and unity for the whole city in a time of racial tension. Howard wrote the screenplay and sent it around to producers, but it tanked, as he put it. He was at the point of telling the coaches that nobody wanted it when Jerry Bruckheimer called. Disney joined the team and the film became a box office hit.

Actors Denzel Washington and Will Patton were selected as the coaches, with many young actors selected to be players. All of the actors were required to attend a football camp for two weeks. While some had never touched a football before (Ethan Suplee, who played big Lewis Lastik, said it was a "horrible torture"), many of the actors had played football in high school or college. (Denzel Washington played football and ran track as well as coached his son's childhood football team.) One night the real Titans players met with the actors and shared stories of how athletics and that 1971 season had made a difference in their lives.

The real-life coaches, Boone and Yoast, are retired today but were on the set for much of the filming. As depicted in the movie, they had different coaching styles. Boone was hard-nosed (do it until you get it right) while Yoast was more laid-back (talk the kids through things). Both felt their styles complemented each other and helped develop a great team with great leaders. Both saw their role as that of guiding and developing young men to become leaders who cared about each other and the diverse world around them. As they saw it, they planted the seed in those young players, who then planted a seed in the community, and all were changed in the process. Yoast, who coached almost fifty years (football, basketball, and track), shares on the DVD what drew him to coaching:

> Until I came out of the service, I wanted to be a minister. I got to looking around and I thought, gee, if I'm in church, if I'm a preacher, I can only reach the kids that come to me at church. And I knew how much I looked up to my coaches, and I thought maybe I could do that. So I wanted to be a coach 'cause I'd get a chance to work with kids like that.

If one compares the movie scenes with real life, one notes how artistic license was occasionally taken in depicting events, as noted above (see "Clip Conversations"). Some changes included:

1. Coach Yoast had four daughters, but Sheryl was the most involved in his coaching. She actually wasn't a tomboy, as depicted in the film, but was a cheerleader and homecoming queen during her high school days. Sheryl Yoast died in 1996 and so never saw *Remember the Titans*. Understandably this film means a great deal to Coach Yoast and his family.
2. Yoast actually did move Petey Jones from offense to defense, but during a practice, not a game. The parents of the kid who was replaced were not very happy with him, even though the replaced kid acknowledged that Petey was better. The parents confronted both Yoast and Boone. The next day Boone was called into the superintendent's office. He wouldn't back down.
3. A toilet stool, not a brick, was thrown into Coach Boone's living room window one night. He did not have a gun, nor has he ever had a gun in his home. He says he never got over that night.
4. The Titans did chant and sing, but they never danced on the football field.
5. There were rival white coaches who would not exchange game films, but no rival coach ever called Coach Boone a monkey. One did call his players "dogs." So he got permission from the school board to give that coach a dog after the game. Boone never did it, but he liked that in the movie his character gives the coach a banana.
6. Several of the characters were created for the film to make it more conflicting and dramatic—Ray Budds, Alan Bosley, Fred Bosley, and Coach Tyrell.
7. Gerry Bertier, very depressed after his accident, came to Coach Yoast's office one day. Coach Yoast told Gerry that he was depressed because he was a competitor and he wasn't competing. He told Gerry about the Wheelchair Games.

Gerry had competed in track (javelin and high jump), so Yoast kidded him that he would have to give up the high jump but that he could compete in javelin and shot put. Yoast coached him all the way to the Wheelchair Olympics.

Denzel Washington won the Best Actor award for the film in the first Black Entertainment Television Awards, and Trevor Rabin won the BMI Film and TV Awards for his music. The movie also won the Image Awards for Outstanding Motion Picture and Outstanding Actor. The film's budget was $27 million—small for today's studio films; all of the actors and producers took pay cuts to make the movie. Its total box office receipts were $124.4 million. It opened with a gross of $20.9 million in the U.S. and kept September 2000 from being one of the worst months for movies ever. Regardless of its revenue, this film will bring ample rewards to anyone looking for a family or youth group film.

17. X-Men

God, Images of the Savior
Identity, Stranger

Both Movies:
Racial Reconciliation
Affirming the Human Spirit, Hope,
Intolerance, Transformation
Courage, Sacrificial Love,
Tolerance, Justice,
Power, Racism

Themes

18. The Hurricane

Faith, Friendship, Love
Anger, Choice, Redemption, Trust

X-Men
U.S., 2000
104 Minutes, Feature, Color
Actors: Hugh Jackman, Patrick Stewart, Ian McKellen, Halle Berry, Anna Paquin, Bruce Davison, Rebecca Romijn-Stamos, Famke Janssen, James Marsden

Director: Bryan Singer
Screenwriter: David Hayter
Rated: PG13 (violence, mild profanity, mature themes)
DVD Features: theatrical trailer and TV spots, art gallery, Hugh
  Jackman's screen test, Bryan Singer interview with Charlie Rose, Fox
  Special: "The Mutant Watch," deleted scenes—separately or through
  the extended branching version, Spanish subtitles

The Hurricane
U.S., 1999
146 Minutes, Feature, Color
Actors: Denzel Washington, Vicellous Shannon, Deborah Unger, Lieve
  Schreiber, John Hannah, Dan Hedaya, Debbi Morgan, Rod Steiger
Director: Norman Jewison
Screenwriter: Armyan Bernstein and Dan Gordon
Rated: R (violence, profanity, mature themes)
DVD Features: theatrical trailer, production notes, commentary by
  director, Spotlight on Location: "The Making of *The Hurricane*,"
  deleted scenes with introductions by the director

Synopsis and Theological Reflection

Several summers ago the Fox Family Network promoted
its fall programming with radio advertisements. Actor Danny
Glover was heard saying, "My heroes aren't from movies and
comic books. They're real people." He was promoting the show
Courage that would showcase real-life heroes. We want to commend to you two movies about heroes—one comic-book and
one real-life, but all reminding us of the same truth.

X-Men hit the theaters in the summer of 2000 with lines of
comic-book aficionados eagerly awaiting the chance to see their
longtime mutant heroes reach the silver screen. And like the
comic book, what they saw was a movie with multiple levels
of meaning.

At its most obvious level, the story of *X-Men* goes something
like this. In a time in the "not so distant future," when gender,
race, and religion don't separate people, mutated characteristics

Xavier (Patrick Stewart) and Magneto (Ian McKellen) discuss their opposing view-points on the future of humankind. *X-Men* (d. Singer, 2000). Photo by Attila Dory. Copyright 2000 Twentieth Century Fox. All rights reserved.

and special powers do. Operating out of fear, a U.S. senator leads the charge to register such mutants so as to protect the world against these "others." This mutant population has two leaders. One, Charles Xavier (Patrick Stewart), believes that humankind will slowly come to accept the superpowered mutants as they are, without fear or prejudice. Thus, he creates a safe place for young mutants to mature and develop their gifts for the betterment of the world. The other mutant leader, Magneto (Ian McKellen), is convinced that regular humans will never accept the mutants and so mutants must violently take control of humankind.

Each leader has his cast of supporters. Wolverine, Storm, Cyclops, Dr. Jean Grey, and Rogue join together with Xavier. Magneto's band of mutants includes Sabretooth, Mystique, and Toad. Their names give you a good idea of what their special powers are. But beyond these powers, the mutants are just like us in their loyalty, fear, love, humor, goodness, and evil. They help us, the viewers, confront our own fears of those different from ourselves.

The *X-Men* comic book creators, Stan Lee and Jack Kirby, brought the comic-book story to life in 1963, the year of the march on Washington during the civil rights struggle. Not surprisingly, bigotry was one of their themes, as well as the common youth angst of not being understood. Lee and Kirby have even indicated that for them, Xavier and Magneto represented the two options available to African-Americans at the time, that of Dr. Martin Luther King Jr. and that of Malcom X. Thus, social issues and pop culture were woven into the story.

The movie depicts the struggle of these mutant camps with wonderful but not overdone effects, subtle humor, smart leaders and loyal followers, a few twists and turns, and a shadowing of our own dark human history (e.g., the Holocaust, McCarthyism, the Ku Klux Klan). But it does even more. Without giving away the ending, suffice it to say that Xavier and his X-Men, though only movie or comic-book heroes, are true heroes. In particular, Wolverine becomes a type of Christ figure, whose sacrificial love proves salvific. And all this from a comic book!

If you want to see an example of a real-life hero who lived in the years through which *The X-Men* comic books sold (1960s to the 1980s), you need to see the movie *The Hurricane*. Denzel Washington plays the part of Rubin (Hurricane) Carter, a talented boxer and a defiant black nationalist who was falsely accused and convicted of a triple homicide in 1967. After nineteen years in prison, fighting each day for his dignity and innocence, Hurricane Carter was acquitted and released in 1985.

While the film has been criticized for its weak script and lack of attention to the actual facts of the case, all agree that it has captured the inspirational story of one remarkable individual. This real-life story portrays human dignity, courage, compassion, and ultimately, justice. As we watch Hurricane Carter on the screen, we stare human dignity in the face, even in the midst of racism. Denzel Washington gives the performance of

Rubin "Hurricane" Carter (Denzel Washington) meets with his friends who are determined to prove his innocence. *The Hurricane* (d. Jewison, 1999). Photo by George Kraychyk. Copyright 1999 Beacon Communications. All rights reserved.

a lifetime (we think that he should have won the Academy Award for Best Actor).

Both *X-Men* and *The Hurricane* remind us that we are all created in the image of God and thus are worthy of respect and care. Almost forty years have passed since these stories first came to the world's attention, yet we struggle with the same tragic, real-life presence of intolerance, whether it be racism, or sexism. We need real-life heroes, and even comic-book ones, to remind us of our sin but also of the potential for goodness within each one of us. While not appropriate for young children, we would encourage youth ministers to see both movies with their high school groups (or parents with their teenagers) and talk about the values portrayed.

Dialogue Texts

When an alien resides with you in your land, you shall not oppress the alien. The alien who resides with you shall be to you as the citizen among you; you shall love the alien as yourself, for you were aliens in the land of Egypt: I am the LORD your God.

Leviticus 19:33–34

As for the assembly, there shall be for both you and the resident alien a single statute, a perpetual statute throughout your generations; you and the alien shall be alike before the LORD. You and the alien who resides with you shall have the same law and the same ordinance.

Numbers 15:15–16

Then he will say to those at his left hand, "You that are accursed, depart from me . . . ; for . . . I was a stranger and you did not welcome me, naked and you did not give me clothing, sick and in prison and you did not visit me." . . . Then he will answer them, "Truly I tell you, just as you did not do it to one of the least of these, you did not do it to me."

Matthew 25:41–43, 45

There is no longer Jew or Greek, there is no longer slave or free, there is no longer male and female; for all of you are one in Christ Jesus.

Galatians 3:28

Some friends play at friendship but a true friend sticks closer than one's nearest kin.

Proverbs 18:24

Surely there is a future, and your hope will not be cut off.

Proverbs 23:18

Discussion Questions

Combo Questions

1. Some have called *X-Men* a sci-fi adventure that taps into our feelings about diversity, tolerance, justice, and hope for a

reconciled world. Perhaps *The Hurricane* could be seen as a sports film that does the same thing. If you had to describe the films and their underlying themes, what would you say and why? In what ways are the movies similar or different in how they tackle issues of intolerance, racism, power, and justice? Does the fact that one film is based on a true story cause you to take its message more seriously than the one based on a comic book, or vice versa? How? Why?

2. The theme of hope is recurrent in both films. Professor Xavier and Magneto begin and end *X-Men* with conversations about hope. When the story begins and they meet, Magneto asks, "Whatever are you looking for?" Xavier responds, "I'm looking for hope." When Xavier visits Magneto in his plastic prison at the end, Magneto asks, "Why do you come here, Charles?" This time Magneto knows the answer, "Ah, yes. Your continuing search for hope." In *The Hurricane*, Rubin Carter has a longstanding battle with hope, going back and forth between hate, defiance, resignation, and trust. What are these movies saying to the viewer about hope? How might you put your theology of hope into dialogue with the characters and their stories?

3. Another theme that both films tackle is the issue of how best to fight intolerance and injustice. Think of Xavier's way of educating, training, and mentoring young mutants to serve the world in its social evolution, vis-à-vis Magneto's desire for revolution to make the world accept them. Likewise, think of the variety of ways Rubin uses through the course of his life to survive in and defeat an unjust world. (He even fights with himself about how to respond.) How have each of their respective experiences influenced how they fight intolerance and injustice? How have you dealt with such evil in your life? Did these movies help you to better understand your and others' views about combating evil? What was Jesus' style in confront-

ing the evil of the world? What little steps can you take to walk in his way?

Clip Conversations

X-Men

1. Chapter 10 [33:33–38:20]—"The Mutant Brotherhood." Magneto says to Senator Kelly, "Are you a God-fearing man, Senator? That is such a strange phrase. I've always thought of God as a teacher, as a bringer of light, wisdom, and understanding. You see, I think what you really are afraid of is me. Me and my kind. The Brotherhood of Mutants. Oh, it's not so surprising really. Mankind has always feared what it doesn't understand. Well, don't fear God, Senator, and certainly don't fear me. Not any more." How would you have responded to Magneto? What does "fearing God" really mean? In your view, what does he have right about God and human beings and what does he have wrong? Again, how has his personal experience led him to such a view? How can we be sensitive listeners to people's pain while pointing them to a loving and just God?

2. Chapter 16 [1:01:50–1:03:10]—"Death of a Mutant." Senator Kelly in his pain and aloneness reaches out to Storm for comfort and understanding. In his last moments what does he ask her? Do you think that her response is an honest one? Have you ever reached out to someone very different from you? What happened? How have fear and perhaps past experiences kept you from being able to trust and love others? How did Jesus break down barriers of fear between people? How can we follow his example?

3. Chapter 24 [1:26:51–1:29:01]—"Logan's Sacrifice." Logan reaches Rogue, but it appears it's too late. How is his act of touch an act of sacrifice? Think of the ways Jesus sacrificially

touched others. How does Rogue forever bear the marks of her redemption/resurrection? How has Logan been changed also?

The Hurricane

1. Chapter 10 [53:10–1:07:20]—"The Hole." The strong language and dark lighting make this scene almost terrifying, but it is for a reason. During his time in "the hole" Rubin fights isolation and the injustice and indignity of his situation. However, perhaps worse are the demons within him who fight for control. Have you ever felt like different parts of you were in a cosmic struggle? Who or what helped you out of such a place? Rubin's first real contact out of "the hole" is with Lt. Jimmy Williams. How does he bring some dignity and humanity into Rubin's situation? How does this give Mr. Carter a strategy to deal with his incarceration? Do you think it was a helpful or effective strategy? As years go by, Rubin is forced to face the reality of doing the time. What personal sacrifices does he make to survive, and at what cost?

2. Chapter 14 [1:33:03–1:46:00]—"Carter's Foot Soldiers." Young Lesra, having read and been inspired by Rubin's story, has begun a relationship with him through letters and visits. But even here Rubin struggles to trust and have hope, pushing Lesra and his Canadian friends away. What happens when Rubin hits rock bottom and calls them? What is he saying to them? How do they respond? How has his story inspired Lesra and the Canadians to live lives of faith, hope, and love? What other heroes are present in this story? What characteristics do these heroes have in common?

3. Chapter 18 [2:12:37–2:15:00]—"Risen from the Dead." Lesra sits with Rubin as they wait for the federal judge's decision on his case. Remind yourself of the stories of Reuben (e.g., Genesis 29:31–35; 37:17–30) and Lazarus (John 11), and then listen to their conversation. What does Rubin emphasize by

reminding Lesra of these biblical characters? How is his current view of the world reflected in his statement, "Hate put me in prison. Love's gonna bust me out"? What kind of spiritual journey has he taken? What helped him to see things in a new light? How has Lesra changed, and does he understand how he has already busted Rubin out? Might we say that Jesus' love busted Lazarus (and us) out of death?

Bonus Material

X-Men

Some of the cast of the film have their own superhero stories. Initially Bryan Singer wanted Russell Crowe to play Wolverine, but Hugh Jackman eventually won the part. (Maybe Aussies make good heroes—think of Mel Gibson.) Rebecca Romijn-Stamos had to endure over eight hours of makeup preparation for her role as Mystique—the scaly, blue-skinned body impersonator. Stan Lee, the *X-Men* creator, makes a cameo appearance as a hotdog vendor on the beach when Senator Kelly emerges like a jellyfish from the sea.

If you like bonus material such as deleted scenes, the DVD of *X-Men* gives you the opportunity to view them separately or integrated into the complete film, with an on-screen symbol to mark when a deleted scene has been inserted. A nifty feature, if the deleted scenes had really been worth watching. Two scenes, "Storm Teaching Class" and "Rogue in Classroom with Bobby and Storm" might be interesting to view and discuss with regard to why they might have been deleted. (Are they heavy-handed in their commentary on intolerance and Christianity?) The Fox Special "The Mutant Watch" also has similar allusions to the church and its language of intolerance. Whether unfair swipes or valid criticism, these scenes didn't make it into the movie for some reason.

X-Men was a hit with the Academy of Science Fiction, Fantasy, and Horror Films, USA. It was nominated for ten Saturn Awards and won six, including Best Science Fiction Film, Best Director, Best Writing, and Best Actor (Hugh Jackman). It was nominated for various other awards for Sound Editing, Costume Design, and Visual Effects. Perhaps the most interesting nomination came from the Political Film Society, in the categories of Human Rights and Peace. The film's budget was $75 million—average for today's studio action films with lots of special effects. Its total box office receipts were $295.6 million, with $157.3 million in the U.S. Some may think that watching a comic-book story does not merit the time or that it is nothing but entertainment, but this sci-fi fantasy allows viewers to enjoy themselves while also causing them to think about intolerance in a new way.

The Hurricane

Director Norman Jewison is well-known for his films, many having to do with social issues. His filmography includes: *Fiddler on the Roof, Jesus Christ Superstar, Agnes of God, A Soldier's Story, Moonstruck,* and *In the Heat of the Night.* He showed *The Hurricane* incomplete (no credits or proper color) at the 1999 Toronto International Film Festival. He had submitted the film as hundreds of pieces splinted together because he had been working on it the previous evening. Before the showing started, he said to the audience, "I'm so nervous that the splints may fall apart."

With its first showing came much acclaim but also some criticism. Some critics claimed that Jewison and the screenwriters compressed time, combined characters, and rearranged events with an irresponsible nonchalance. Others felt this artistic license had nonetheless maintained the integrity of the story of Rubin Carter's life. Jewison himself hoped that the film would also be seen "from the standpoint of what it has to say about us as a people."

What are some of these rearranged events and compressed characters? Carter was actually convicted of three muggings prior to his murder trial. In real life there was no bad cop character like Della Pesca. Between his two convictions, Carter was released from prison for four years. He did not speak at his federal court hearing, and he eventually married one of the Canadians, Lisa Peters. There is no doubt that Rubin Carter was an angry man for much of his life. The film doesn't hide this side of him, but it does try to bring into focus for the viewer the reasons, justifiable or not, for his anger. It also doesn't hide the transformation he underwent throughout his life. If you want to read more about this journey, you can get Carter's memoirs, *The Sixteenth Round*, or the Canadians' story of their journey with Carter, *Lazarus and the Hurricane*. (Note: They were actually a community of nine people, with three being most active in his appeal to the court.)

Denzel Washington, a deeply committed Christian, wanted to play the part of Rubin "Hurricane" Carter even before the screenplay was in development. He got the part, and one year before production started he began training—physically, mentally, and emotionally. He lost from forty to sixty pounds (depending on sources you read) and became a pretty good fighter. He worked with retired professional fighter Jerry Claybon, and they sparred close to two hundred rounds. Though he tried to capture this physical aspect of Rubin Carter, he was equally committed to portraying Carter's emotional and spiritual journey. He wanted the viewer to see the search within himself that Carter undertook.

Like the *X-Men* DVD, this one also has deleted scenes recorded (but not in an integrated way). They are worth seeing for themselves but also because Norman Jewison, who has a somewhat rare final cut authority on all his films, explains why the scenes were cut. You may agree with him on some and not on others. The first deleted scene is poignant and worth discussion. (Possible discussion questions: What is your definition of human dignity? At what cost do we let people touch us? Is it worth the sacrifices we might need to make? What cost did Jesus pay for becoming human? How did he help others fulfill their God-given humanity?)

The Hurricane garnered several nominations and awards, but it might best be remembered for the awards it wasn't given. While many believe that this may have been Denzel Washington's finest performance ever, he was nominated but did not win the Oscar or the Screen Actors Guild award for Best Actor. He did, however, win the 1999 Golden Globe and Image awards for his portrayal. Two other Golden Globe nominations were received for Best Film (drama) and Best Director. The film's total U.S. box office receipts were just $51 million—hardly stupendous or miraculous given Hollywood's box office hits these days. But on the other hand, the film is a miracle. The "miracle of his redemption" is how the real Rubin Carter talks about his story. It is this journey of the human spirit that is worthy of anyone's viewing.

Forgiveness

19. Smoke Signals

U.S., 1998
88 Minutes, Feature, Color
Actors: Adam Beach, Evan Adams,
    Irene Bedard, Gary Farmer,
    Tantoo Cardinal, Tom Skerritt
Director: Chris Eyre
Screenwriter: Sherman Alexie
Rated: PG13 (adult language and themes, domestic violence)
DVD Features: theatrical trailer

> **Themes**
>
> **Forgiveness**
> *Community, Friendship,*
> *Reconciliation within Families,*
> *The Lord's Supper,*
> *The Power of Story*
> Affirming the Human Spirit, Death,
> Healing, Identity, Truth

Synopsis and Theological Reflection

The Covenant Church in which I (Rob) grew up was predominantly Swedish (though we did have one messianic Jew, a Chinese matriarch and her talented clan, and several Armenian families). When my mother, who is Cherokee and Irish, started attending the church around 1930, she was the only non-Swede. Not wanting her culture to be lost, she took our whole family on Easter vacations to Arizona to visit Indian reservations and Native American archaeological sites. Growing up with a healthy consciousness that we were part Native American was not easy. Few cared about the modern-day Indian then, and little has changed since.

It should come as no surprise, then, that it is rare to find a movie about contemporary Native Americans. Audiences will pay to see cowboy and Indian fare based in the nineteenth century, but few in our culture have any real interest in exploring what it means to be an Indian in white America today.

Victor Joseph (Adam Beach) and Thomas Builds-the-Fire (Evan Adams) wait for the bus to Arizona. *Smoke Signals* (d. Eyre, 1998). Photo by Jill Sabella. Copyright 1998 Miramax Films. All rights reserved.

That the film *Smoke Signals* was so well received by audiences (albeit small) and critics alike is therefore quite extraordinary. The movie even won two awards at Robert Redford's 1998 Sundance Film Festival.

Billed as the first feature movie entirely written, directed, and acted by Native Americans, *Smoke Signals* was adapted for the screen from four short stories by Sherman Alexie out of his collection *The Lone Ranger and Tonto Fistfight in Heaven*. Alexie is quoted in *Time* magazine as saying, "I love the way movies have more power than books. They continue the oral tradition, the way we all sit around the fire and listen to stories." Here, indeed, is a story to see and hear.

The film opens on the Fourth of July, 1976. It tells the tale of two modern-day Coeur d'Alene Indians, Victor Joseph and Thomas Builds-the-Fire, who twenty years later leave their Idaho reservation to go by bus to retrieve the ashes of Victor's alcoholic father. Arnold Joseph has died in Arizona years after abandoning his family, and forgiveness does not come easily. Victor is good-looking, self-righteous, and stoic. He has sealed himself off in anger since his father left him as an adolescent. Thomas—geeky, happy, and forever talkative—is the storyteller trying to understand his friend's pain (and perhaps his own). It is Arnold Joseph who binds these otherwise dissimilar twenty-year-olds together. He is not only Victor's father; he also saved the infant Thomas from a fatal house fire that orphaned him that Fourth of July evening.

From such a skeletal plot description, one might presume the movie to be dark and sentimental; it is not. Humor abounds. The weather report on K-REZ always begins, "It's a good day to be indigenous," and its traffic report typically says, "One car went by earlier." Frustrated with Thomas's nonstop talking, Victor tells him to "get stoic. Look like a warrior." Thomas accuses Victor of learning his Indianness from watching *Dances with Wolves*. In this movie, we see a younger generation of Native Americans poking fun at themselves.

Smoke Signals is a genre road picture whose structure needs only a destination to work. Otherwise, the story allows for freedom and improvisation along the way. In this movie, the need to recover the father's ashes is the excuse for the young men's bus trip to Arizona. But the real movement occurs as the youths discover life's meaning and possibilities through their growing friendship. Dialogue is the heart of the movie, but it is never preachy. Rather, the movie uses humor and a fondness for Indian culture to help its viewers better understand both today's Native Americans and ourselves.

Through the use of storytelling so typical of Indian culture, *Smoke Signals* weaves together fantasy and realism in a series of flashbacks and fast-forwards, often narrated by Thomas. In the process not only are Thomas and Victor able to accept their past and present, but we as viewers are better able to discover our stories as well. The director, Chris Eyre, says the movie is a "universal story about fathers and friends and forgiveness." He has used the tradition he knows best (Native American), but the movie is meant to transcend culture. Its final soliloquy is a moving voice-over of a poem by Dick Lourie:

> How do we forgive our fathers?
> Maybe in a dream. . . .
> Do we forgive our fathers in our age or in theirs?
> Or in their deaths?
> Saying it to them or not saying it? . . .
> If we forgive our fathers, what is left?

These are questions for any time or place.

However, *Smoke Signals* is more than just a metaphorical story with universal meaning; it is also a Native American movie. The movie is political despite itself; it is about getting to know the American Indian in our midst. We are shown typical ways that Native Americans have learned to cope with the largely indifferent if not hostile world around them—anger, storytelling, alcohol, and community. In *Smoke Signals*, no overarching answers are presented, but insight is achieved nonetheless. And we do get a glimpse of the neighbor in our midst.

Dialogue Texts

You will forget your misery; you will remember it as waters that have passed away.

Job 11:16

And forgive us our sins, for we ourselves forgive everyone indebted to us.

Luke 11:4

The disciples said to him, "Where are we to get enough bread . . . to feed so great a crowd?" Jesus asked them, "How many loaves have you?" They said, "Seven, and a few small fish." Then ordering the crowd to sit down on the ground, he took the seven loaves and the fish; and after giving thanks he broke them and gave them to the disciples, and the disciples gave them to the crowds. And all of them ate and were filled.

Matthew 15:33–37

While they were eating, Jesus took a loaf of bread, and after blessing it he broke it, gave it to the disciples, and said, "Take, eat; this is my body."

Matthew 26:26

Put away from you all bitterness and wrath and anger and wrangling and slander, together with all malice, and be kind to one another, tenderhearted, forgiving one another, as God in Christ has forgiven you.

Ephesians 4:31–32

Discussion Questions

1. *Smoke Signals* is a Native American twist on the road-trip form. (Think of such stories/films as *The Odyssey*, *The Wizard of Oz*, *Easy Rider*, *Thelma and Louise*, or *Finding Nemo* in which, through the course of taking a journey from one physical location to another, the characters discover new things about themselves and the world.) Victor and Thomas are on a journey from their reservation in Coeur d'Alene, Idaho, to Phoenix, Arizona. What sorts of things do they learn along the way about themselves, each other, and the world? How does getting Arnold Joseph's ashes from Susie Song (their "destination") bring further understanding? How does the return trip help to solidify their newfound understandings? What is the real journey for each of them?

2. Along the journey the viewer is presented with various ways of dealing with loss and death. How does Arnold Joseph cope with his own powerlessness and the effects of the fire that took Thomas's parents? How does Victor deal with his father's alcoholism and eventual abandonment of the family? How does Thomas live with the fact that Arnold Joseph saved him from the

fire that took his parents? How do Victor's mom and Thomas's grandmother deal with their losses? Finally, how does Susie Song help Arnold and Victor begin to live into and beyond their losses? With which character (and his or her way of responding to life's losses) did you most empathize and why?

3. What difference does it make that this is a Native American film? How does it help us see beyond the stereotypes of American Indians present in other films? How does it use humor in this regard to reeducate the viewer as to the struggles of Native Americans (see chapter 12 [38:48–42:57]—"John Wayne's Teeth")?

4. How important is it that Thomas's stories are not always based on facts but instead are woven together from his life experience and his imagination? Is there still truth in the fiction he creates? What are the filmmakers saying about the power of story? Is this a uniquely Native American perspective or more universal? How have the people of God through the centuries viewed story?

Clip Conversations

1. Chapter 2 [00:30–4:45]—"Born of Smoke and Ash." Listen to Thomas Builds-the-Fire's voice-over. If this film is a road-trip movie, why does it start this way? What do we learn about this community, the power of story, and our two young protagonists from the event that tied their lives together? What other character is most important in setting up the journey and why?

2. Chapter 6 [13:20–18:00]—"On the Road." Victor and Thomas talk to their mom and grandmother about their possible road trip. Victor's mom uses her fry bread as a way to talk to Victor about his decision. Why do you think she does that instead of just telling him what to do? What is she saying to

him through this object lesson? How might you apply this to your own life? How can the church be the kind of community Arlene Joseph is talking about? (You might also discuss Thomas's story of Arlene's fry bread—chapter 14 [45:10–51:50]—and the way it is depicted as almost sacramental within the community. Why do you think the filmmakers used such an allusion to the Lord's Supper?)

3. Chapters 17 [1:03:03–1:08:55] and 19 [1:12:50–1:16:20]—"The Wreck and the Run" and "Going Home." Victor and Thomas head home to Idaho. They argue vehemently about Arnold Joseph. In that argument, what do we learn? How is their respective pain expressed? Could you relate to their pain? They come upon a car crash, and Victor runs for help. How does Victor's run for help function in his own healing? Out of the hospital (and the sheriff's office) they continue on their journey home. What is different about each of them now? Listen to the song, "Father and Farther," that is playing while they drive. (Sherman Alexie actually wrote the lyrics for the song.) What are the filmmakers telling the viewer about Victor and his father, and perhaps about other fathers and sons or mothers and daughters?

4. Chapter 21 [1:20:30–1:23:05]—"Forgive Our Fathers." Again Thomas Builds-the-Fire narrates by reciting the Dick Lourie poem "Forgiving Our Fathers" from his book *Ghost Radio*. How has the journey changed Victor? He got his father's ashes, but what else did he receive in the process? How does Victor and Thomas's journey speak to your journey? How can the church be a place that allows people to make journeys of friendship and forgiveness?

Bonus Material

As noted above, Sherman Alexie, who wrote *Smoke Signals*, is a Coeur d'Alene Indian who has gained national attention for his writing—eight collections of poetry, two novels, and two short story collections. The *New Yorker* called him "one of the best American fiction writers under forty," and he has won numerous awards for his writing. This is quite an astounding outcome for a child who was born hydrocephalic. At six months he underwent brain surgery but was not expected to survive. When he did survive, the doctors told his parents that he would most likely live with severe mental retardation. The rest is history. As Tamara J. Jaffe-Notier noted in her 2001 interview with Alexie for *Door* magazine, "He appears to have sustained just enough brain damage to make him horribly funny and creative, for which all of us can be thankful."

Sherman Alexie didn't play in a church basketball league, but he did play basketball regularly and even once went to a Christian basketball camp in the Northwest. He describes himself as growing up Catholic and being a recovering Catholic who's had to learn a lot about grace and forgiveness.

As viewers note, he uses allusions to Catholic liturgy and theology, which he values. His wife, also a Native American, has a master's degree in theology and worked with Young Life at one point. When asked in the *Door* 2001 interview about the connection between humor and the spiritual life, Alexie responded, "God is funny . . . I just feel it. I'm never happier than when I'm making people laugh about serious subjects. I think people are more open to new ideas and thoughts, changes, when they're laughing."

Smoke Signals was made for $2 million. After winning the Audience Award and the Filmmakers Trophy at the Sundance Film Festival, Miramax picked the film up for distribution. It was reported that Alexie had wanted the film to be called "What it Means to Say Phoenix, Arizona," but Miramax chose to market it with a more "Indian-sounding" title (stereotypes die slowly). The film also garnered nominations or awards at various other film festivals and among other film organizations. Total box office earnings were roughly $7 million.

20. Antwone Fisher

U.S., 2002
120 Minutes, Feature, Color
Actors: Derek Luke, Joy Bryant,
   Denzel Washington, Salli Richardson,
   Earl Billings, Viola Davis, Novella Nelson
Director: Denzel Washington
Screenwriter: Antwone Quenton Fisher
Rated: PG13 (adult language and themes, child abuse, brief violence)
DVD Features: theatrical trailer, commentary by director Denzel
   Washington and producer Todd Black, "Meeting Antwone Fisher"
   featurette, "The Making of Antwone Fisher" featurette, "Hollywood
   and the Navy" featurette, Spanish subtitles and dubbing

> **Themes**
>
> **Forgiveness**
> *Celebration, Dreams/Hopes,*
> *Family, Healing*
> Abuse, Anger, Friendship, Identity,
> Love, Parents, Suffering, Trust

Synopsis and Theological Reflection

Woe to one who is alone and falls and does not have another
to help.

Ecclesiastes 4:10b

Tears of joy are always a rare treat at the movies. They are
also usually hard-won—the result of our identification with a
character who transcends extraordinary circumstances, but not
without cost or continuing struggle. The movie *Antwone Fisher*
brought such tears to our eyes. Here is a movie that will inspire
even the most cynical; a true-life story that portrays a hard-won
hopefulness despite life's hopelessness.

The result of the work of three gifted men, this movie is must
viewing for all high schoolers and adults. *Antwone Fisher* is not
only the name of the movie, it is the name of the screenwriter.
His autobiographical story has been brought to the screen by
Denzel Washington in his auspicious directorial debut and by
newcomer Derek Luke, whose performance in the title role
brings a quiet presence to the screen that is at once heartbreak-
ing and compelling.

Antwone (Derek Luke) sits in Dr. Jerome Davenport's (Denzel Washington) office refusing to talk. *Antwone Fisher* (d. Washington, 2002). Copyright 2002 Fox Searchlight. All rights reserved.

The movie is a coming-of-age story. Seeking to reclaim his past in order to live into his future, Antwone Fisher tells us his story. Born inside a prison two months after his father was killed by a former girlfriend, never claimed by his mother once she was released from jail, beaten and humiliated by his foster mother, a preacher's wife, and cast out into the street, Antwone can only dream of the family he has never had. Unwanted, unloved, abandoned, abused, Antwone becomes sullen and uncommunicative, prone to uncontrollable outbreaks of anger. Yet he is all the more tragic because of his perceived goodness. He wants to overcome his demons; he cares for his friends; he is sensitive as an artist and writer; he desires to love and be loved. He deserves more; anyone deserves more! What is wrong with us as a society that such pain can be present in the lives of some—especially our children?

As the movie opens, Antwone, a navy seaman, has been assigned to a Navy psychiatrist (Dr. Jerome Davenport, who is played by Denzel Washington) for anger management lest he get bounced out of the armed services. Davenport slowly breaks through Antwone's defenses, and he begins to tell his story. As he recovers his past, which we see through a series of flashbacks, Antwone also begins to live into his future. And so do we; we come to care for him. His is a story of past heartbreak and present courage, of social dysfunction and personal resilience.

Yet this movie is not really about someone pulling himself up by his bootstraps. As the African-American preacher J. Alfred Smith has reminded us, some individuals don't even have boots. Bootstraps are not enough. It is only the tough love of his counselor and the tender love of his girlfriend, Cheryl, that together provide the context in which he can find wholeness. Given the verbal abuse of his foster family, Antwone finds it difficult to trust his counselor. Their relationship through most of the movie is both awkward and fragile. Yet as trust is mutually given, it proves redemptive—not just for Antwone, but for Davenport as well. Similarly, given the sexual abuse he has experienced, Antwone is shy and awkward with the opposite sex. Antwone is a virgin and little more than a kiss is ever shown on the screen as Antwone and Cheryl (Joy Bryant) begin to date. Yet their hard-won and vulnerable affection makes their gentle kisses seem all the more sensual. Here is a love that is real and deep. They care for each other, and we are moved.

Antwone Fisher is not a movie for children. The story involves child abuse and a shooting. Yet it is intelligently told with restraint, emotional honesty, and even some humor. Denzel Washington's confident grasp of the story has allowed him to use a simple, straightforward storytelling technique that concentrates on the characters and avoids either graphic sexuality or violence. His own acting ability has perhaps given him the tools to help his two young leads explore a depth of personhood not often captured on the screen. And the fact that the story is based in real life only adds to the power of their portrayals.

The movie begins with Antwone's dream of a family banquet, and its ending does not disappoint. The hero's desire for a father ends with a substitute father discovering his own need for a son. His search for his roots produces unexpected dividends and an alternate celebration. And his and Cheryl's reciprocal love suggests that a new family is being born. There is an optimism to the story that is hard-won. Families are complex and complicated organisms that often inflict pain and crush spirits, but they also can renew and redeem. We in the family of God should remember this message and model it to a hurting world: "For if they fall, one will lift up the other" (Eccles. 4:10a).

Dialogue Texts

Then Joseph could no longer control himself, . . . and he cried out. . . . Joseph said to his brothers, "I am Joseph. Is my father still alive?" But his brothers could not answer him, so dismayed were they at his presence. . . . Israel said, "Enough! My son Joseph is still alive. I must go and see him before I die." . . . All the persons of the house of Jacob who came into Egypt were seventy.

Genesis 45:1, 3, 28; 46:27b (the Joseph story, Genesis 37–50)

For if they fall, one will lift up the other; but woe to one who is alone and falls and does not have another to help.

Ecclesiastes 4:10

Do not judge, and you will not be judged; do not condemn, and you will not be condemned. Forgive, and you will be forgiven; give, and it will be given to you. A good measure, pressed down, shaken together, running over, will be put into your lap; for the measure you give will be the measure you get back.

Luke 6:37–38

Bear with one another and, if anyone has a complaint against another, forgive each other; just as the Lord has forgiven you, so you also must forgive. . . . And let the peace of Christ rule in your hearts.

Colossians 3:13, 15a

And the angel said to me, "Write this: Blessed are those who are invited to the marriage supper of the Lamb."

Revelation 19:9

Discussion Questions

1. The film *Antwone Fisher* has touched all but the most hardened cynics with its inspirational, true story. Why do you think that happened? How does the film touch the viewer's head, heart, and gut? Which scene moved you the most and why? If you were to describe the movie to a friend, what would you say the key themes are? Would you recommend it? Why or why not?

2. Antwone Fisher's journey to home and family was not an easy one. Given his horrific past, he needed help to get there. Both Dr. Davenport and Cheryl Smolley walk with him, even when he tries to push them away. What things do they do even when Antwone is not ready to trust them? How must they all learn that there is no quick fix to Antwone's problems (see chapter 10 [30:02–34:41]—"Slipping Up")? What can the Christian community learn from these characters and their story about the healing of deep wounds and the path to shalom? How can we best serve those with such pain in their lives and model the hope and peace we have in Christ?

3. Through flashbacks we see the unfolding of Antwone's story. How did you feel to find out that his abusers were part of the Christian community? How would you feel about the church, or even Jesus, if you had experienced what Antwone experienced at the hands and mouth of Mrs. Tate? How does Dr. Davenport begin to make sense of their treatment of him? How does Antwone react to his explanation, and what did you think of their conversation (see chapter 9 [25:47–30:02] —"Feeling Powerful")? The book to which Dr. Davenport refers is by John W. Blassingame, titled *The Slave Community*. How can we as followers of Christ understand evil—its causes, its consequences, and the restoration of people who have been touched by it?

4. *Antwone Fisher* marks Denzel Washington's debut as a director. Film critics have noted how he focused on the story rather than on special effects and on the characters' feelings rather than on graphic scenes. He himself speaks of his use of restraint, of letting some things go to the imagination of the viewers. Do you think he succeeded in drawing the viewer in by not putting everything on screen, or was he avoiding hard issues, as some critics claimed?

Clip Conversations

1. Chapter 1 [00:00–03:06]—"Antwone's Dream." The film opens with a small boy wandering through a cornfield. He comes upon a barn. The doors are thrown open, and he is invited into a great feast with many people spanning numerous generations. They are all waiting for him to start the meal, as a big plate of pancakes is set before him. A bell rings, a shot is heard, some faces flash, and we see Antwone waking from his dream. How does this scene set the stage for the themes of the movie?

2. Chapters 19 [1:07:37–1:11:06] and 20 [1:11:06–1:14:11] —"Thanksgiving" and "Who Will Cry." Antwone arrives at Dr. Davenport's house to celebrate Thanksgiving. What things does Antwone especially notice and appreciate? How is this normal family, arguments and all, a refreshing experience for him? How is it a painful experience? He gives the doctor a gift—a poem. How does his poem show the extent of his healing thus far? According to Dr. Davenport, how much further does he need to go? How does his poem also speak to the wounds of Dr. Davenport and his wife? How does it speak to you?

Who will cry for the little boy, lost and all alone?
Who will cry for the little boy, abandoned without his own?
Who will cry for the little boy, he cried himself to sleep?
Who will cry for the little boy, who never had for keeps?
Who will cry for the little boy, who walked the burning sand?

Who will cry for the little boy, the boy inside the man?
Who will cry for the little boy, who knew well hurt and pain?
Who will cry for the little boy, he died and died again?
Who will cry for the little boy, a good boy he tried to be?
Who will cry for the little boy, who cries inside of me?

3. Chapter 30 [1:47:32–1:50:46]—"Welcome to the Family." Somewhat sadly, Antwone returns from meeting his mother for the first time. His newfound auntie's house is filled with his relatives, all waiting to meet him and give him some love. She opens the dining room doors for him to see a table laden with food (including pancakes!), even more generations of his family, and Cheryl waiting. As he enters, an old matriarch of the family beckons him. As she tenderly holds his face she says, "Welcome." Everyone piles in as the homecoming feast begins. Roger Ebert, in speaking of his experience of this film, said, "I do not cry easily at the movies. . . . I have noticed that when I am deeply affected emotionally, it is not by sadness so much as by goodness." What did you think and feel as you watched this scene?

Bonus Material

The film *Antwone Fisher* was written by and about the real Antwone Fisher. His life story basically follows the film, and he credits the Navy for helping him to begin to deal with his past hurts and anger. It wasn't until he was working as one of the guards at the main gate of Sony studios that he began writing his life story. One day a limousine chauffeur asked him what he was doing. When he explained, the man told him that they were offering a free screenwriting course at the Bethel AME Church in South Central Los Angeles. Antwone took the class from Chris Smith and began writing longhand on yellow legal pads. Chris mentioned to his old college roommate, producer Todd Black, that one of his students had an incredible story. Todd met Antwone and heard his story. He gave Antwone an office and a computer, taught him how to use it, and paid him to write full-time on his screenplay.

Meanwhile Black pitched the story to the head of Fox studios, but he met resistance because no one really believed the screenplay could be done. Forty-one drafts (typed with two fingers) and a year later, they had a screenplay, and Fox bought it. Antwone credits the writing of the screenplay and working with Todd as part of his healing.

Many of the cast and crew had their own stories connected to the film. Derek Luke (Antwone in the film) was working at the Sony gift shop when he auditioned for the role. He and Antwone had actually become friends, but he never mentioned this in his audition. Denzel Washington chose this script to be his directorial debut because of the strength of the story and the spirit of Antwone Fisher's character. Given his leads were young, inexperienced actors, Washington encouraged them to write a journal about their characters so that they knew them from the inside out. Likewise, he wanted them to understand something of the psychology of abuse and the power of redemption—concurrent themes in the film.

The real Antwone Fisher is married now and has two young daughters. Besides the screenplay, he has published his memoirs, *Finding Fish*, and the book, *Who Will Cry for the Little Boy?* He is a crusader about foster care and adoption. Both of his foster brothers went to prison. His younger brother has been released, but his older brother is serving a sentence until 2007. Given their and his experience, he also spends time speaking to kids at risk, in juvenile hall or wherever he is invited. He met his mother at age thirty-six and has had little contact with her since. When his oldest daughter was born, he took her to meet her grandmother. His mother cursed at the child, and "that was the end of that," said Antwone. "Sometimes you have to let things go" is a phrase that Antwone has learned to live with.

Antwone Fisher was made for $12.5 million, with U.S. box office earnings reaching just over $21 million. It garnered various nominations or awards among some film organizations, such as the Chicago Film Critics Association, the National Board of Review, and the Writers Guild of America. It won Humanitas, Image, and Independent Spirit awards. However, it did not receive even one nomination for an Academy Award. It just goes to show, awards and box office receipts are sometimes poor indicators of whether God will show up and speak to us when we go to a film.

Community
and Friendship

21. About a Boy

U.S./Britain, 2002
100 Minutes, Feature, Color
Actors: Hugh Grant, Nicholas Hoult,
Toni Collette, Rachel Weisz
Directors: Paul Weitz and Chris Weitz
Screenwriters: Peter Hedges, Chris Weitz, Paul Weitz
Rated: R (profanity, adult themes)
DVD Features: theatrical trailer, production notes, cast and filmmakers,
commentary with directors, deleted scenes, "Spotlight on Location:
The Making of *About A Boy*," music videos by Badly Drawn Boy,
"Santa's Super Sleigh" (the complete lyrics), "The English to English
Dictionary"

Community and Friendship
*Affirming the Human Spirit,
Self-Centeredness*
Children, Family, Humor, Isolation

Themes

Synopsis and Theological Reflection

> No man is an island, entire of itself;
> every man is a piece of the continent, a part of the main.
> If a clod be washed away by the sea, Europe is the less,
> as well as if promontory were,
> as well as if a manor of thy friend's or of thine own were.
> Any man's death diminishes me, because I am involved
> in mankind.
>
> John Donne, *Devotions* (1624)

The way I see it, every man is an island.

But the great thing is, there's never been a better time in history to be an island. Even fifty years ago, for instance, they didn't have daytime TV, or videos, or CDs, or home espresso makers,

Will (Hugh Grant) and Marcus (Nicholas Hoult) spend the afternoon together in front of the TV. *About a Boy* (d. Weitz & Weitz, 2002). Copyright 2002 Universal Pictures and StudioCanal. All rights reserved.

or glossy magazines with questionnaires about how cool you were. . . .

Sure I was an island, but I was a pretty cool island. I was Ibiza.

Will Freeman, *About a Boy* (2002)

Most people know of John Donne, the remarkable English poet, philosopher, and preacher of the seventeenth century. Few people know Will Freeman, but they know a few folks like him. Many people missed the small 2002 film *About a Boy* because it debuted the same weekend as the *Star Wars* prequel, *Attack of the Clones*. *About a Boy* tells the story of Will "Free-man" (Hugh Grant), an extremely shallow and self-absorbed swinging single who meets Marcus (Nicholas Hoult), a twelve-year-old boy who is anything but shallow and the *uncoolest* kid in his school. As the title suggests, this is the story of a boy, rather, about two "boys" and the effect they have on each other's lives. Will teaches Marcus how to be a kid, and Marcus helps Will to finally grow up.

Will, the thirty-eight-year-old boy, is living off the substantial royalties of "Santa's Super Sleigh," a Christmas song his father wrote before Will was born. He's never had a job or a relationship for more than a few days. Marcus, the other boy, is navigating a leftover-from-the-sixties hippie single mom, Fiona (Toni Collette), who battles depression. The two meet when Will starts dating women from a single parents' support group (he's faking that he has a child so he can pick up single moms) and Marcus is sent to spend the day with a single neighbor (Will's date) and her child. While the date ends badly (they kill a duck at the pond with Fiona's loaf of homemade health bread that actually resembles a hockey puck, and they return to Marcus's home to find Fiona has attempted suicide), Marcus and Will are in each other's lives for the long haul.

Marcus soon figures out Will's selfish philosophy and lifestyle and decides to change it. Besides, he and his mother can use some help. As he says to Will, "Two people aren't enough; you need a backup." Watching Marcus wear down Will is just one of the many humorous pleasures of the film. Eventually, but kicking and screaming most of the way, Will sees that life without another is meaningless and that "once you open your heart to one person, you open it to others." *About a Boy* is sweet but also often bittersweet, for it deals with the human condition in a realistic way. Both comedy and drama come from the characters and their situations, for such is life.

Directed by Paul Weitz and Chris Weitz (*American Pie*), *About a Boy* is based on the book by Nick Hornby (*High Fidelity*) with the screenplay by Peter Hedges (*What's Eating Gilbert Grape*) and the Weitz brothers. Not all will be comfortable with some of their other work, but *About a Boy* should not be missed. These are talented filmmakers. In talking about his film, Paul Weitz concluded, "I think the heart of the film lies in the strong mix of comedy and emotion. It's extremely funny but tackles very

profound themes about isolation, about family, and about love."
It was nominated for several awards, including two Golden
Globes for Best Motion Picture, Musical or Comedy, and Best
Performance by an Actor, Musical or Comedy.

Why did critics like this movie? They liked it because it's
not sentimental but rather gritty and true. As one critic stated,
"People are jerks, but they still need each other. And through
each other they can become more whole." Why did we like it?
Perhaps for some of the same reasons, but also because it made
us imagine the church as a place where people, regardless of
their baggage, are made more human, more whole, by coming
together. If our culture is yearning for connection in a sea of
isolation, shouldn't the church be known for its contagious community? The church needs to invite the world to a place where
no person is an island and where you have all the backup you
need. We have Christ and his body—the saints past and present
through the ages, even John Donne. Now that's backup and a
story worth telling!

Dialogue Texts

Then the LORD God said, "It is not good that the man should be
alone."

Genesis 2:18

A friend loves at all times, and kinsfolk are born to share
adversity.

Proverbs 17:17

Two are better than one, because they have a good reward for
their toil. For if they fall, one will lift up the other; but woe to one
who is alone and falls and does not have another to help. Again,
if two lie together, they keep warm; but how can one keep warm
alone? And though one might prevail against another, two will
withstand one. A threefold cord is not quickly broken.

Ecclesiastes 4:9–12

Bear one another's burdens, and in this way you will fulfill the
law of Christ.

Galatians 6:2

Discussion Questions

1. *About a Boy* starts with Will congratulating himself that he is
an island, and a "pretty cool island" at that. He has his gadgets,
so he doesn't really need others to mess him up with responsi-
bilities or obligations. Marcus, on the other hand, after having
experienced his mum's attempted suicide, realizes that he and
his mum need help—"need backup." The twin poles of the film
are set in place. Put these two characters and their beliefs about
relationships into conversation with the biblical texts above.
What is the film's message regarding a human being's need for
relationship? What does the Bible teach?

2. The film is about two boys, one learning to be a kid and
the other learning to be an adult. What scenes in particular
show how Will helps Marcus be a kid? Why does Marcus need
these experiences? Why does he need Will? Marcus is sometimes light-years ahead of Will emotionally. What scenes or
voice-overs in particular reveal that Will is learning, or at least
questioning himself, because of his relationship with Marcus?
What is he learning?

3. How do Marcus and Will change over the course of the
film? What acts by Will evidence that he is living into relationships and into the commitments and sacrifices they entail?

Clip Conversations

1. Chapter 8 [29:47–35:08]—"Cool Uncle Will." Through
voice-over Will is giving us his philosophy of a day, that is,

how an unemployed bachelor spends his day productively. As he leads the viewer through his day, what are you thinking? While he's at the hair salon, Will's theory is disrupted by a call from Marcus, who wants to get together again. Aghast, Will tries to put him off until he figures out that he'd be using up some of his "units of time" by being charitable. He agrees to meet Marcus and his mom. Having completed these charitable units of time, what does Will actually realize about himself? Does his life "mean anything"? Why or why not?

2. Chapter 12 [52:20–58:10]—"Christmas." Describe Christmas dinner at Marcus's home—through his eyes and then through Will's eyes. Are there any glimpses of how they might both be changing? Nick Hornby, the writer of the novel *About a Boy*, in another similarly chaotic scene of family and friends (not included in the film) writes, "Will couldn't recall ever having been caught up in this sort of messy, sprawling, chaotic web before; it was almost as if he had been given a glimpse of what it was like to be human." How are both Will and Marcus becoming more human?

3. Chapter 19 [1:33:50–1:36:12]—"No Man Is an Island." Compare Will's voice-over at the beginning of the movie with his voice-over at the end. What is Marcus thinking? If Marcus and Will represent something of the contemporary world's yearning for community, how can the church authentically model community for this postmodern world?

Bonus Material

As noted in the production notes to the shooting script, *About a Boy* was published in 1998 and was Nick Hornby's third novel, after *Fever Pitch* and *High Fidelity* (these also were made into films). The novel sold more than one million copies in Britain alone, and foreign rights were sold in more than twenty countries. It was a number one bestseller in the U.K. and also hit number two on the *Los Angeles Times* bestseller list.

Nick Hornby served as one of the executive producers of the film. However, numerous chapters in the book were cut out of the film and the ending was changed. The directors did this to keep the focus on the two main characters and to use a setting with which the viewer was already familiar (London), which is not the case in the novel. They thought they stayed true to Hornby's ending by not really having an ending. As they put it, "And if it is an ending, we were hoping not for a Hollywood Ending or even a Happy Ending but, to coin a phrase, an Okay Ending, which is a good place for these characters to find after all they've been through." We are not sure we agree. Hornby's missing chapters are worth reading, and we found his ending better. Check it out.

Robert De Niro's Tribeca Productions optioned the rights to the book in 1998 as it was going to print. Tribeca found a British producing partner in Working Title Films (which had done Hornby's book *High Fidelity*). The Weitz brothers became involved because Chris had read the novel on vacation and loved it. Some were concerned that the Weitz brothers might not be up to the task, since they were mostly known for their light teen hit *American Pie*. Hugh Grant, though a fan of *American Pie*, was even concerned. But he quickly learned that "although capable of fabulous infantilism, they're also extremely serious and learned people." For you see, Chris Weitz was schooled at St. Paul's, London, and Cambridge University.

Hugh Grant was signed on to the film even before the directors because he loved the novel and wanted to play the part of Will. He even tried buying the rights for his own production company. Nicholas Hoult was cast from hundreds of kids who tried out for the part. Previously he had only had several small television roles. It was a dream come true for Nicholas. His mom had to drag him away every day when shooting ended. At the end of shooting all of Nicholas's scenes, he cried because he was so upset that the experience had come to an end. But when the filmmakers gave him a PlayStation 2 in appreciation for his wonderful work in the film, his tears stopped!

Music was another important aspect of the film. The directors listened to Badly Drawn Boy's album, "Hour of the Bewilderbeast," while they worked on the script. They pitched the idea to the producers to use the artist, a.k.a. Damon Gough, for the film. He came on board early, allowing him to come to the set, see dailies, and be shown cut footage during shooting of the movie. In this way they could time certain sequences to his music instead of the other way around.

About a Boy was nominated for Golden Globes in both Best Actor and Best Motion Picture, Musical or Comedy, categories. It was also nominated for Best Adapted Screenplay by the Academy of Motion Picture Arts and Sciences, the Writers Guild of America and BAFTA (the British Academy). With a budget of $27 million, its worldwide gross was $125 million ($41 million in the U.S.). Showing this film to your youth group would be a wonderful way to start a conversation about the peer pressure to fit in that many junior high and high school youth feel. By laughing *with* Will and Marcus, we all might see how much "no man is an island" and how much we need each other.

22. *Italian for Beginners*

Community and Friendship
Loneliness, Prayer,
Renewing the Church
Affirming the Human Spirit,
Brokenness, Celebration,
Clergy, Faith, Food,
Hope, Love, Materialism

Themes

Denmark, 2001
112 Minutes, Feature, Color
Actors: Anders W. Berthelsen,
  Peter Gantzler, Lars Kaalund,
  Annette Stovelbae,
  Ann Elenora Jorgenson, Sar Indrio Jensen
Director: Lone Scherfig
Screenwriters: Lone Scherfig
Rated: R (profanity, sexual scenes)
DVD Features: Dogme 95 Manifesto

The Italian class students take a field trip to Venice. *Italian for Beginners* (d. Scherfig, 2001). Copyright 2000 Miramax Films. All rights reserved.

Synopsis and Theological Reflection

To the least and lonely, such is the good news of love. And the least and the lonely come in all shapes and sizes, as Danish writer-director Lone Scherfig shows us in the lovely film *Italian for Beginners*. As one movie critic swooned (and movie critics rarely do swoon), she "has made a film so unabashedly hopeful that it actually makes the heart soar." But we're getting ahead of ourselves, for this hope is not pie-in-the-sky, nor is it easily experienced. The characters move from loneliness to community in slow and sometimes painful steps. But isn't that how life is for most of us?

Italian for Beginners is actually a romantic comedy with three romances bundled into one. The connecting thread is that all of the characters live in the same Danish town and all attend the local Italian for Beginners class. There are eventually nine students total, but we enter the lives of six. We meet Jorgen Mortenson, the friendly, gentle assistant manager of the local hotel, as he receives the order to fire the hotel's restaurant manager, Halvfinn, his troubled friend. Halvfinn is generally rude to everyone including his waitress, Giulia, a beautiful Italian immigrant. Upon losing his job, however, Halvfinn is hired as a fill-in to teach the evening Italian class he attends, for he is the best of the students. Jorgen has become so taken by Giulia's simple spirit that he is already enrolled in the class so he can learn to speak to her in Italian. And Giulia, in order to see the shy Jorgen, eventually joins as well.

To these three students is added Andreas, a newly licensed theological student and temporary resident at the hotel. He has been sent to the town to pastor a local congregation that is dying due to the bitterness of the previous pastor. He arrives in his Maseratti, hoping people won't notice just how lonely he is since his young wife's death. Karen is the local hairdresser, and all of the main characters end up in her shop at one point or another. She too is struggling, given her alcoholic mother who is dying. Finally, we have Olympia, a clumsy, bakery-store worker who lives with her abusive father. Such a ragtag group would hardly seem a promising class, but by the movie's end they (and we) have learned much about both life and love (as well as a little Italian!).

As the movie gradually reveals unsuspected connections between the characters and their interactions allow romances to bloom, the viewer is drawn into the preciousness of life, with all of its pain and joy. The actors are masterful in making us feel their characters' common experience of loneliness, be it Giulia, unable to communicate in Danish, or Pastor Andreas preparing for a service by reciting his sermon: "It is in loneliness that God seems farthest away. But God is here . . . in compassion, in friendship, between us . . . in love, in every moment . . . in the arm you slip around the waist of your beloved." He then silently and alone weeps in his hotel room. Or we watch as Jorgen shares his "problem with women" with the pastor, only to "pastor" Andreas with his gentleness and care. And when Karen and Olympia are asked if they need someone to be with them in times of loss, they each respond, "I'm used to being alone." The beauty and poignancy of these lives is stunning, as if, to quote one critic, "They're lit from within, emanating exquisite sadness, yearning and carefully guarded hope." It is as if by showing their earthly brokenness, the director makes their romantic transcendence even more breathtaking.

It's not just romantic love that binds the wounds, however; it is the love of a newfound community—the connectedness to others on the journey—that creates new possibilities. Along with its deglamorization of the swinging single life, the movie shows us the possibilities and hope of community. As the classmates join together in a meal at the end of the film, we see the affection that has bloomed in the midst of their respective problems. The problems remain, but they pale in comparison to the love and care shown to each other. Hope for the future saturates the air, but it is a battered optimism, one filled with enough irony to make the happy ending both desired and earned.

At one point in the story, Giulia is praying to God, reminding him that he came into the world for the humble and poor. She includes herself and her newfound friends in that group. And yes, Jesus did come for the least of us. He came to a motley crew of twelve and showed them a new way to live with each other, ushering in a new community of love and service. It is such a gospel that Andreas also models for his struggling parish. The result is new possibilities for a congregation that seemed to have little promise or future. Whether among couples, classmates, or congregants, the simple lesson is clear: Love can prove transformative. Jesus comes again today—calling the least of us to faith, hope, and love. But the greatest of these is love.

Dialogue Texts

Some friends play at friendship but a true friend sticks closer than one's nearest kin.

Proverbs 18:24

There is nothing better for mortals than to eat and drink, and find enjoyment in their toil. This also, I saw, is from the hand of God; for apart from him who can eat or who can have enjoyment?

Ecclesiastes 2:24–25

Two are better than one, because they have a good reward for their toil. For if they fall, one will lift up the other; but woe to one who is alone and falls and does not have another to help. Again, if two lie together, they keep warm; but how can one be warm alone? And though one might prevail against another, two will withstand one. A threefold cord is not quickly broken.

Ecclesiastes 4:9–12

For I was hungry and you gave me food, I was thirsty and you gave me something to drink, I was a stranger and you welcomed me, I was naked and you gave me clothing, I was sick and you took care of me, I was in prison and you visited me. . . . Truly, I tell you, just as you did it to one of the least of these who are members of my family, you did it to me.

Matthew 25:35–36, 40

[Love] bears all things, believes all things, hopes all things, endures all things.

1 Corinthians 13:7

Discussion Questions

1. Think about how the movie starts and the film's home-video feel (e.g., no special lighting, no background music, a handheld camera). How did you feel as you watched the characters? Did this feeling change by the end of the film? How does this style enhance or detract from the story and the characters?

2. Through the course of the film we learn that several characters are learning to live with loss in their lives—loss of loved ones, loss of power, loss of physical capabilities, or even the loss

of the presence of God. With the loss comes loneliness, guilt, and pain, but sometimes it also brings relief. Both Karen and Olympia lose a parent. How did you feel when these two characters died? How did their deaths release Karen and Olympia to something new—with each other and with others? Notice the hymn, "This Blessed Day," that is sung at both the funerals. What is the director saying to the viewer about some kinds of loss? Do you agree?

3. The film ends with a meal in Venice. What does the trip to Italy mean in each of their lives? How is each of the characters different at this point? How are they caring for each other? What things haven't changed? Why does Andreas not need his Maseratti anymore?

Clip Conversations

1. Chapter 3 [17:20–25:00]—"Which Way the Wind Blows." Pastor Andreas is preparing his sermon. He speaks of loneliness and when we perceive God's absence. Discuss his response to these ultimate questions of loss and life. "But God is here . . . in compassion, in friendship, between us, inside us, in love, in every moment, in the arm you slip around the waist of your beloved." Do his words sound authentic; did you get the feeling that he has truly wrestled with these questions and is on a journey himself? How does his response foreshadow the dinner in Venice? How can the church model authentic community?

2. Chapter 8 [59:27–1:08:40]—"Through the Holidays." Relationships are deepening as various characters confide in and encourage each other. Prayer is even mentioned as a possible way to deal with life's ups and downs. (Notice the juxtaposition of the full Christmas service and Andreas's Christmas dinner alone, until he finds Jorgen in the kitchen.) In fact we see and hear Giulia praying as she works. What is revealed in her simple

prayer? What happens after she prays? Given how prayer is portrayed here, how is the director revealing her own view of prayer? What do you think about prayer?

3. Chapter 9 [1:08:40–1:12:50]—"The Meaning of Loss." Again the director is placing side by side moments of joy and hope with moments of hard realism, confession, and disagreements. Here we see Andreas's visit to Rev. Wredmann's home. It begins with Christmas greetings and ends with Andreas shouting at the pastor to get on with his life. Discuss their conversation. How has loss affected them both? Why do you think they have reacted so differently?

Bonus Material

Italian for Beginners falls into the romantic comedy genre, but its story is far from the traditional formula. There is more going on than two-dimensional characters falling in love. These people are real, with real problems, dilemmas, and pain (impotence, alcoholism, drug addiction, emotional abuse, fetal alcohol syndrome, death, grief, fear, and faith). The love they eventually share is, thus, even more remarkable.

Italian for Beginners won the Silver Berlin Bear Jury Prize at the Berlin Film Festival and was nominated for Best Picture at the 2001 European Film Academy. Its total box office receipts were over $15 million. It was made following the aesthetic principles of the Dogme 95 filmmakers, who insist on natural lighting, the use of color film, handheld cameras, filming on location, no props or sets, and only sounds or music that are created on location. In addition, these principles prohibit traditional genre films and films that are not based in real time (e.g., no flashbacks allowed) or use superficial action such as murders, weapons, etc. The last of the ten principles states, "The director must not be credited." The actual Dogme 95 Vow of Chastity, as it is called, ends with this statement: "Furthermore I swear as a director to refrain from personal taste! I am no longer an artist. I swear to refrain from creating a 'work,' as I regard the instant as more important than the whole. My supreme goal is to force the truth out of my characters and settings. I swear to do so by all the means available and at the cost of any good taste and any aesthetic considerations."

Obviously the Dogme 95 filmmakers are a unique (read "idiosyncratic") group, flying in the face of Hollywood filmmakers. Thus, the movie provides a different type of film experience, one unlike a major studio film. Though it might take some getting used to the style, it is well worth the effort.

Faith

23. Simon Birch

U.S., 1998
113 Minutes, Feature, Color
Actors: Ian Michael Smith, Joseph Mazzello, Ashley Judd, Oliver Platt, David Strathairn, Jim Carrey
Director: Mark Steven Johnson
Screenwriter: Mark Steven Johnson
Rated: PG (mild and brief profanity, mature themes)
DVD Features: theatrical trailer

Themes

Faith
Embracing Our Vocation,
Friendship,
Negative Images of the Church,
Sharing Our Faith
Affirming the Human Spirit, Death,
Family, Role of Clergy,
Sacrificial Love

Synopsis and Theological Reflection

> Before I formed you in the womb I knew you,
> and before you were born I consecrated you;
> I appointed you a prophet to the nations.
>
> Jeremiah 1:5, opening quotation
> in *A Prayer for Owen Meany*

I am doomed to remember a boy with a wrecked voice—not because of his voice or because he was the smallest person I ever knew, or even because he was the instrument of my mother's death, but because he is the reason I believe in God.

> Quoted in *Simon Birch*; suggested
> by the novel *A Prayer for Owen Meany*

Being lovers of books *and* films, we couldn't resist *Simon Birch*, a film adaptation (in a very loose sense) of John Irving's novel *A Prayer for Owen Meany*. We say this despite the fact that seven of the ten critics we surveyed praised the novel but called the

Joe (Joseph Mazzello) and Simon (Ian Michael Smith) share a deep friendship as they each discover their destiny. *Simon Birch* (d. Johnson, 1998). Photo by Alan Markfield. Copyright 1998 Hollywood Pictures Company. All rights reserved.

film a "promising failure." There are those times (and *Simon Birch* is an example) when a film does not fully capture the power of the novel. In *Simon Birch*, the story's power is lost in part because the novel's explicitly Christian worldview is diluted. (The above quote from the film actually continues in the novel, "I am a Christian because of Owen Meany.") However, the basic story of two twelve-year-old best friends (both social misfits in a small, New England town in the mid-1960s) trying to understand life is kept intact. In the telling, the film wonderfully deals with faith, fate, and friendship. Thus, we felt that while the over-five-hundred-page novel might never make it to your bedside nightstand, the film *Simon Birch* should make it to your video/DVD player.

Born a dwarf, Simon (played by three-foot-one-inch-tall Ian Michael Smith who actually suffers from Morquio syndrome) is declared a miracle by the doctor delivering him. And Simon never lets anyone forget that *he is a miracle*, more than the mere sum of his parts. Moreover, he is sure that God has a plan for his life (and everyone else's!), much to the consternation of those around him—his parents, his classmates, his Sunday school teacher, and even the local reverend. His best friend, Joe (played by Joseph Mazzello), is also somewhat of an oddity. But in his case, it has nothing to do with physical appearance. He's different than all the other kids because his mother (played by Ashley Judd) has raised him out of wedlock, much to the shock of the whole town, and without divulging the identity of the father.

Thus, the two boys' contexts and quests set the stage. Joe longs to find his father. Simon is determined to find God's plan for his life. Together, the two boys celebrate and mourn the mysteries of their respective searches. And in the process Simon continues to challenge himself and others to believe. "I want to know there is a reason for things. I want you to tell me God has a plan for me, for all of us." When not only Reverend Russell, but most of the town, is unable and even afraid to trust God as Simon does, it is up to him to communicate faith to all, and particularly to Joe. "I have faith; the problem with you is you don't have faith. Faith is not in a floor plan." Only a real friend could challenge another to faith in such a way, and the result is Joe's spiritual and emotional growth.

Simon Birch is an unabashedly sentimental tearjerker, much less complex and nuanced than the novel. The two boys succeed in their quests, although in somewhat unpredictable ways. As Joe narrates at the end of the movie, "With Simon's help I found my real father." But his words carry far more meaning than that of his biological father. And Simon, convinced that "I'm God's instrument; there are no accidents," does indeed become a hero in the hands of the Creator.

The complexity of the movie's plot has been reduced from the novel, but the characters are nonetheless winsome. Their banter and escapades are often raucously funny (the Christmas pageant with Simon as the baby Jesus is a combination of a Sunday school teacher's worst nightmare and slapstick). As Roger Ebert reflected about this film, "We go to the movies for lots of reasons, and one of them is to seek good company." Simon and Joe are so likeable, you are glad to be eavesdropping on them.

Watch *Simon Birch* with your family and you will have plenty to talk about regarding the themes of family, of dealing with the loss of a loved one or with physical disabilities, and of trusting in God's plan for each one of us. But most of all you will be in good company!

Dialogue Texts

Before I formed you in the womb I knew you, and before you were born I consecrated you; I appointed you a prophet to the nations.

Jeremiah 1:5

But I do not count my life of any value to myself, if only I may finish my course and the ministry that I received from the Lord Jesus, to testify to the good news of God's grace.

Acts 20:24

Consider your own call, brothers and sisters: not many of you were wise by human standards, not many were powerful, not many were of noble birth. But God chose what is foolish in the world to shame the wise; God chose what is weak in the world to shame the strong.

1 Corinthians 1:26–27

However that may be, let each of you lead the life that the Lord has assigned, to which God called you.

1 Corinthians 7:17

I therefore, the prisoner in the Lord, beg you to lead a life worthy of the calling to which you have been called, with all humility and gentleness, with patience, bearing with one another in love, making every effort to maintain the unity of the Spirit in the bond of peace.

Ephesians 4:1–2

We know that all things work together for good for those who love God, who are called according to his purpose.

Romans 8:28

Discussion Questions

1. As noted above, both the novel and film have an explicitly religious tone. The whole atmosphere of the film is imbued with religious elements: the opening scene in the cemetery, the Sunday school class, the role of the Episcopal priest, Rebecca's funeral, and the Christmas pageant. How might these elements be conversation points with non-Christian friends? How might they instruct us as Christians? Of course the greatest spokesman for God is Simon, who never stops reminding people of the presence and power of God—sometimes humorously and, finally, by giving his life for others. What did you learn from Simon about sharing your faith?

2. Compare and contrast the characters in the film. Which characters show goodness, beauty, and/or truth? Which characters, though socially acceptable, show little of these characteristics nor much generosity of spirit? Did you connect with Simon? Why or why not? What's so special about his relationship with Joe? How do the characters grow, especially Simon and Joe but also Reverend Russell and Ben Goodrich?

3. After Rebecca's death, Simon leaves Joe all of his baseball cards. Joe in turn gives Simon his armadillo. Both are entrusting the other with their most precious possession, as a sign of abiding friendship and love. As they talk (chapter 10 [40:33–45:07] —"A Gift In Return"), we see how each one is dealing with

the death of the person they loved so much. How do they both say some things that are true about the situation? How is Joe challenged by what Simon says? What does it mean to be an instrument of God? How does Joe come to understand Simon's point of view?

4. In the end, who is Joe's biological father, but who has become his *real* father? Why did Joe choose Ben Goodrich? What fatherly characteristics had Ben shared with Joe? Would you have chosen similarly? Why or why not? What glimpses do we get as to the type of father Joe has become? Bonus question: What does the armadillo at Simon's grave mean?

Clip Conversations

1. Chapter 2 [00:30–3:55]—"Opening Credits." Joe, as an adult (Jim Carrey), explains why he will always remember his friend Simon. How does this opening scene give us a glimpse into Simon's purpose? Think about your own coming to faith. Was there someone important in your journey to God? How might God want to use you in someone else's life?

2. Chapter 8 [26:50–33:40]—"Coffee and Doughnuts." Simon starts making comments in the worship service about the extracurricular activities of the church. Later, Reverend Russell meets with him, and Miss Leavey chastises him further. Rebecca intervenes and thanks Simon. Why are many of the adults so threatened by Simon? On the other hand, why is Rebecca so grateful for Simon? Have you known people who, like Simon, are unabashedly vocal about their faith? How did they make you feel? How can we be unabashed about our faith in our own postmodern context?

3. Chapters 16 [1:06:50–1:09:10] and 18 [1:15:20–1:22:00]—"Reverend Russell's Rules" and "Punishment." Both these clips

revolve around nuggets of conversation that raise the question, "Does God have a plan for us?" Why can't Reverend Russell tell him that God has a plan for him? How do you see Simon as a prophet to Reverend Russell and the whole church community? Do you agree that God has a purpose for everyone? Why or why not?

Bonus Material

Simon Birch was panned by many critics for its failure to capture the complexities of John Irving's novel and for its sentimental tone. However, as noted above, when seen in its own light, even being sentimental, the film is worth recommending. Roger Ebert even gushed, "Simon Birch is an unabashedly sentimental tearjerker. Either you stand back and resist it, or you plunge in. There was something about its innocence and spunk that got to me, and I caved in."

On websites of viewer reviews, the film also got high marks. Many saw it as a testament to the resilience of faith. Others said it was worth seeing just to see and hear Simon Birch. Both Joseph Mazzello and Ian Michael Smith won awards for Best Young Actor, for they gave wonderful performances. Its total box office receipts were $19 million. Neither a box office hit nor of critical acclaim, but in its own way, Simon Birch is a delightful way to have a conversation about faith. (And it just might inspire you to read A Prayer for Owen Meany, which is one of our all-time favorite novels!)

24. *Tender Mercies*

U.S., 1983
89 Minutes, Feature, Color
Actors: Robert Duvall, Tess Harper,
Betty Buckley, Ellen Barkin, Allan Hubbard,
Wilford Brimley
Director: Bruce Beresford
Writer: Horton Foote
Rated: PG (adult language and themes)
DVD Features: theatrical trailer; "Miracles and Mercies," featuring
recent interviews with the cast and crew

Faith
Affirming the Human Spirit,
Baptism, Grace, Holy Spirit,
Life as a Gift, Salvation,
Transformation
Joy, Loneliness, Love,
Second Chances, Sharing Our Faith,
The Stranger, Work

Themes

Synopsis and Theological Reflection

Tender Mercies, written by Texas playwright Horton Foote, tells the story of a has-been country singer and songwriter who has sunk as low as the bottom of his whiskey bottle. The movie begins with Mac Sledge collapsing after a drunken brawl, only to awaken two days later to find himself at a dilapidated motel/gas station in the middle of nowhere in rural Texas. The motel/gas station is run by Rosa Lee, a widow who is trying to make a living while raising her young son, Sonny. Offering Mac a job as the motel handyman in order to pay off his bill, Rosa Lee even more importantly provides Mac with quiet strength, simple faith, and straightforward acceptance. As a result, Mac is able to escape from the wilderness of a lost voice, a lost career, and a lost family, and in time he is reborn.

The secret to Mac's new life is the undeserved grace of Rosa Lee. Though she is reserved and seldom smiles, her *tender mercies* are nevertheless regenerative. Often the two adults eat in silence. When dialogue does take place, it is lean and terse. Life has been hard for both of them, and Mac has failed utterly. But for Rosa Lee, there is neither preaching nor condemnation. As the two learn slowly to talk to each other, they each share their pain. For example, just as Mac gains enough confidence to begin

Mac (Robert Duvall) and his new wife, Rosa Lee (Tess Harper), together with her son, Sonny (Allan Hubbard). *Tender Mercies* (d. Beresford, 1983). Copyright 1983 Universal City Studios. All rights reserved.

writing again, one of his songs is rejected. Rosa Lee is there to offer support in her quiet, straightforward way: "It's bound to be hard on you. . . . I love you. When I thank the Lord for his tender mercies, you and Sonny head the list."

There is nothing sensationalized about Mac's transformation. Neither a Hollywood romance with a fancy wedding nor a miraculous conversion with immediate results and storybook ending is scripted. In fact, the marriage that does happen and Mac's acceptance of Christ, which does take place, both happen off camera. Only the appearance of a ring on his finger and a simple baptism at the local church signal for the viewer that Rosa Lee's Christian faith and steady love have proven transformative for Mac.

Two of Mac's country Western songs (two written by Duvall himself) give voice to his life story. The one that Mac writes and then sings with his new band says, "If you'll just hold the ladder, baby, I'll climb to the top." Not great words, but a profound insight nonetheless—one that Mac has personally experienced. Given Rosa Lee's confidence in him, given her unconditional love, Mac has the faith to climb out of the tomb. Moreover, what happens relationally for him also takes place spiritually. Rosa Lee's tender mercies become a window to God's tender mercies.

As the film ends, Mac is singing a ballad he had sung to his daughter as a child but which he has long suppressed: "On the wings of a snow white dove, He sends his pure white love." It is ultimately the Holy Spirit that brings new life to Mac. There are few movies in Hollywood that better portray the wonder of God's gift of salvation through his Spirit than this one.

C. S. Lewis, in his autobiography *Surprised by Joy*, describes the fragile and elusive presence of grace in his life. Lewis could not produce it on command; when he tried to grasp it, it faded in his hand like a picked flower. But the quiet reality of grace, which produced joy in the ordinary events of life, proved so compelling that it sent him on a search for God.

Lewis's conversion was hardly climatic; it happened quietly as he drove to the zoo one day. In his book, Lewis goes to great lengths to separate the source of that joy—God himself—from our experience of it. As the psalmist reminds us, "The LORD is good to all: and his tender mercies are over all his works" (Ps. 145:9 KJV). There might or might not be fireworks, but these experiences are only our response to that grace—those tender mercies—that is given to us by God. Duvall and Foote understand that the miracle of grace is more important than any titanic result. And their *Tender Mercies* is the compelling result.

Dialogue Texts

The LORD is good to all: and his tender mercies are over all his works.

Psalm 145:9 KJV

Have mercy on me, O God, according to your steadfast love; according to your abundant mercy blot out my transgressions. Wash me thoroughly from my iniquity, and cleanse me from my sin.

Psalm 51:1–2

How can we who died to sin go on living in it? Do you not know that all of us who have been baptized into Christ Jesus were baptized into his death? Therefore we have been buried with him by baptism into death, so that, just as Christ was raised from the dead by the glory of the Father, so we too might walk in newness of life.

Romans 6:2–4

Work out your own salvation with fear and trembling; for it is God who is at work in you, enabling you both to will and to work for his good pleasure.

Philippians 2:12–13

Discussion Questions

1. You probably can't have a movie about a country Western singer in rural Texas without hearing some country tunes in the movie. However, in this case the music (some of it written and sung by Robert Duvall himself) is integral to the story we see visually. Think about the opening and repeated song, "It Hurts

to Face Reality." How does this song reflect the story of Mac's life and others in the film? Check out the progression of songs in the film, from the above to "Jesus Saves," to "Fool's Waltz," to "Wings of a Dove," to "If You'll Hold the Ladder (I'll Climb to the Top)," to the final song, "You Are What Love Means to Me." How do they give voice to Mac's transformation?

2. While our attention is drawn to Mac and his journey, Rosa Lee is in fact the catalyst for his redemption. She has high standards but is never judgmental. She lives a life of quiet love and discipline—from singing in the church choir, praying, and reciting the Psalms (she recites Psalm 145:9 and Psalm 25:4–5 [check out verse 6 also]) to her enjoyment of the simple pleasures in life such as town dances, hanging laundry in the expanse of God's creation, and helping others, whether Mac or his runaway daughter, Sue Anne. How does Rosa Lee's living out of her faith allow God's tender mercies to touch and transform Mac? How do we, as viewers, see and experience God's tender mercies in new ways through her? How might she be a model both for our own discipleship and for our friendship evangelism?

3. Driving home after Sonny and Mac's baptism, Sonny looks in the rearview mirror to see if he looks any different. He then asks Mac whether he feels different, to which Mac replies, "Not yet." Sonny asks, "Do you think I look any different?" Mac only answers with another, "Not yet." How is this "not yet" especially true? St. Paul uses the expression "being saved" rather than "saved" in 1 Corinthians 1:18 and 2 Corinthians 2:15. Both Mac and St. Paul know that conversion and faith are an ongoing process and not just a sudden, miraculous event. Reflect on your own conversion experience and life in Christ. Where are you in the process of maturing in Christ?

4. In fact, faith is often tested and shaped by hard times. How does Mac react to the tragedy that besets him later in

the film? How does his reaction show us his conversion is real and honest? What has contributed to your spiritual development? How have tragic or hurtful experiences impacted your faith? Did you experience a deepening of faith after the pain or numbness subsided? Or are you still in the honest questioning and real struggle stage? Are there other Christians (Rosa Lee folks) who might struggle with you into the light and peace of God's presence? How can the church be a place that lovingly (not judgmentally) sits with folks during these times of painful growth into faith?

Clip Conversations

1. Chapter 9 [30:20–36:38]—"Tender Mercies." Here we see and hear Rosa Lee's conversation with Mac, telling him that he is at the top of the list of God's tender mercies to her. What are those tender mercies in your life? How have you expressed your thanks for them? To God? To people? (You might consider keeping a "tender mercies" journal that you regularly share with God and others.)

2. Chapters 14 [52:30–58:00] and 15 [58:00–1:02:12]—"Sue Anne" and "Wings of a Dove." Mac's daughter comes to visit him and asks him about a song he used to sing to her—"On the Wings of a Dove." Why do you think Mac lied to her about knowing the song? Of what or whom was he afraid? Have you ever been afraid to live into the changes (transformation) happening in you? What or who helped you overcome your fear?

3. Chapter 16 [1:02:12–1:06:30]—"Baptism." Sonny and Mac's baptism and the drive home. Have you been baptized? If so, share the story of it with the group. How did it change you, and how are you not yet changed?

Bonus Material

As the actors and crew reflected on their experience of making *Tender Mercies* (see DVD), many commented on the profound effect the film had on their own lives. Horton Foote himself grew up in rural Texas until as a young adult he went off to New York to become an actor. The blend of toughness and gentleness in the film comes from his firsthand knowledge of and respect for the simplicity of life and the people of rural Texas. He chose to coproduce the film with Robert Duvall, whom he considers to be one of the world's best actors and whose acting is "always full of revelations."

Initially some critics believed that Horton Foote wrote the film for Robert Duvall because he always had wanted to play a country Western singer. However this wasn't the case. But the film did give Duvall the chance to be a country singer for a moment, even writing and singing some of the songs in the film. His portrayal of Mac was one filled with understanding and appreciation for common people. He credits Foote's honest screenplay as a perfect vehicle for this portrayal.

Tess Harper credits the film and Horton Foote with the ability to deal with the humanity in all of us, while adding that he helps you "see into peoples' souls." She was constantly struck by the vastness of the landscape in which they worked and suggested that the combination of Foote's screenplay and Bruce Beresford's direction perfectly illuminated "a little piece of life in the vastness of creation."

Finally, Allan Hubbard, who played Sonny, shares on the DVD that not only the film but also his relationship with Robert Duvall shaped him. His love for guitar playing (he currently is a guitar instructor) was born on the film set. Robert Duvall's playing and spending time teaching him chords and other basics sent Allan on a lifelong vocation. One month after the film finished production he turned ten years old. Robert Duvall came back for his birthday party and gave him his first guitar.

Tender Mercies was nominated for five Academy Awards (including Best Picture of the Year). It won two—Robert Duvall for Best Actor and Horton Foote for Best Original Screenplay. This was actually quite astonishing because when the film opened early in the year, it opened in only three theaters (one each in New York, Chicago, and Los Angeles) for two months. It then disappeared until the nominations came out ten months later. Its total box office receipts were a modest $8.4 million. Hardly the typical makings of an Oscar winner, but thankfully viewers and critics recognized what a gem this movie is.

Faith and Doubt

25. The Third Miracle

U.S., 1999
120 Minutes, Feature, Color
Actors: Ed Harris, Anne Heche,
Armin Mueller-Stahl, Charles Haid,
Michael Rispoli, James Gallanders
Director: Agnieszka Holland
Screenwriters: Richard Vetere and John Romano
Rated: R (brief profanity, mature themes)
DVD Features: theatrical trailer, commentary by director, isolated
music score, Spanish subtitles

Themes

Faith and Doubt
Clergy, Cost of Discipleship,
Embracing Our Vocation,
Miracles, Saints
Choice, Negative Images of the
Church, Obedience to God,
Sharing Our Faith

Synopsis and Theological Reflection

Something interesting happened in Hollywood as the millennium approached. A number of adult dramas were released, all of which took the Christian faith with new seriousness. *The Green Mile, The End of the Affair, Dogma, The Big Kahuna, The Third Miracle*—these R-rated films invited moviegoers to consider God and the effect of his presence in their lives. True, the church and its hierarchy were still lampooned—but then we often deserve what we get. However, the reality of God, the centrality of faith, and the importance of obedience were embraced. These movie stories at times had salty language, graphic violence, and/or explicit sexuality. They are not for everyone—certainly not the young. But the passion with which these movies portray issues of faith and doubt suggests a new openness in moviemakers to consider Christian belief.

Father Frank (Ed Harris) visits the site of a miracle. *The Third Miracle* (d. Holland, 1999). Photo by Pierre Vinet. Copyright 1999 Sony Pictures Classics. All rights reserved.

Of these five movies, readers will be most familiar with *The Green Mile*. Its use of Christ imagery to tell the story of a black prisoner wrongly imprisoned for the death of two young girls will bring tears to your eyes. (We have heard from numerous pastors who have preached sermons based on the movie, for they see it as one of the best "Jesus movies" recently made.) Graham Greene's *The End of the Affair* tells the story of a prayer that is answered and the subsequent price this extracts. Belief in the efficacy of prayer is taken seriously, as is the importance of fulfilling your vows to God.

Kevin Smith's *Dogma* made headlines across the country for its "sacrilegious" portrayal of the Catholic Church. But what was almost lost in the scuffle over this Gen X movie was its radical commitment to the Christian God as the source of all life and goodness. Smith says he made the movie to challenge his friends who are "cultured despisers of religion" to consider the Christian faith. *The Big Kahuna*, starring Kevin Spacey and Danny Devito, portrays three salesmen of industrial lubricants at a convention who struggle over life's ambiguities and argue whether God has anything to say about their lives.

This leaves us with the last movie of the group—*The Third Miracle*. Most of you will no doubt say, "I've never heard of it." This is a pity, for it might just be the best of the group. Released in limited theaters late in December 1999, it never got the general marketing it deserved despite wonderful reviews. Thankfully, you can find it at your local video store.

Set in Chicago in 1979, the movie tells the story of a Catholic priest, Frank Shore, who has left his church assignment and is living in a hotel for transients and eating at a soup kitchen with a cross-section of society's rejected. Father Frank was a postulator, a priest assigned by the church hierarchy to investigate claims of miracles and sainthood. In the process of having to disprove a man's supposed heroic virtue, Frank also destroyed the faith of a whole parish that had come to believe in the miracles of this man. Frank's church superiors were pleased he had exposed such superstition for what it was, but the weight of destroying the sincere faith of ordinary people causes Frank to question his own.

When the church comes calling again, Frank is compelled not only to investigate the faith and good works of another possible saint but his own as well. The movie thus becomes both a spiritual pilgrimage and a detective story, with a romance thrown in to boot.

Ed Harris, who plays Frank Shore, is utterly convincing in his portrayal. Cursed by skepticism, hounded by his superiors, and tempted by sex, he refuses to succumb, instead choosing to be faithful to God and his church. And the temptations are real. The chemistry between Frank and Roxanne (Anne Heche) is almost combustible. The concern of his superiors for the church to be thought of as modern and appropriately unsuperstitious is intimidating. And the tragic events surrounding his own call to ministry would challenge the faith of most of us. We agonize with Frank and sense his struggle. We also celebrate with him.

For someone to be beatified in the Catholic Church in the 1970s, canon law required that the person be pure and that three miracles occur as a result of his or her life and ministry. As the story unfolds, and it is a good one, there are indeed two miracles that become documented. It is not clear, however, what the third miracle is. Maybe it is the miracle of faith itself—a faith that is reborn in Frank and a faith that will be strengthened in moviegoers as well.

Many Christians are looking for ways to talk about their faith with friends, colleagues, and family who no longer attend church regularly, or never did, and yet might be open to discuss spiritual experience. You might try inviting a neighbor or friend over to see *The Third Miracle*. It will stimulate a wonderful discussion over a cup of coffee afterwards. Not only will it afford you the occasion of sharing something of the Christian story with others, it might even be the occasion for *your* faith to be strengthened. We know; it happened to us.

Dialogue Texts

Blessed are the poor in spirit, for theirs is the kingdom of heaven. . . . Blessed are the meek, for they will inherit the earth. . . . Blessed are the merciful, for they will receive mercy. Blessed are the pure in heart, for they will see God.

Matthew 5:3, 5, 7–8

I believe; help my unbelief!

Mark 9:24

Now faith is the assurance of things hoped for, the conviction of things not seen.

Hebrews 11:1

Let us hold fast to the confession of our hope without wavering, for he who has promised is faithful. And let us consider how to provoke one another to love and good deeds.

Hebrews 10:23–24

Discussion Questions

1. How might the Beatitudes be brought into conversation with this movie? How are they a measure of true sainthood? How do they compare to Father Short's or Archbishop Werner's view of sainthood? How would you describe a saint? From what we know from the movie, how did Helen O'Regan live out her faith? Given your definition of sainthood, was she a saint?

2. Do miracles still happen in today's world, or are they just superstition and the work of con artists? At a prerelease screening of *The Third Miracle*, an audience of sophisticated, urban, mostly young, unchurched viewers asked this question. Even though the film staff had prepared their own questions to ask the audience, the viewers would have none of it. They wanted to talk about whether such miracles and faith could happen today and, as the film appears to ask, whether miracles are ever wasted. If you had been in the theater that night, how would you have entered into the conversation about miracles? Have you ever experienced a miracle? How did you know it was a miracle? When you have shared the experience with others, how have they reacted?

3. How have Father Frank and Roxanne each changed through the course of the film? From your perspective, what is the most significant miracle in the film? Is there a third miracle portrayed?

Clip Conversations

1. Chapter 11 [45:35–49:20]—"Frank's Confession." Frank goes to the confessional of his friend John. He asks him, "Where does faith go? . . . How does faith get away from you, John?" He shouts at God, "I'll give up, I'll give up everything. . . . I just want it to be true . . . !" How does John respond (with words and/or by his actions)? What lessons can we learn, good or bad,

from John about how to respond to a fellow Christian's doubts? How would you respond to a friend struggling with doubt?

2. Chapter 13 [54:10–57:50]—"Bargain with God." Frank shares with Roxanne how he was called into the priesthood. What strikes you about what he says? How did you feel? How has his life been shaped by miracles and tragedies? Have you ever bargained with God? What happened? What did you feel?

3. Chapter 18 [1:10:15–1:17:30]—"Frank's Decision." Frank meets Roxanne to tell her that he's recommending her mother for sainthood. She asks, "Should I be happy?" He says, "No, well, I didn't think you would be happy." Why? What does this decision represent in Frank's life vis-à-vis his faith and Roxanne? Roxanne is justifiably hurt, but what is Frank feeling? From your perspective, is this an honest depiction of his faith at this point in the film? Think of a time that you made a costly decision because of your faith commitment. How did you feel?

4. Chapter 28 [1:51:40–1:54:25]—"Three Years Later." A little boy with an angelic voice sings, "Before your eyes the world unfolds. Let me dissolve my hatred. So I can know you, so I can know you. Let me sacrifice my fear. So I can see you, so I can see you." Frank has just said a first communion mass for a group of children and enjoys posing for a picture with them. How does this haunting song connect with Frank's journey in the film? How does the end of the film bring his journey to some closure?

Bonus Material

Director Agnieszka Holland is a practicing Catholic. When she read the screenplay she was deeply touched because it took faith seriously. She says that the protagonist, Frank Shore, is struggling, "as I am struggling," to have faith in today's world, with so many problems, suffering, materialism, etc. She also was fascinated with other questions. What does it mean to be a saint? What kind of saint does the church need today? What does the Catholic Church mean to people today? Thus, one of her motivations for making the film was to portray issues of faith and religion in a positive and compelling way. She decided this would not be possible unless she could get Ed Harris, with whom she had worked before, to play the part of Frank Shore. She sent him the script, and he liked it. They both felt that portraying the story was the "occasion to spend several months of our lives going through some kind of spiritual journey."

Filming of the first scene, the bombing of Bystrica, took place in Slovakia, just one week before the actual bombing began in the former Yugoslavia. Very few effects were used in the making of the film. Holland wanted to try to portray the miraculous, the dimension of faith, through the characters' emotions, not through special effects (as opposed to the over-the-top thriller *Stigmata*, which came out about the same time). As reviewer Chuck Rudolph wrote, "What's ultimately best about *The Third Miracle* is how small and quiet a film it is." Holland changed the time period from the 1990s, which the book uses, to the 1970s because John Paul II changed the rules in 1984 regarding the number of miracles needed for official sainthood. Previously three miracles were needed for canonization; today, only one miracle is needed.

A film about the Catholic Church and its workings necessarily includes lots of priests. Holland tried to have the various characters represent the different faces of the church—political, pastoral, economic, spiritual. She did not want a one-dimensional, stereotypical portrayal of the church. Holland also included some of her own life in the characters. For example, the name Father Paul Panak, the priest at St. Stanislaus Church where Helen O'Regan had worshipped, came from the name of Holland's childhood nanny, Paulina Panak.

The film was made on a relatively small budget, and total box office receipts were just over $2 million—not worth making for most studios. Nevertheless, you will be glad that *The Third Miracle* was made and that miracles continue in the kingdom of God.

Holland finishes her commentary on the movie by thanking the viewer and wishing for him or her a miracle.

26. *Signs*

27. *K-PAX*

Confession
Grief, The Randomness of Life

Both Movies:
Faith and Doubt
Miracles
Death, Evil, Family, Friendship,
The Mystery of Life, Wonder

Healing, Images of the Savior,
The Beauty of Creation

Themes

Signs
U.S., 2002
106 Minutes, Feature, Color
Actors: Mel Gibson, Joaquin Phoenix, Cherry Jones, Rory Culkin, Abigail Breslin, Patricia Kalember, M. Night Shyamalan
Director: M. Night Shyamalan
Screenwriter: M. Night Shyamalan
Rated: PG13 (brief violence, mild profanity, mature themes)
DVD Features: "Making Signs"—six production featurettes, deleted scenes, storyboards: multi-angle feature, M. Night Shyamalan's first alien film

K-PAX
U.S., 2001
123 Minutes, Feature, Color
Actors: Kevin Spacey, Jeff Bridges, Mary McCormack, Alfre Woodard, David Patrick Kelly
Director: Iain Softley
Screenwriter: Charles Leavitt
Rated: PG13 (brief violence, adult language and themes)
DVD Features: commentary by director; making-of featurette; alternate ending; deleted scenes; "The Making of K-PAX," pictures by Jeff Bridges; Spanish subtitles

Morgan (Rory Culkin) and Bo (Abigail Breslin) tell their father, Graham Hess (Mel Gibson), about aliens. *Signs* (d. Shyamalan, 2002). Photo by Frank Masi. Copyright 2002 Touchstone Pictures. All rights reserved.

Synopsis and Theological Reflection

As the first anniversary of 9/11 approached, the film capturing the attention of many was M. Night Shyamalan's *Signs*. A sci-fi thriller with both heart and humor, the movie helped many deal with life's ongoing terrors by portraying two significant resources available to us. Viewers felt both the importance of family—of turning to those close to us—and the importance of faith—of belief in a God who signals his presence and power even through the chaos of life. *Newsweek*'s David Ansen rightly titled his review of the film, "Families, Fear and Faith."

The story is a straightforward one, told without much of the pyrotechnics and quick cuts of the typical summer adventure flick or sci-fi thriller. Think more of Hitchcock or Spielberg's *E.T.*

than *Mission Impossible 2*. Most of the action takes place within the small, rural farmhouse where Graham Hess (Mel Gibson) and his children live. An Episcopal priest, he has lost his wife in a freak car accident and with her his faith. But as the story unfolds (strange signs appear in the cornfield of his farm and aliens attack), Graham moves back toward faith despite himself, and we cheer for him. Life simply is more than random circumstance; it has a spiritual core that cannot be denied even in adverse circumstances.

As we watched *Signs*, we often found ourselves on edge, and so did others. We heard whispered behind us, "I never thought cornstalks could be so terrifying." But we all felt more than just fear. We came to care for Graham and his children, even to root for them as they were terrorized. Our empathy for this family was real. We were amazed at how the director created an alternate, yet believable, world of coincidences. Our emotions jumped back and forth like a yo-yo as we entered into the story.

As in his first megahit, *The Sixth Sense*, Shyamalan has used those closest to us, our children, to explore how we might respond to the evil we experience. Can we get so caught up with what life takes away that we ignore what is most precious to us? Can the innocence and trust of children lead us? Is life simply a chain of random incidents without meaning or spiritual significance, or is there a deeper reality that fills us with wonder and hope, even given the contradictions? Bad things happen to good people. How should good people respond?

Signs was not the first sci-fi movie to explore such themes after 9/11, however. Kevin Spacey's movie exploring life's meaning and spiritual possibilities, *K-PAX*, came out just after the World Trade Center disaster. Again, the story is not simply about the disconcerting presence of the mysterious; it is also about the transforming power of relationships.

Like *Signs*, *K-PAX* mixes humor, suspense, and loving relationships into an engaging story. A traveler named PROT arrives in New York claiming to be an alien from the planet K-PAX. Sent to a mental hospital for observation and diagnosis, he is discovered

PROT (Kevin Spacey) and his psychiatrist, Dr. Mark Powell (Jeff Bridges), meet in the hospital garden. *K-Pax* (d. Softley, 2001). Photo by Suzanne Tenner. Copyright 2001 Universal Studios. All rights reserved.

to have a baffling knowledge of the universe, as well as a saintlike capacity to bring healing to his fellow patients. PROT also can see light that the normal human cannot see, and he likes to eat bananas whole, skin and all! As the movie unfolds, his psychiatrist, Dr. Powell (Jeff Bridges), is drawn more and more to believe in PROT, even if he can't intellectually accept his story. At the movie's end, we are left vaguely uncertain whether PROT is a mentally deranged person—the tragic consequence of a grizzly homicide—or an evolved being—an extraterrestrial. Or could he be both?

As with *Signs*, the power of this sci-fi movie is not in its fast pace or its special effects. *K-PAX* has neither. Rather the movie finds its twin center in the importance of relationships and the reality of mystery. The bond established between the two leading characters not only causes viewers to question science's ability always to provide the answer (the astronomer and the psychiatrist are equally unable to explain PROT and what he knows), but it also turns us toward that which is precious in life—our family and our faith. PROT, the mysterious outsider, a kind of Christ figure, causes Powell to reconnect with his estranged family. Those in the mental hospital are healed as they put their trust in PROT. Life has a wonder and significance that goes beyond what our workaday world can provide.

As we continue post 9/11 to question the loss of life and the reality of evil, Christians might take a lesson from these Hollywood films. Life's meaning is not found first of all in what we can make (even a World Trade Center) or in what we can figure out (why does evil happen?) but in faith and family.

Dialogue Texts

Therefore I will not restrain my mouth; I will speak in the anguish of my spirit; I will complain in the bitterness of my soul.

Job 7:11

What is the Almighty, that we should serve him? And what profit do we get if we pray to him?

Job 21:15

Father of orphans and protector of widows is God in his holy habitation. God gives the desolate a home to live in; he leads out the prisoners to prosperity.

Psalm 68:5–6

Let those who are wise give heed to these things, and consider the steadfast love of the LORD.

Psalm 107:43

Enjoy life with the wife whom you love, all the days of your vain life that are given you under the sun, because that is your portion in life and in your toil at which you toil under the sun. Whatever your hand finds to do, do with your might; for there is no work or thought or knowledge or wisdom in Sheol, to which you are going.

Ecclesiastes 9:9–10

Light is sweet, and it is pleasant for the eyes to see the sun. Even those who live many years should rejoice in them all; yet let them remember that the days of darkness will be many. All that comes is vanity.

Ecclesiastes 11:7–8

Blessed are the poor in spirit, for theirs is the kingdom of heaven. . . . Blessed are the meek, for they will inherit the earth. . . . Blessed are the merciful, for they will receive mercy. Blessed are the pure in heart, for they will see God.

Matthew 5:3, 5, 7–8

For I am convinced that neither death, nor life, nor angels, nor rulers, nor things present, nor things to come, nor powers, nor height, nor depth, nor anything else in all creation, will be able to separate us from the love of God in Christ Jesus our Lord.

Romans 8:38–39

Discussion Questions

Combo Questions

1. Both *Signs* and *K-PAX* belong to the science fiction category of films. However, both the films turn the type on its head. Much is left to the viewer's imagination rather than splashing

everything on the screen. There is a minimal use of special effects. Finally, the characters' deep relationships with each other actually birth new understanding for them and the viewer. Kevin Spacey called *K-PAX* a sci-fi fable. If you had to describe the films, what would you say and why? Then, in what ways are the movies similar or different in the way they create their sci-fi worlds? What themes do they have in common? Which film would you consider the better film and why?

2. The theme of family is recurrent in both films. Both Graham Hess and Dr. Mark Powell are caught in their own worlds of grief, doubt, or workaholism such that they have trouble relating to their families at times. Yet they both come to see the gift they have been given. Do you think their struggles were portrayed with honesty? Who or what helped them to appreciate their families? Why is it that death often puts perspective on our relationships with loved ones? Have you ever felt estranged from your family? Did these movies help you see your family in a different light?

3. Another theme that both films tackle is faith/belief and doubt. M. Night Shyamalan speaks of his film being a metaphor for faith—of a conversation between God and one man. However, the conversation takes place through other characters too, such as his children, his brother Merrill, Officer Caroline Paski, or even Ray Reddy, the man who accidentally killed his wife. Kevin Spacey talks of *K-PAX* as asking the fundamental question, "Can we believe—do we have the capacity for belief—beyond what we know?" Again, various other characters add their voices to the debate, such as Steve, Dr. Powell's brother-in-law, when he says, "I don't know what I believe, but I know what I saw." These films invite the viewer to join the conversation, so jump in. Does it matter what or whom you believe in, or is the important thing just belief? Is life random, or do things happen for a purpose? Why do bad things happen to good people? Do miracles happen? What is the relationship between faith and

reason/science? After seeing the film with friends, if they asked you, "Was Jesus who he said he was or just delusional like PROT?" how would you respond?

4. Compare the endings of both films. One is quite ambiguous (Is PROT an alien or a seriously ill man?), while the other is perhaps too tightly resolved. How did the endings work in their respective films? Did they have integrity? As a viewer did you feel satisfied, challenged, or cheated?

5. Take a look at the dialogue texts above and put each one into conversation with one or both of the films. Obviously, some are better partners than others. An obvious text from *K-PAX*, 1 Corinthians 13, was not included. However, you might ask what other things are happening on the psych floor while the patient is reading the text. What do you think the filmmakers are saying? And what of the scene when the patient asks PROT if he would be able to take his Bible to *K-PAX*? Is this a sympathetic reading of the love passage?

Clip Conversations

Signs

1. Chapter 5 [20:32–25:40]—"Breaking News." Having heard the news report about the crop circles, Graham takes his family to town to get "their minds on everyday things." In town, each family member does his or her errand before gathering at the local pizza parlor for dinner. While each has interesting or funny interactions with local people (don't be afraid to enjoy the humor or campiness—remember it's a sci-fi film!), Graham's conversation with the teenager in the pharmacy depicts one side of faith for many people—the fear of judgment. Why is she making such a confession now, and why to him? Do you think her confession is portrayed honestly? Or is the filmmaker playing with a religious form to remind us of the ways we cope

with fear? Is the scene sympathetic? What other small glimpses in the film (characters' words or actions) depict faith?

2. Chapter 10 [39:30–48:50]—"Fourteen Lights." The family has been riveted to the television as reports come in regarding the extraterrestrials. With the kids asleep, Merrill asks Graham for a little comfort as he wonders if this is the end of the world. Graham gives his "people break down into two groups" speech. What exactly does he tell his brother? Do you agree with his explanation of people? He says to Merrill, and the viewer, "You just have to ask yourself, what kind of person are you? Are you the kind that sees signs? Sees miracles? Or do you believe that people just get lucky? . . . Is it possible that there are no coincidences?" After you've discussed those questions, think about Merrill's response, "I'm a miracle man," and Graham's response, "There is no one watching out for us. We are all alone." How do each of their life experiences impact how they see the world? Is that true of you too?

3. Chapter 18 [1:18:42–1:25:56]—"Locked in the Basement." The aliens try to reach the family as they hide in the basement and actually grab Morgan for a brief, terrifying moment in the dark. Saved from their clutches but thrown into an asthma attack, Morgan lays on his father's chest gasping for air. Graham alternates between trying to calm his child and help him breathe, and venting his anger at God. Is this scene a turning point in Graham's faith? Why? Listen to the words he says to his son, "Don't be afraid of what's happening. Believe it's going to pass. Believe it. Just wait. Don't be afraid. . . . Believe. . . ." Are these words a prayer? Who might be talking to whom (besides Graham talking to Morgan)?

K-PAX

1. Chapter 5 [23:32–36:20]—"A Lot Like Home." Trying to understand PROT better, Dr. Powell asks about his home on K-

PAX. In the process, he's given a lesson in listening, the rest of the universe, and the "stupidity" of human ways. What do you think of PROT's understanding regarding an eye for an eye vis-à-vis Jesus? The rest of the chapter contains scenes juxtaposing Dr. Powell's "normal/sane" life with PROT's "delusional" life. Who has time for the people around him? Who is the healer? Who understands the mysteries of the universe? As film critic James Berardinelli wrote in his review of the film, "It doesn't take a religious scholar . . . to see similarities between PROT and Jesus." What other similarities or differences do you see?

2. Chapter 15 [1:38:13–1:47:08]—"Connected." PROT's announced departure date is the next day. As patients party and turn in their essays to win that chance to go with him to K-PAX, Dr. Powell offers PROT a bon voyage drink. As the doctor wonders about visiting K-PAX, PROT encourages him to see the beauty around him on earth. What specifically does he tell the doctor? How has their relationship helped the doctor see his need for connectedness? With what possibilities does PROT challenge Dr. Powell? Which possibility do you believe at this point?

3. Chapter 17 [1:51:30–1:55:10]—"This Time Is All You Have." We see Dr. Powell talking to a catatonic Robert Porter (but is that a smile on his face after hearing of his fellow patients?). Then we hear PROT's voice, as his last bit of wisdom is shared with the good doctor, "I wanna tell you something, Mark, something you do not yet know that we K-PAXians have been around long enough to have discovered. The universe will expand, then it will collapse back on itself, then it will expand again. It will repeat this process forever. What you don't know is that when the universe expands again, everything will be as it is now. Whatever mistakes you make this time around, you will live through on your next pass. Every mistake you make, you will live through again, and again, forever. So my advice to you is to get it right this time around. Because this time is all you

have." What do you think of his wisdom? What is he saying? Is PROT a poster child for reincarnation or more like Qoheleth, the writer of Ecclesiastes, who wants us to enjoy life as the gift that it is? (See Dialogue Texts above and Eccles. 1:3–9.)

Bonus Material

Signs

M. Night Shyamalan is currently considered one of the truly great, young filmmakers. *Newsweek* called him "Hollywood's hottest new storyteller" and the "next Spielberg." Born in Madras, India, in 1970, Shyamalan was raised in an affluent suburb of Philadelphia and attended Catholic and Episcopal schools. Though both his parents were doctors, he became interested in filmmaking at age eight when he was given a Super-8 camera. By the time he was seventeen, he had made forty-five home movies. Since his blockbuster hit and critical success, *The Sixth Sense*, and his screenplay for *Stuart Little*, Shyamalan has been sought after for such things as writing the fourth chapter in the Indiana Jones adventures and directing the third Harry Potter film. He has declined in order to work on his own projects.

The DVD is wonderful for those interested in knowing more about this director/screenwriter because it has great bonus material about him, from the mundane to the sublime. You can start by looking at a clip from the first alien movie he made when he was a teenager. From there you can listen to Shyamalan's vision about writing and filmmaking—create stories that have meaning ("head"), connect with the individual but express universal themes ("heart"), and give the viewer a "roller coaster ride" ("gut"). This philosophy is similar to Jon Boorstin's (see our chapter "Finding God in the Movies: An Introduction" under the subheading "Unpacking the Story"). Listening to his "theology" of film, we were struck by how he definitely sees himself as an artist, asking us to use our imagination, allowing us to interpret his work in a personal way. He wants to show us a way, not tell us what we should think. He's an artist, not a preacher.

Mainly the DVD will tell you about the making of *Signs*—the events (actual crop circles appearing in the 1980s), people (Hitchcock with his less-is-more style), and stories (movies like *Invasion of the Body Snatchers*) that gave inspiration to the project. Everything from the technical aspects of computer graphics to the process of choosing the location, to ways of motivating actors, to interesting stories about filming are shared. Of note is that filming started two days after the 9/11 events. The cast and crew began their work together by having a candlelight vigil. Immediately they went into shooting the scheduled scene—perhaps the most emotional one of the film (Graham Hess talking to his dying wife). Given this start and the fact that most of the crew had worked together on both of Shyamalan's previous films, a strong sense of community was noted on the DVD featurette.

Like Woody Allen, Mike White, and Kevin Smith, Shyamalan has always cast himself in his movies—in leading roles when he was a teenager to barely noticeable parts in his more recent blockbusters. In *Signs* he brought his participation to a new level with a small but important role as the man who accidentally killed Graham Hess's wife. A bit nervous, he placed the photo of the cast's candlelight celebration in one pocket and into the other a photo of his grandfather, who had died the day before they filmed his confession scene. Other personal connections between the director and film include his daughter's own artwork being used as Bo Hess's drawings in the film and the stories of the children's births being the actual birth stories of Shyamalan's own children. (A not so personal tidbit is that the role of Graham Hess was originally written as an older character. Both Paul Newman and Clint Eastwood were offered the role but turned it down.)

Signs was nominated for various awards including the Saturn award for Best Science Fiction Film. Its budget was $72 million, which was far surpassed by its total box office receipts of $407 million, with almost $228 million in the U.S. alone.

K-PAX

Though the stars of *K-PAX* were just as well-known as the stars of *Signs*, the director of the film, Iain Softley, has nowhere near the name of M. Night Shyamalan (though it may be marginally easier to say). Softley has spent much of his career making documentaries and music videos in England. His first feature film work began in 1992 with *Backbeat*, a film exploring the early days of the Beatles. Softley's films previous to *K-PAX* include *Hackers* (a cult classic) and *The Wings of the Dove*, which earned four Academy Award nominations. Though less famous, Iain Softley is an accomplished director also.

K-PAX received two nominations, one from the Academy of Science Fiction, Fantasy and Horror Films, USA (Best Actor), and one from the Image Awards. The budget for this film was $48 million (obviously Kevin Spacey and Jeff Bridges don't come cheap, as the film had no real special effects). The film's total U.S. box office receipts were just $50 million, and roughly another $4 million abroad. These numbers are hardly stupendous given Hollywood's box office hits these days (especially in comparison to a film like *Signs*). But who knows, perhaps in K-PAXian dollars that is a great sum of money.

Living Our Faith

28. The Year of Living Dangerously

Australia, 1982
114 Minutes, Feature, Color
Actors: Mel Gibson, Sigourney Weaver,
Linda Hunt, Michael Murphy, Bill Kerr,
Paul Sonkkila, Bembol Roco
Director: Peter Weir
Screenwriter: Peter Weir, C. J. Koch, David Williamson
Rated: PG (mature themes, brief profanity and violence, sexual scenes)
DVD Features: theatrical trailer, Spanish subtitles and dubbing

Living Our Faith
Being Prophetic, Compassion,
Images of the Savior,
Justice, Poverty
Clash of Cultures, Grief,
Sacrificial Love, Service

Themes

Synopsis and Theological Reflection

Our experiences in a movie theater can range from pure entertainment, to art, to a divine moment. *The Year of Living Dangerously* was a divine moment in my (Cathy's) life—a moment of conversion.

In 1982, out of college and into my first job as a real estate appraiser at Bank of America, I saw the film *The Year of Living Dangerously*. The film, which is several stories within a story, is by Australian Peter Weir. (His other films include *Fearless, Witness, Dead Poet's Society, The Truman Show*, and *Master and Commander*—all worth seeing, and each will ignite great discussion.) *The Year of Living Dangerously* is, on one level, about Indonesia in 1965 and President Sukarno's tightrope walk between the poverty of his people and the revolutionary call of the communists. It is also a love story between Guy (Mel Gibson), an Australian journalist, and Jill (Sigourney Weaver), a British embassy attaché. Like other Weir films, it is also about standing

Guy Hamilton (Mel Gibson) and Billy Kwan (Linda Hunt) walk the streets of Jakarta. *The Year of Living Dangerously* (d. Weir, 1982). Copyright 1982 MGM/UA Entertainment Co. All rights reserved.

in the intersection or clash of cultures (in this case, East and West). But these various stories only set the context for what spoke to me most in the film.

Billy Kwan (played by actress Linda Hunt—her stunning portrayal won an Oscar) is a half-Chinese, half-Australian cameraman who is literally and figuratively the eyes for those around him. He shows Guy the heart of Jakarta—the slums and back alleyways filled with the poverty and pain of the people. Having seen, Guy nevertheless responds that a journalist must expose the structures, not get personally involved. But Billy doesn't let him off the hook. Rather he quotes Tolstoy, who is quoting Luke 3:10, "What then must we do?" Billy tells Guy that Tolstoy sold all he had to relieve the suffering around him. Guy is not persuaded, but neither is Billy dissuaded.

Through most of the movie, we see Billy trusting in Sukarno's leadership for structural change and at the same time being involved in personal acts of compassion as he supports a young prostitute and her child. It is only when Billy's "family" is destroyed—the child dies from drinking polluted water—that he questions his role. He sobs as he pounds out on his typewriter "What then must we do?" and decides he himself must challenge the government. He hangs a sign that reads

SUKARNO FEED YOUR PEOPLE

He is then murdered by the president's police. When Guy and Jill find him dead on the street, they once again begin to see.

"What then must we do?" I left the theater with that phrase and the agonizing eyes of the children of Jakarta burned onto the screen of my mind. In Luke 3, we first hear this question as John the Baptist is preaching repentance and calling the people to bear fruit worthy of their conversion. When the crowd doesn't get it and asks, "What then must we do?" he tells them to live ethically and generously: "Whoever has two coats must share with anyone who has none; and whoever has food must do likewise." Or to tax collectors, "Collect no more than the amount prescribed for you" (vv. 11, 13). In Luke 4, we hear Jesus echoing the same ethic and compassion as he begins his ministry with these words: "The Spirit of the Lord is upon me, because he has anointed me to bring good news to the poor. He has sent me to proclaim release to the captives and recovery of sight to the blind, to let the oppressed go free" (v. 18).

A combination of people, events in my life, and the Holy Spirit had prepared me to see this film. It became a turning point, a recovery of sight. The next week I returned to my project at work, appraising a hospital, but I saw the world differently. Within weeks I applied for a leave of absence and within months left for Mexico to work as a short-term missionary. Six months after my return, I resigned my position to start my own appraisal business in which I would work only thirty hours a week so I could give myself to the youth of my church and community, to the financial and political struggle to build a shelter for women and children in my city, and to study in the area of cross-cultural theology and ministry. The last twenty-two years have included a variety of tasks, jobs, ministries, and people. And it seems that Billy Kwan's, Tolstoy's, and the Bible's question still rings in my ears, "What then must we do?" I pray that the Spirit will guide me in the years to come as I seek to be more responsive to that question and obedient to Christ.

Dialogue Texts

But seek the welfare of the city where I have sent you into exile, and pray to the Lord on its behalf, for in its welfare you will find your welfare.

Jeremiah 29:7

He has told you, O mortal, what is good; and what does the Lord require of you but to do justice, and to love kindness, and to walk humbly with your God?

Micah 6:8

John said to the crowds that came out to be baptized by him, . . . "Bear fruits worthy of repentance. . . ." And the crowds asked him, "What then should we do?" In reply he said to them, "Whoever has two coats must share with anyone who has none; and whoever has food must do likewise. . . . Do not extort money from anyone by threats or false accusation."

Luke 3:7–8, 10–11, 14

When he [Jesus] came to Nazareth, . . . he went to the synagogue. . . . He stood up to read, and the scroll of the prophet Isaiah was given to him. He . . . found the place where it was written: "The Spirit of the Lord is upon me, because he has anointed me to bring good news to the poor. He has sent me to proclaim release to the captives and recovery of sight to the blind, to let the oppressed go free, to proclaim the year of the Lord's

favor." . . . Then he began to say to them, "Today this scripture
has been fulfilled in your hearing."

Luke 4:16–19, 21

Discussion Questions

1. Peter Weir is a master at portraying the collision between
cultures and how persons struggle to fit in their world. (See the
discussion of *Fearless* for a further consideration of Weir's style
and overarching themes.) Describe the following characters
as to their values and motivations for being in Indonesia: Guy
Hamilton, Billy Kwan, Jill Bryant, Kumar, Peter Curtis, Col.
Henderson, and Wally. What makes Guy and Billy similar in
that they are "not at home in the world" (Billy's words)?

2. Billy Kwan tells Guy, "I can be your eyes." To Peter Curtis,
who is raving about how cheaply prostitutes can be gotten, he
says, "Starvation is a great aphrodisiac!" Note Peter's response:
"Keep it up, Billy. Keep it up. We'll nail you to the old cross!"
What kind of figure is Billy—a prophet, a savior? How does his
death bring redemption to Guy?

3. How does Guy change throughout the film? What does he
begin to see? After Billy's death, how is his blindness fitting (cf.
Acts 9:8–9)? What final act of Guy's shows that he has turned
from his old values?

4. In a movie filled with powerful scenes, which one made a deep
impression on you? How has this film helped you to see in new
ways? What have you learned about caring for those who suffer
or taking responsibility to help relieve suffering in the world?

Clip Conversations

1. Chapter 4 [4:55–11:30]—"The Streets of Jakarta." Having
just arrived, Guy walks the streets of Jakarta with Billy, seeing

the horrible poverty and starvation and experiencing the Indonesians' disgust for the West. They discuss possible reactions to the overwhelming problems. Billy quotes Tolstoy, quoting Luke 3 (see Dialogue Texts), and adds, "Well, I support the view that you just don't think about the major issues. You do whatever you can about the misery that's in front of you. Add your light to the sum of light." What is Guy's response? Does Billy accept his answer? With similar scenes in our own country, how do you wrestle with a response?

2. Chapter 9 [33:35–40:00]—"Trusting Billy." For the first time we see how Billy actually walks the talk he gave Guy. He brings food, a toy, and money to a prostitute and her sick son. Afterwards, in his bungalow he reflects on the woman and, again, on the Luke text. He writes, "We must give our love to whomever God has placed in our path." What do you think of his response? Think about who God has put in your path. Is there someone who is in need of your compassion or acts of justice?

3. Chapter 20 [1:28:25–1:32:23]—"A Shattered Faith." Billy has visited the woman and boy only to find that the little one has died. Out of anguish he rails against the Western journalists and argues with Guy. Back at his typewriter, he weeps. Consumed with anguish he asks, "What then must we do?" What does Billy do and what are the consequences? Compare what happens to him with what the people wanted to do to Jesus after his speech in the temple in chapter 4 of Luke. What is similar? What is different?

Bonus Material

As noted in the discussion of *Fearless*, Peter Weir is inspired by music to create and make his stories into film. In *The Year of Living Dangerously* we see this played out with the piece "September" from *Four Last Songs* by Richard Strauss, performed by Kiri Te Kanawa. This haunting solo carries us through two scenes in the film. We hear it first when Billy plays it for Guy, who sits in Billy's bungalow yearning for Jill. (Guy has fallen in love with her, but she is fearful to enter into a relationship with him.) Then we hear it again when Billy is wracked with sorrow for the child who has died. In both cases the music helps us to feel the depths of love these men have experienced.

Weir is also known for taking on social issues, and he wanted the film to accurately portray the immensity of the situation in many poor countries. Thus, he filmed in the Philippines, that is until the crew was forced to leave after receiving threats from the Islamic community. He and his crew then had to recreate on a movie lot the squalor, poverty, noise, heat, and emotion of Indonesia in 1965.

The Year of Living Dangerously was nominated for one Academy Award and one New York Film Critics Circle award. Both awards were for Best Supporting Actress, which Linda Hunt won for her stunning portrayal of a half-Chinese, half-Australian man. The film also was a competing film at the 1983 Cannes Film Festival. The film's budget was a mere $6 million, and its total box office receipts were just over $10 million. Though certainly not noteworthy by Hollywood standards, the small budget and receipts seem only fitting for a film about poverty.

29. *Patch Adams*

U.S., 1998
120 Minutes, Feature, Color
Actors: Robin Williams, Daniel London, Monica Potter, Philip Seymour Hoffman, Bob Gunton, Michael Jeter, Harold Gould, Irma Hall

Living Our Faith
Compassion,
Embracing Our Vocation,
Home, Healing, Service
Creativity, Grief, Humor,
Nature of God, Suffering

Themes

Director: Tom Shadyac
Screenwriter: Steve Oedekerk
Based on the Book: Gesundheit: *Good Health Is a Laughing Matter*, by
   Hunter Doherty Adams and Maureen Mylander
Rated: PG13 (mature themes and humor, brief profanity)
DVD Features: production notes, cast and filmmakers' bios, theatrical
   trailer, outtakes, director's commentary, and "The Medicinal Value of
   Laughter"

Synopsis and Theological Reflection

During one of our early sabbaticals from teaching, we were writing and enjoying life in a small town outside of Malaga, Spain. There in the land of Cervantes, all films are dubbed into Spanish; subtitles are rarely used. While Cathy, being fluent in Spanish, loved this, Rob had to put his moviegoing on the back burner for three months (difficult for someone who gathers not only enjoyment but employment from the study of film).

One Saturday afternoon, Cathy joined some local friends (a Colombian missionary family living in Spain) to see *Patch Adams*. We had seen it in the States, but you hear new things through another language, so off she went. They laughed; they cried; they saw themselves in the film. When Cathy asked Efy (the family's eight-year-old soccer aficionado) what his favorite part of the film was, he answered without missing a beat, "My favorite part was when Patch said to God, 'Talk to me.' And God did talk to him. He sent him a butterfly as a message."

"Let the little children come to me, and do not stop them; for it is to such as these that the kingdom of heaven belongs" (Matt. 19:14). Somehow kids have gotten it, and this film has touched even many adult viewers. Hundreds of email messages came in on chat lines about the film and how they could really relate to the horrors of healthcare these days, and about their need for a hero like Dr. Patch Adams. However, the critics panned the movie as "shamelessly sentimental" or "emotional fascism." Other criticism has come from an occasional doctor who has

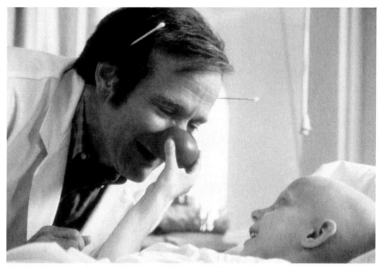

Patch Adams (Robin Williams) with child in hospital. *Patch Adams* (d. Shadyac, 1998). Copyright 1998 Universal Pictures. All rights reserved.

seen the film and taken offense. How could lay viewers and professional critics or practitioners be at such odds? Perhaps the professionals have misdiagnosed the point of *Patch Adams*.

Producers Mike Farrell (of the popular TV series *M.A.S.H.*) and Marvin Minoff wrote in the *Los Angeles Times* that the film is not an "attack on medical practitioners" but rather "a wacky but concerned assault on a medical establishment gone awry." Absolutely! For you see, the film is a true story about one man's pilgrimage through the healthcare system.

The movie starts with Patch having to commit himself to a mental institution. The callous treatment he receives there inspires him to reach out to his fellow patients with kindness and laughter. In the process, he is healed. Having experienced how humor can aid health, he decides to enter medical school so he can give his life to helping others. Unfortunately, medical school turns out to be a mixed bag; the nurses and patients love him, but his superiors are offended by his free spirit, unbridled enthusiasm, and clowning around. With the lines drawn, we are headed for a predictable showdown and a predictable winner.

So why see *Patch Adams*? Because you'll smile while thinking about healthcare. And if you're like many Americans, we bet you haven't had those two experiences together for quite some time. Most of us struggle to get our healthcare providers to be responsive, and we are the lucky ones. Millions of people in our country don't have health insurance and go without the healthcare services they need. That's what the critics missed when they saw *Patch Adams*. They failed to recognize how desperately people yearn for medical treatment that is relationship-driven, service-oriented, and hope-filled. And it's not just patients; many doctors yearn for this also.

Our church is in a denomination called The Evangelical Covenant Church, and we're blessed in this denomination to have many saints and even a few Patch Adamses. Stories are told of Dr. Teddy in Zaire or Dr. Mildred Nordlund in China, and anyone who hears these stories knows that these were amazing doctors who loved their patients. Today, doctors such as Richard Trinity, a small-town general surgeon who serves on the World Mission Committee of our denomination, or pediatrician Jamie Knauss, who also teaches in the children's Sunday school program at our church, care for patients with humor and compassion. In our own family, we have Uncle Paul (Dr. Paul W. Johnston), a retired surgeon who had patients, nurses, and students singing his praises. We can all think of those women and men who are called to be instruments of God's healing and embody many of the insights we see in *Patch Adams*.

"See what others don't see. See life in a new way each day," says one of Patch's first friends in the psychiatric hospital. "We need to really listen to people and to take our eyes off our own problems by serving others," Patch admonishes his fellow students. Jesus often saw what others didn't see and listened to people as he served the hurting around him. Dr. Patch Adams isn't Jesus, nor are our beloved doctors, but they do have the capacity to be "little Christs" to all those who come their way. *Patch Adams* shows us a glimpse of that possibility in the midst of our tears and laughter.

Dialogue Texts

A cheerful heart is a good medicine, but a downcast spirit dries up the bones.

Proverbs 17:22

Even in laughter the heart is sad, and the end of joy is grief.

Proverbs 14:13

Therefore I will not restrain my mouth; I will speak in the anguish of my spirit; I will complain in the bitterness of my soul. . . . What are human beings, that you make so much of them, that you set your mind on them, visit them every morning, test them every moment?

Job 7:11, 17–18

They entered the house of Simon and Andrew. . . . Now Simon's mother-in-law was in bed with a fever, and they told him about her at once. He came and took her by the hand and lifted her up. Then the fever left her. . . . That evening, at sundown, they brought to him all who were sick or possessed with demons. . . . And he cured many who were sick with various diseases, and cast out many demons.

Mark 1:29–32, 34

Do not deceive yourselves. If you think that you are wise in this age, you should become fools so that you may become wise. For the wisdom of this world is foolishness with God.

1 Corinthians 3:18–19

Discussion Questions

1. Despite all the panning by critics, many people have found the film *Patch Adams* inspiring. Perhaps the viewer is emotionally manipulated by stereotypes, pranks, and tear-jerking scenes, but there is also much to discuss regarding humor, healing, the nature of God, and how we deal with human suffering. Let's begin

with the topic of humor. How important is humor and laughter to living out your Christian faith? What truth did Patch live out about laughter in the face of pain and death? Why does laughter feel so good? Share one of your most laughter-filled experiences. (Check out chapter 5 [27:37–45:00]—"Doctor Clown"—and/or the outtakes on the DVD to have a laugh together. Even the cast and crew had moments of uncontrollable laughter.)

2. Dean Walcott is certainly a one-dimensional poster child for healthcare devoid of compassion. In his speech to the incoming medical students he says that he must "train the humanity out of you to make you something better: a doctor." Though exaggerated, how do this character and the film tap into our worst nightmares about our healthcare system? How do Patch's friends at the diner echo some of your feelings and experiences? How does this picture compare to the picture we have of Jesus and his ministry of healing in the Gospels? What role can the church play to keep the human, as well as the divine, touch in healthcare?

3. After Carin's death, Patch is angry with God. How is Patch like a modern-day Job in his complaint toward God? What other biblical characters complained to or bargained with God? What changes Patch's complaint into renewed faith and action? What do you think the director and screenwriter were saying to the viewer about the nature of God and the nature of human suffering? (Though low-key about their personal lives and faith, both the director and the screenwriter are Christians, so some of their theology is coming out in the film.)

Clip Conversations

1. Chapter 1 [00:00–9:40]—"The Troubled Mind." Listen to Patch's voice-over as we first see him riding on a bus. What is he searching for, and how is his search a universal one? How

do his words set the stage for the entire film? How is the hospital one step toward home or the right path for Patch? Who or what experiences at the hospital help him most along this journey?

2. Chapter 2 [9:40–16:35]—"Look Beyond." Patch approaches another patient at the hospital—genius/crazy man Arthur Mendelson. What does Arthur teach Patch? How does Patch apply his natural gift for humor and compassion, and his lesson from Arthur, to his roommate, Rudy? How does this lesson and its application free Patch to live into his gifts? How did Jesus look beyond appearances or the circumstances of those he met? How can the church be an encourager of looking beyond as we serve in the world?

3. Chapter 15 [1:39:28–1:46:30]—"Patch's Appeal." What strikes you most about Patch's plea to the medical board and his student colleagues? How might you put in dialogue the following words from Patch's speech with biblical texts?

> Death is not the enemy. . . . If we're going to fight a disease, let's fight one of the most terrible diseases of all—indifference. . . .
> You treat a disease—you win, you lose. You treat a person, I'll guarantee you'll win no matter what the outcome. . . .
> I wanted to become a doctor so I could serve others, and because of that I've lost everything; I've also gained everything.

Bonus Material

The story of how Hunter "Patch" Adams's journey came to the movie screen is a long one filled with strange connections and serendipities. Trying to raise money for his Gesundheit Institute, Adams decided to write a book. When the book came out in 1993, he found himself being interviewed on radio and TV. This media attention soon brought phone calls from Hollywood producers and directors. Adams even made a trip to

Hollywood to meet with one of those interested movie teams and was totally turned off by their commercialism and slick pitch. He needed to make money for his dream hospital, but he didn't want to sell his soul.

For advice, he turned to Mike Farrell, whom he had met on the *M.A.S.H.* set years before. (Adams had served as an advisor to the 1972–1983 TV series.) When Farrell read the book, he knew that he wanted to work on the project himself. Soon Steve Oedekerk was brought on to write the screenplay, and producer Barry Kemp brought Universal Studios into the equation. After the script was developed, director Tom Shadyac was approached. He was immediately interested. "I thought it was a fascinating story that talked about a theme that is very close to me, which is how humor can be used as a tool in healing." He agreed to do the film, but only if Robin Williams would agree to play the part of "Patch Adams." They got Williams, and filming began in February 1998.

Filming took place primarily in three locations. First, production designer Linda DeScenna created a twenty-thousand-square-foot hospital set at sound stages on Treasure Island in the San Francisco Bay. The filming then moved to North Carolina, where the University of North Carolina was used as a double for the Virginia Medical University, and the historic Biltmore Estate was the setting for the future Gesundheit Institute.

While the movie presents a condensation of events and experiences, and the characters are often composites of people in his life, the film portrays or extrapolates from actual events and experiences in Hunter "Patch" Adams's life, from his balloon parties (which he has orchestrated more than thirty times for friends or patients), to a bathtub filled with noodles (which turned into 25,000 pounds of noodles in a portable swimming pool in the movie), to performing like a clown. The movie tried to capture the essence of this man's humor and compassion. His philosophy isn't just jokes for jokes' sake but rather to help others. On the DVD, Adams states that he has always been about an environment and staff that are happy, funny, loving, cooperative, and creative. And he believes that with those five qualities "great medicine would happen whether you were cured or not." Adams's approach (1970s) predates more recent research on endorphins and healing, as well as the book by Norman Cousins, *Anatomy of An Illness* (1979), in which Cousins, the editor of *Saturday Review*, wrote of his use of humor to successfully fight his own cancer.

In true Patch Adams style—showing humor and compassion to others—the cast and crew joined together to work with the San Francisco Make-A-Wish Foundation. Several children who were undergoing cancer treatment appeared in the film (scenes in the pediatric ward). In this interaction, it appears that the giving and humor went in all directions. The kids' parents remarked that the experience lifted their spirits. The presence of the sick children and their laughter and joy also helped the cast and crew really experience the power of combining humor and compassion in the treatment of patients.

Within months of the movie's release, over two thousand medical professionals had offered their services to the Gesundheit Institute, which Adams founded and which continues his work today. You can find out about the institute and its mission "to bring fun, friendship and the joy of service back into health care" by logging on to http://www.patchadams.org.

Patch Adams was nominated for various awards, including an Oscar for its music, an American Comedy Award, and a Golden Globe for Best Motion Picture—Comedy/Musical. Robin Williams was nominated for Golden Globe, Golden Satellite, and American Comedy awards. While many critics booed the work, people all over the world were walking into theaters by the droves to experience it. Box office receipts worldwide were $200 million, with $135 million just in the U.S. Let's hope some of those dollars went to helping Hunter "Patch" Adams build his dream hospital.

Images
of the Savior

30. *The Spitfire Grill*

Themes

Images of the Savior
*Forgiveness, Grace,
Healing—Wounded Healer,
Salvation*
Brokenness, Goodness of Creation,
Food, Friendship, Redemption,
Sacrificial Love, The Stranger, Trust

U.S., 1996
116 Minutes, Feature, Color
Actors: Alison Elliott, Ellen Burstyn,
Marcia Gay Harden, Will Patton,
Kieran Mulroney
Director: Lee David Zlotoff
Screenwriter: Lee David Zlotoff
Rated: PG13 (mild profanity, mature themes)
DVD Features: theatrical trailer

Synopsis and Theological Reflection

Even though you may never have heard of it, *The Spitfire Grill* is one of those must-see movies. The film, though widely praised, was also labeled by a few critics as "proselytism in disguise." Perhaps it is, but so then are all films that seek to affect their viewers—that is, any film worth seeing.

The movie tells the story of Percy Talbott who comes to Gilead, Maine, to find a job after finishing her prison term. Percy is given work by Hanna, the owner of a diner, The Spitfire Grill, and is befriended by Shelby, Hanna's niece by marriage. A rocky but genuine friendship ensues between the women, and their relationship forms the center of the film. There are good men in the story, including Joe, who accepts Percy without judging her former life and seeks to understand her continuing pain. But the movie's power and meaning come from the interaction between the three women.

Percy (Alison Elliott), Shelby (Marcia Gay Harden), and Hanna (Ellen Burstyn) work together to keep the Spitfire Grill going. *The Spitfire Grill* (d. Zlotoff, 1996). Photo by Eric Lee. Copyright 1996 Castle Rock Entertainment. All rights reserved.

Early in the story, when Hanna falls and breaks her leg, Percy takes over the diner with the help of Shelby. Percy can't cook, but she is willing to learn, and the two younger women keep the restaurant in business. One evening as Percy is allowed by Hanna to rub lotion on her tender leg, she asks the older woman, "You suppose if a wound goes so deep, the healing of it might hurt as bad as what caused it?" Here in microcosm is the question of the film, for Gilead, too, is suffering from a wound. All of the citizens of this small hamlet have been deeply hurt. Their hopes have been shattered by the disappearance of Hanna's talented son, Eli, who represented their future. He has failed to return from Vietnam. Their wound needs treatment, but it will prove painful.

It is Percy who acts as a balm to bring spiritual healing and new possibility to Gilead. At first, Percy simply substitutes for Hanna in running the cafe and in providing food for a needy recluse. But the wound is deep. Healing can come only as it is pierced ("Percy-ed") through sacrificial love and forgiveness. Reconciliation does take place, but it is not without its heavy price.

The Spitfire Grill was warmly received by viewers and critics alike. Made on a modest budget (about $6 million) by a Roman Catholic organization in Mississippi, it was the surprise hit at Robert Redford's Sundance Film Festival in 1996, winning the Audience Award. Castle Rock Entertainment then purchased it for $10 million—a record price at the time for a Sundance film.

However, the film has not been without its controversy. Some critics, after learning of its religious sponsorship, had second thoughts about its value. They wondered if the film contained hidden propaganda, though they had trouble knowing what to criticize. (The film has little mention of God, and the town's one church is empty.) This is not the explicit religiosity of The Ten Commandments, but the message of redemption shines through nonetheless. Not all in the larger society seem willing to accept the film's indirect spiritual gift, particularly if it comes from a Christian organization. Yet most viewers are taken by it.

Perhaps we can understand the value of The Spitfire Grill by recalling the fiction of another indirect storyteller. It has been fifty years since C. S. Lewis sought to overcome the narrow secularity of our modern age by writing children's stories. He was concerned that modern women and men were being cut off from our roots and our destiny and were in danger of becoming little more than "trousered apes."

The purpose of Lewis's Chronicles of Narnia was to give a new generation of readers the taste and feel of truth—to baptize their imagination. In this way, Lewis hoped to assist others beyond the tiny, windowless universe they had mistaken for reality. A good story, thought Lewis, should do more than offer an engaging plot or merely produce excitement. (We suspect Lewis would have been critical of such films as Independence Day and Mission Impossible. What might he have thought of the movies made based on his colleague Tolkien's trilogy, The Lord of the Rings?)

In a good story, plot is important, but particularly as a net to catch something else. The story should mediate something more or other than what we are conscious of in our day-to-day existence. In the *Chronicles of Narnia*, Aslan, the lion (who is a Christ-figure), explains to the children that he has brought them to this distant place so that having experienced him there, they might be able to recognize Aslan in another guise where they live.

What Lewis did for his generation through fiction—the baptizing of their imaginations—others are attempting in our day through the use of film. A wonderful example of this is *The Spitfire Grill*. (*Places in the Heart, X-Men 2*, and *The Lord of the Rings* also come to mind.)

Like Aslan, Percy Talbott is an unlikely Christ-figure who by coming to Gilead "ends winter" and "makes the wounded whole." Like Christ, Percy experiences rejection and is thought to have a questionable reputation. Yet through her life, Percy is able to pierce through to the core of the small town, exposing its hurts and the need for her healing balm. It is indeed painful, but Percy heals both a family and a town. Truly she is a "balm in Gilead."

Rent *The Spitfire Grill* by all means! Here is a film you might want to view with a neighbor who has not experienced the redeeming love of Jesus. It is a film that can initiate discussion with your teenager or a colleague from work. You do not need to make the Christ imagery explicit in your discussion with others. The producers worked hard to create an indirect representation of the Christian story. The film is meant to be preliminary to the gospel. You will have other occasions for more explicit witness. For the moment, let the shape and feel of God's truth work its charm in your life and in the lives of those around you. You might find your imaginations baptized.

Dialogue Texts

For the hurt of my poor people I am hurt, I mourn, and dismay has taken hold of me. Is there no balm in Gilead? Is there no physician there? Why then has the health of my poor people not been restored?

Jeremiah 8:21–22

He heals the brokenhearted, and binds up their wounds.

Psalm 147:3

For while we were still weak, at the right time Christ died for the ungodly. Indeed, rarely will anyone die for a righteous person—though perhaps for a good person someone might actually dare to die. But God proves his love for us in that while we still were sinners Christ died for us.

Romans 5:6–8

If we confess our sins, he who is faithful and just will forgive us our sins and cleanse us from all unrighteousness.

1 John 1:9

We know love by this, that he laid down his life for us—and we ought to lay down our lives for one another.

1 John 3:16

Discussion Questions

1. After critics found out that the film had been financed by the Sacred Heart League of the Catholic Church, Lee David Zlotoff, the director, went on record denying that *The Spitfire Grill* had any spiritual message. Would you agree? Did he overreact? How are the names of the characters evocative of biblical stories and themes? What other religious symbols did you notice in the film? In what ways do you see Percy as a Christ-figure? How is she a wounded-healer in need of forgiveness and grace herself?

2. The power of the movie lies in Percy's growing relationships, first with Hanna and Shelby and then with Johnny B.

How does each of the women change through the course of the film? How does Johnny B. change? How does the viewer see that trust engenders trust in each of these relationships? How might this lesson be applied to your own life?

3. Even though the film focuses on the life of Percy Talbott and her relationships with a few key individuals, it is also about a town. How do Percy's eyes see the wondrous creation that is Gilead (e.g., Percy's view of Joe's "worthless" trees)? How is this grace infectious? How are the townspeople drawn into the healing grace that the women have started to experience? How do the townspeople live and share grace with each other? How does the end of the film show their continued desire to extend grace? How might our church communities model such grace?

Clip Conversations

1. Chapters 15 [55:45–58:15] and 16 [58:15–59:50]—"New Name: Johnny B." and "Picture This." The relationship between Percy and the "man in the woods" takes a giant step forward even without face-to-face contact. How does Percy show her trust and respect for Johnny B.? How does he respond? How does the awesomeness of nature and Johnny B.'s own woundedness allow Percy to share her grief with him? They are wounded healers to each other. What lessons can we learn from their example?

2. Chapter 17 [59:50–1:02:55]—"Wounds that Run Deep." Percy helps Hanna put ointment on her broken leg. She wonders out loud about some wounds and their healing. How did Hanna respond? What do you think she was thinking about? How would you have responded to Percy? What has been your experience with the healing of personal wounds? Has it been effortless and painless? How have wounds and their painful healing helped you to better understand and offer balm to others?

3. Chapter 23 [1:17:50–1:23:38]—"Out in the Open." Johnny B., in his way, invites Percy to his home. Again she is touched by his creativity. She wanders out singing "There Is a Balm in Gilead." How do they each extend trust and receive grace to/from each other? Hanna's response is hardly one of grace. Why does she react the way she does?

4. Chapter 26 [1:30:50–1:35:00]—"Percy's Past." Shelby finds Percy in the empty church, where she confesses to Shelby what she's done. Why do you think Percy went to the church; for what was she searching? How would you have responded if Percy had shared her story with you? What have you learned in your own life (through personal experience, the teachings of the Bible, or the movement of the Holy Spirit through your local community) about God's forgiveness? Why did she feel guilty—for killing her stepfather or for not saving her child? How do Hanna and Percy share this pain of not being able to save their children? How does Percy ultimately save Johnny B.? How does Claire's letter at the end of the film pick up on this salvation theme?

Bonus Material

Gilead is a fitting name for the town that provides Percy refuge. The biblical Gilead was a place of refuge for people in danger. Jacob went to Gilead when he fled from Laban (Gen. 31:21–55), and David went there during Absalom's revolt (2 Sam. 17:22–29).

As noted above, *The Spitfire Grill* won the Audience Award at the Sundance Film Festival in 1996. With a budget of $6 million, the profits (over $3 million) received from the movie's sale to Castle Rock Entertainment allowed the Sacred Heart League to build a school in rural Mississippi. The movie's total box office receipts eventually totaled about $13 million.

Marcia Gay Harden, who played Shelby, went on to win in 2000 the Academy Award for Best Supporting Actress for the film *Pollock* (and was nominated in the same category for *Mystic River* in 2004). Will Patton, who played Nahum, went on to portray coach Bill Yoast in *Remember the Titans,* also in 2000 (see the earlier discussion of that movie).

The movie was actually filmed in northeastern Vermont, which has more farmland than central Maine. There is a wonderful shot, for example, of Lake Willoughby Gap. Our Maine acquaintances tell us that the accents of most of the characters are likewise foreign to upstate Maine, but we suspect only those who are New Englanders will notice.

This film is small and simple in its beauty, but it is well worth viewing and discussing. Percy points us to Jesus and his model of sacrificial love.

31. *The Iron Giant*

U.S., 1999
80 Minutes, Feature, Color, Animated
Voices: Jennifer Aniston, Eli Marienthal, Harry Connick Jr., Vin Diesel, Christopher McDonald, James Gammon, Cloris Leachman, John Mahoney
Director: Brad Bird
Screenwriter: Tim McCanlies and Brad Bird
Based on the Book: *Iron Giant,* by Ted Hughes
Rated: PG (brief cartoon violence—excellent for children)
DVD Features: theatrical trailer, making-of documentary, music video

Themes

Images of the Savior
Affirming the Human Spirit, Nonviolence, Play, Prayer, Sacrificial Love
Choice, Goodness of Creation, Freedom, Imagination, The Stranger, War, Wonder

Synopsis and Theological Reflection

Forget *Runaway Bride,* forget the last James Bond movie, and forget *The Blair Witch Project.* These movies might have done well at the box office, but 1999 was the year for animation. As Ken-

The Iron Giant (voice of Vin Diesel) holds Hogarth (voice of Eli Marienthal) in his hand. *The Iron Giant* (d. Bird, 1999). Copyright 1999 Warner Bros. All rights reserved.

neth Turan of the *Los Angeles Times* wrote that year, "We have just experienced probably the most impressive year for feature animation in the history of motion pictures."

Toy Story 2, Tarzan, South Park, Pokémon, Princess Mononoke, Stuart Little, Fantasia—these were all major releases in 1999. And the best of the group (though the least recognized by moviegoers) was one you probably have never even heard of, *The Iron Giant*. This film is a must, not only for five- to ten-year-olds but also for adults. C. S. Lewis once said, "A children's story which is only enjoyed by children is a bad children's story." *The Iron Giant* is a great story for both adults and children.

The story is adapted from Ted Hughes's children's book, *The Iron Man*. Director Brad Bird gave the original British story an American twist, setting it in a small town in Maine during the height of the Cold War with its ever-present paranoia and tension. Sputnik circles the globe, newspaper headlines regularly declare the threat of a Russian invasion, and bomb shelter drills are frequently practiced in the local school. Young Hogarth overhears the talk of invasion (from Russia and/or space) and goes on a hunt to find the invader.

What he finds is a fifty-foot tall metal man—an Iron Giant. But this big hulking thing that mysteriously arrives from outer space is curiously childlike too, gentle and receptive. Only when threatened does his enormous capacity for blind destruction emerge. Together with Dean, a friendly junkyard owner and scrap-metal artist, Hogarth tries to keep the Iron Giant happy (his diet is metal) and hidden. This proves a bit difficult given the giant's voracious appetite and his playfulness, which includes such things as a cannonball dive into a lake, draining it of all water. Nevertheless, life is good, that is until an obsessed federal agent, Kent Mansley, comes to town.

Calling in the army to destroy this suspicious enemy, the agent would destroy the town in order to save it from the metal monster. Hogarth, on the other hand, reminds the Iron Giant that though designed to be a massive moving gun, "You don't have to be a gun. . . . You are who you choose to be. . . . You choose." And the giant chooses the way of loving sacrifice.

With Hogarth and the Iron Giant, we join in the winsome mystery of friendship. A childlike wonder, imagination and re-sourcefulness, a trust in each other, and most importantly, a faith in the goodness of the other's soul sustain their love for each other. What we first think of as a metal monster, even a weapon of destruction, becomes a dear companion. In some ways this film is an animated *E. T.* While some of the film's humor and references to the 1950s are aimed at adults, its message of love, acceptance, and nonviolence is accessible to all ages. This film goes against the tide of the thrill of violence in many films by its blatant affirmation of peacemaking.

In addition to its simple, touching story, the animation of *The Iron Giant* is unlike many of the others mentioned above. It is unpretentious, reminding you of the old Saturday cartoons. It is a perfect match with the story and a refreshing alternative to many of the high-tech, high-glitz productions produced by Disney and others.

Having heard of *The Iron Giant* but initially scratching it off our long list of to-see movies, we owe our viewing of this film to our good friend, Tim Allen, himself an accomplished animator at Disney. After viewing it, we shared together how we were totally captured by the winsomeness, the power, and the meaning of this movie. Something at our core was touched. He said it much better than we could: "I am amazed at what this film says. I am amazed at how delightfully it says it. And I am amazed that it got made at all. It is a rare achievement—animated or otherwise."

Dialogue Texts

Some friends play at friendship but a true friend sticks closer than one's nearest kin.

Proverbs 18:24, cf. Proverbs 17:17

This is my commandment, that you love one another as I have loved you. No one has greater love than this, to lay down one's life for one's friends.

John 15:12–13

Do not envy the violent and do not choose any of their ways; for the perverse are an abomination to the LORD, but the upright are in his confidence.

Proverbs 3:31

If it is possible, so far as it depends on you, live peaceably with all.

Romans 12:18

We know love by this, that he laid down his life for us—and we ought to lay down our lives for one another.

1 John 3:16

Discussion Questions

1. Most film critics raved about this film, some for its animation (classic 2-D hand-drawn animation for all of the human characters combined with 3-D computer graphics for the Iron Giant)

but most for its story and writing. One critic, James Berardinelli, wrote, "*The Iron Giant* teaches lessons about friendship, tolerance and sacrifice, all without turning preachy." What can we learn about friendship and sacrificial love from putting Scripture and the film in conversation? Taking the biblical texts above, dialogue with these themes. How might we better understand human nature and the choices we make? (Don't we all have a gentle giant and a Rambo within ourselves?) How might this film be a starting point in the conversation between peacemakers and those eager to protect our country from the threat of violence?

2. This children's story raises the question of the relationship between machines and humans. The Iron Giant remembers that Hogarth saved him from being electrocuted. Likewise, he is curious about Hogarth's world and seems to have a conscience. Is he solely a machine or more? How could this film's message be put in dialogue with Psalm 8 (e.g., verse 4, "What are human beings that you are mindful of them?")?

3. With a missile headed straight for the town, the Iron Giant chooses to be other than a giant gun. He says to Hogarth, "I fix. Hogarth, you stay. I go. No following." His last act is one of sacrifice for Hogarth, to which the boy responds, "I love you." As the Iron Giant flies off to obliterate himself and the missile, he repeats Hogarth's earlier words to him, "You are who you choose to be," to which he contentedly adds, "Superman" (chapter 28 [1:13:55–1:16:35]—"The Giant's Choice"). How is the Iron Giant a kind of savior figure? How was his act of sacrifice on Hogarth's (and the town's) behalf similar to or different from Jesus' sacrifice for us? How is the ending of the film like a resurrection?

Clip Conversations

1. Chapter 11 [27:20–29:55]—"Hands On." Hogarth and the Iron Giant have definitely become friends. Due to a little train

adventure, some of Iron Giant's mechanical parts have been lost. In fact, one of the giant's hands is wandering through Hogarth's home. During dinner with his mother, Hogarth tries to keep his mom from seeing the hand. He even prays an elaborate prayer so she keeps her eyes closed while the hand is in the kitchen. What do you think of Hogarth's prayer? In Hollywood portrayals of prayer that you have seen, what do they get right? What do they get wrong?

2. Chapter 19 [48:05–50:02]—"Come On In!" Hogarth, Iron Giant, and Dean are hanging out together at the lake. Just enjoy, no questions. You might share in the group about the time you first tried something daring, or the last time you "went for it" like a big kid.

3. Chapter 20 [50:02–53:55]—"Soulful Under the Stars." Hogarth and the Iron Giant find a beautiful deer in the woods. Moments later they hear a shot and are saddened when they find that two hunters have killed the deer. Hogarth tells his friend that guns kill. "It's bad to kill. But it's not bad to die." Hogarth then talks with the Iron Giant about the soul. Even though what he shares is more Platonic (i.e., the soul and the body are too sharply separated) than biblical, it still is quite a moment for a cartoon to tackle such a topic. What is rightly recognized is that we are spiritual as well as material beings. How would you talk about this spiritual dimension with someone you meet for the first time? What language does the Bible use to describe humankind's spiritual reality? (For a start, see Gen. 2:7, Jesus' teaching in Matt. 22:37, or Paul's words in 1 Thess. 5:23.)

Bonus Material

The Iron Giant might sound familiar since the story was originally written by Ted Hughes and published in 1968 in England as *The Iron Man.* The children's book inspired a 1989 album by Pete Townshend of The Who. The album then inspired a play at London's Old Vic. Finally, Warner Brothers, home to the Superman copyright, picked up the rights to the screenplay. Pete Townshend was also the executive producer of the film.

Brad Bird, best known for his work on the series *The Simpsons,* jumped at the chance to write the screenplay and direct the film. He pitched the idea to Warner Brothers with the question, "What if a gun had a soul?" He wanted the film to have an old world feeling, like a Brothers Grimm fairy tale, so he used elements such as traditional animation techniques (except for the Iron Giant, which is CGI), and a score of instrumental music performed by the Czech Philharmonic.

Many of the names of the characters and places come from the worlds of animation and comedy. Frank and Ollie, the two trainmen interviewed after the derailment, are caricatures of Disney classic animators Frank Thomas and Ollie Johnston, and these men also perform the voices for their characters. Frank and Ollie are also lifelong train enthusiasts and have extensive scale model railroads in their backyards like Walt Disney used to have. Bird Landing is a reference to director Brad Bird. Hogarth comes from comics illustrator Burne Hogarth, best known for the Tarzan adventure comic. Annie and Hogarth's last name pays homage to author Ted Hughes. Floyd Turbeaux is actually one of the characters Johnny Carson used to do on his show to lampoon the National Rifle Association.

The Iron Giant won numerous awards. At the Annies (the "Oscars" for animation) the movie garnered fifteen nominations and won nine, including awards for Writing, Animating, Directing, and Theatrical Feature. Numerous film critics' associations picked it as the best animated feature of the year. The British Academy of Film and Television gave its Children's Award for Best Feature Film to the makers of *The Iron Giant.* Total box office receipts worldwide were $30.5 million. Its U.S. receipts were disappointing, especially given the across-the-board kudos it received. Critics and viewers alike proclaimed that it would be "a contemporary classic" . . . "to be watched over and over." No wonder it also won the Saturn Award for Best Home Video Release. So enjoy this great children's story, even if you are an adult.

Renewing
the Church

32. *Sister Act*

Renewing the Church
Living Our Faith,
Nature of the Church,
Negative Images of the Church,
Worship
Service, The Stranger

Themes

U.S., 1992
100 Minutes, Feature, Color
Actors: Whoopi Goldberg, Maggie Smith,
Kathy Najimy, Mary Wickes, Harvey Keitel,
Wendy Makkena
Director: Emile Ardolino
Screenwriters: Paul Rudnick, Nancy Meyers, Robert Harling, Carrie
Fisher, Jack Epps Jr., Jim Cash, Eleanor Bergstein
Rated: PG (mild profanity, adult situations)
DVD Features: theatrical trailer, two movie videos, "Inside Sister Act"

Synopsis and Theological Reflection

Recently we revisited *Sister Act*, which first caused us to smile
and tap our toes years ago. Seeing it again only reinforced our
desire to commend its vitality. In particular, the movie portrays
how it is possible to renew a church.

Now before you laugh us off, hear us out. Perhaps picturing
Whoopi Goldberg as the agent of church renewal is a stretch for
you. Her character, Deloris van Cartier, a lounge singer who later
becomes Sister Mary Clarence to hide from the mob in "the last
place on earth they would look for her," is an even less likely
candidate. Yet from the opening scene of Deloris as a young girl
in Catholic school naming the apostles—"John, Paul, George
. . . Ringo . . . or Elvis?"—we suspect that she will return to her
roots somehow and bring new life to them.

Not exactly thrilled with her situation of having to hide
out as a "penguin" in a convent attached to a dying urban

Sister Mary Clarence (Whoopi Goldberg) and Sister Mary Patrick (Kathy Najimy) trade some dance steps with neighborhood girls. *Sister Act* (d. Ardolino, 1992). Photo by Suzanne Hanover. Copyright 1992 Touchstone Pictures. All rights reserved.

church, Deloris is befriended by two of the nuns. However, her unorthodox ways (leading her sisters to a bikers' bar in the neighborhood) get her into trouble and the Mother Superior assigns her the task of directing the off-key, offbeat, and off-putting choir. Sister Mary Clarence has her hands full, but combining her lounge singing and Catholic school experience, she leads the choir in a new type of sacred music. Their Sunday choral pieces include "My God" ("My Guy") and "I Will Follow Him."

The choir brings new, alive worship into this church where the priest had cried out to his small but faithful flock, "Something has gone wrong here. Where is faith? Where is celebration? Where is everyone?" But Sister Mary Clarence and her choir do more than bring new life to worship; they bring new life to the neighborhood. They break out of their insulated and isolated life in the cloister and march into the needs, dreams, problems, and joys of the people in their midst. From food lines

to car repair, from painting projects to jumping rope or dancing with the "unreachable" youth in the neighborhood, they
bring their worship of a loving God into the streets. Soon the
neighborhood catches the vision (and the sound!) and starts
packing the pews.

Worship and mission, worship and service, worship and outreach—whatever you choose to call them, these are two key
ingredients of a vital community of disciples. Writing from his
cell in a Nazi prison, Dietrich Bonhoeffer wondered how best to
renew a church that had all the right words but lacked spiritual
life and vitality. His answer: "prayer and righteous action." We
doubt Sister Mary Clarence read Bonhoeffer, but she learned
his point by trial and error. Our worship, drawing close to God
in penitence and praise, should propel us into the world, living
the Good News. And our outreach and service should compel
us to worship the One without whom our own poverty would
engulf us.

Now certainly Disney did not plan for this movie to be a
possible resource for church renewal specialists, but most reviewers understood that engaged worship and ministry in the
neighborhood were key to St. Catherine's renewal. Granted not
all church communities have a "Sister Mary Clarence," but that
does not matter because it is the Holy Spirit who will empower
our worship and service.

Try it out. How about a leadership or church retreat during which you view the movie and have a frank conversation
about the health and vitality of your church? While you may
think that Sister Mary Clarence's goal of getting "butts in the
seats" may be a bit crass, perhaps we care too little about
the church being an inviting place for friends and neighbors.
Create vital worship—and this does not have to include Mo-
town hits nor preclude Mozart's hits—and reach out in your
context.

Sister Act was panned by some critics as being too "predictable,
with stereotypical characters and a plot that strains credulity."
But others saw it as the sleeper hit that summer, since it was

"funny, up-beat, a film you could take your kids or your grand-parents to." As you can tell, we side with the latter and add our "amen" to its message for us, the church.

Dialogue Texts

[Jesus] said to him, "'You shall love the Lord your God with all your heart, and with all your soul, and with all your mind.' This is the greatest and first commandment. And a second is like it: 'You shall love your neighbor as yourself.'"

Matthew 22:37–39

Clap your hands, all you peoples; shout to God with loud songs of joy. For the LORD, the Most High, is awesome, a great king over all the earth.

Psalm 47:1

Make a joyful noise to God, all the earth; sing the glory of his name; give to him glorious praise.

Psalm 66:1

For I was hungry and you gave me food, I was thirsty and you gave me something to drink, I was a stranger and you welcomed me, I was naked and you gave me clothing, I was sick and you took care of me, I was in prison and you visited me. . . . Truly I tell you, just as you did it to one of the least of these who are members of my family, you did it to me.

Matthew 25:35–36, 40

Discussion Questions

1. Compare Mother Superior's welcome of Sister Mary Clar-ence to the welcome put forth by Sister Mary Patrick and Sister Mary Robert. What feelings are at the root of their different reactions? What keeps you from reaching out to new people?

How might we respond more like the young nuns when people come into our fellowship or community?

2. Compare the choir's singing early on in the film with their performance at the end of the movie. Though somewhat far-fetched that such improvement could happen so quickly and dramatically, why do you think the choir has changed? With what kind of vision for worship and service has Sister Mary Clarence challenged the choir members? How have the nuns themselves changed?

3. Over the years Hollywood has made lots of money from its portrayal of nuns, or rather, their stereotypes. What stereotypes did you notice in the film regarding nuns, religion, the church, etc.? Was the portrayal honest and sympathetic as well? (Note: While this film focuses on the movement of the nuns out from their convent to the neighborhood, there are orders who remain "active in prayer" behind their cloister walls.)

Clip Conversations

1. Chapter 10 [30:36–32:40]—"A Small Congregation." Bishop O'Hara greets a very small congregation this morning and many others. He wonders what has gone wrong. "Where is faith? Where is celebration? Where is everyone?" What are some of the reasons you think there are so few people attracted to his church? Are there any similarities to your congregation? How might renewal come to your community? Might God be calling you to be a Sister Mary Clarence?

2. Chapter 18 [57:50–1:04:05]—"Reaching Out." The choir, under its new leadership, has just sung for mass. While the congregants, and even neighbors who come in off the street, have been moved by the celebration, Mother Superior is not pleased. She and Sister Mary Clarence discuss in a somewhat

comical way the nature of the church. What two perspectives about church are represented here? How does your church talk about its mission in the world? The next scene is of the nuns hitting the streets. What sorts of things are they doing in their neighborhood? How are they received? What are they receiving as they serve in the neighborhood? How does this outreach infect their own lives and their worship?

3. Chapter 21 [1:11:20–1:14:05]—"That Makes Two of Us." Sister Mary Clarence is called to Mother Superior's office for a phone call. They talk about the reality of the neighborhood and being obsolete in its midst. This is the question of the ages for the church. How can the Good News be communicated in a way that is heard by the culture—by people outside the church? What should be unchangeable, and what can be always updated to the times?

Bonus Material

Sister Act is somewhat corny and predictable but nevertheless entertaining. But even critics of the movie asked the question, "Does the church want to be relevant in a postmodern world?" The film has a simple message: The church needs both to be engaged in the world and to be engaged in its worship. Christians need to enter in fully, whether it is in worship and celebration or in service to those around them. And when joined together, worship and outreach will bring new life both to the church and to others. (You might show this film at a leadership event or retreat at your church and have a conversation about its message.)

Sister Act was nominated for two Golden Globes in the Comedy/Musical categories of Best Film and Best Actress. It also won two NAACP Image awards for Best Actress and Best Film. The estimated budget was $20 million. Its total box office receipts were over $180 million. It definitely was a summer sleeper. Many credit this to the upbeat story and comedic talent of Whoopi Goldberg. (The lead role was originally planned for Bette Midler.) Whatever its charm, let it work on you.

33. *Chocolat*

U.S., 2000
121 Minutes, Feature, Color
Actors: Juliette Binoche, Lina Olin,
   Johnny Depp, Judi Dench, Alfred Molina,
   Carrie-Anne Moss, Leslie Caron,
   John Wood
Director: Lasse Hallstrom
Screenwriter: Robert Nelson Jacobs
Based on the Book: *Chocolat*,
   by Joanne Harris
Rated: PG13 (brief profanity, sexual scene)
DVD Features: theatrical trailer, commentary by director and
   producers, deleted scenes, "The Costumes of *Chocolat*," production
   design featurette, "The Making of *Chocolat*," Spanish subtitles

Themes

Renewing the Church
Community, Food, Forgiveness
Freedom, Goodness of Creation,
Healing, Living Our Faith,
Negative Images of the Church,
The Nature of God, Transformation
Affirming the Human Spirit,
Celebration, Clergy, Creativity,
Grace, Hypocrisy, Joy,
Love, Passion for Life, Redemption,
The Stranger, Tolerance

Synopsis and Theological Reflection

When cacao beans, the basis for chocolate, were brought to Europe for the first time, its magical taste so impressed Swedish naturalist Linnaeus that he gave it the botanical name "Theobroma cacao," or "food of the gods." It should come as little surprise then that fellow countryman Lasse Hallstrom, in his film *Chocolat*, has used chocolate as both metaphor and occasion for a town's redemption. In a story reminiscent of *Babette's Feast* (another Scandinavian film), Hallstrom has created a fable about the transformative power of food in the life of a village.

Armande (Judi Dench) visits Vianne (Juliette Binoche) in the chocolate shop. *Chocolat* (d. Hallstrom, 2000). Photo by David Appleby. Copyright 2000 Miramax Films. All rights reserved.

Set in a small town in France in the 1950s, the movie tells the story of Vianne Rocher (Juliette Binoche), a free-spirited mother wandering the world with her daughter, Anouk, and the legacy of her Central American mother. That legacy is a passion to bring healing and life to people through her chocolate treats. The ancient recipes contain a special chili, which ignites a passion for life—thick hot chocolate, chocolate bon-bons, chocolate covered nuts and coffee beans, chocolate cake, etc. Given such images, the M&Ms and Milk Duds that one could purchase at the movie snack bar had little appeal. They seemed like sacrilege.

Vianne arrives in the village to open her *chocolaterie*. In a town shaped by rules that are enforced by the church and mayor, her mission is not an easy one, however. It is the beginning of the season of Lent, and the townspeople have been admonished to forsake any pleasure during the forty days leading up to Easter. Though Christian on the surface, the town is hurting and lonely from its severe denial of the goodness of life. One woman is beaten by her drunken husband and survives the pain by acting crazed before her neighbors. A lonely widower is afraid to speak to the widow he admires in town. A young boy with a gift for drawing is almost crushed under the weight of a controlling mother. Even the young parish priest is forced to carry out his fifty-year predecessor's penchant for religious conformity and the mayor's pain-denying personal discipline. All of them must, above all, conform to the rules of the church and village. As Easter approaches, it is apparent that life is hardly lived in the light of the resurrection.

Through Vianne's patient persistence and care for the townsfolk, however, several individuals experience new life—through her chocolate, yes, but also through her belief in them and their unique value. Vianne revels in who they are and affirms their gifts. She teaches, encourages, disciples, and loves each one of them, and of course she dispenses her chocolate. When gypsies float into town on river barges, she even embraces them. (Johnny Depp plays the leader of these traveling "river rats.") This is the last straw for the mayor, who proclaims a war on immorality. Almost broken by the mayor's constant attacks, Vianne decides to leave town before Easter. But her small group of disciples comes together to create chocolate treats in her stead. The moment she discovers them in her kitchen—expressing their love not only for her but for each other and enjoying their newfound abilities—is truly an epiphany. The delight of community is always something to behold.

Some might ask, "Why is it that in fables like this the church so often is portrayed as rigidly harsh?" Roger Ebert asked such a question in his otherwise favorable review of this movie. And viewers can criticize this movie for once again falling prey to caricature. (It should be noted, however, that in the novel on which the film is based, the chief opponent to Vianne is the pastor, not the mayor. Screenwriter Robert Nelson Jacobs and Lasse Hallstrom, the director, have toned down the story's anticlerical or antichurch bias.) But such a critique also shields us, disciples of Jesus and churchgoers, from what has been all too often the truth. Many of us can tell our own stories of rigid practices that have continued to be enforced in Christian communities long after they have lost their meaning. The disciplines of Lent can be wonderfully redemptive, but wooden practice kills the abundant life Christ came to bring us. Discipline needs wisdom and above all love if its refining fire is to shape and mold us anew.

This fable does more than provide a critique of the church, however. More importantly, *Chocolat* portrays the transformative power of something of which we have a long tradition—a shared meal. Jesus and his disciples at their Last Supper, the agape meal of the early church, and our own celebration of the Eucharist all predate this movie. Movies like *Chocolat* and *Babette's Feast* remind us anew of food's importance in creating community.

When our colleague and friend, David Augsburger, was asked to write an article on chocolate for *The Complete Book of Everyday Christianity* (InterVarsity Press), his friends smiled. He is a lover of chocolate (people line up for invitations to his gourmet dinners), but what could be theological about chocolate? After all, our cakes are called "chocolate decadence" and "devil's food." Tongue in cheek, but with more than a tinge of truth, David put into words what Hallstrom has portrayed in this movie so winsomely: Chocolate's "essential purpose is the creation of community, of joint experiences of joy, of celebrating the goodness of creation." (After all who wants to eat a piece of chocolate cake alone?)

In *Chocolat*, chocolate is not missing from the community's Easter celebration, nor should it be from ours. When our daughters were younger, we hid chocolate Easter eggs to celebrate Christ's gift of life. Our theology was better than we knew.

Dialogue Texts

You shall also love the stranger, for you were strangers in the land of Egypt. You shall fear the LORD your God; him alone you shall worship; to him you shall hold fast, and by his name you shall swear.

Deuteronomy 10:19–20

For freedom Christ has set us free. Stand firm, therefore, and do not submit again to a yoke of slavery.

Galatians 5:1

For you were called to freedom, brothers and sisters; only do not use your freedom as an opportunity for self-indulgence, but through love become slaves to one another. For the whole law is summed up in a single commandment, "You shall love your neighbor as yourself." If, however, you bite and devour one another, take care that you are not consumed by one another.

Galatians 5:13–15

Beware of practicing your piety before others in order to be seen by them. . . . And whenever you pray, do not be like the hypocrites; for they love to stand and pray in the synagogues and at the street corners, so that they may be seen by others. . . . When you are praying, do not heap up empty phrases as the Gentiles do; for they think that they will be heard because of their many words. Do not be like them, for your Father knows what you need before you ask him.

Matthew 6:1, 5, 7–8

Discussion Questions

1. *Chocolat* is a film in which chocolate is a character, as present in the story as any of the other characters. Another character is the north wind. How do chocolate and the north wind function in the film? What do they symbolize in the lives of the other characters? What other movies are similar to *Chocolat* in this way?

2. In the film, Vianne befriends many of the marginalized of the town. Think of her relationships with Armande, Josephine,

Guillaume and his dog Charlie, Luc, and Roux. How does she begin a relationship with each of these individuals when they are initially suspicious of her and her ways? What might we as Christians learn about befriending those who have been hurt by or are suspicious of the church?

3. Though Vianne and her chocolates bring much healing and renewal to the townspeople, there are some things they can't heal or change. When Vianne is confronted with the reality of Armande's illness, she asks why she wasn't told about it before. Armande responds, "Is this a chocolaterie or a confessional?" Again, the juxtaposition of the church's and the world's power is clear. How has the church helped or hurt Armande? How has the chocolaterie helped her? But what aspects of her life can it not heal? Who else is in need of healing in this film? How are the heroine and villain similar?

Clip Conversations

1. Chapter 1 [00:00–5:00]—"Opening Credits: A Tranquil Village and the North Wind." Is the movie meant to be taken literally? What is its organizing principle or theme? Do you feel it is fair or heavy-handed in its portrayals of the church, tradition, and freedom?

2. Chapter 11 [51:38–59:06]—"A Guaranteed Problem." Serge comes to Josephine with flowers and an apology for his long-term beating of her. He says, "God has made me a new man." Josephine is touched by his apology but can't accept that he has really changed. Discuss their conversation. How is God portrayed in this scene? How do we know that, in fact, Serge hasn't changed? How can we as Christians bring Good News about God, forgiveness, and change into dark situations in which breaking old patterns is indeed difficult?

3. Chapter 15 [1:16:16–1:27:20]—"Exquisite Indulgences." Armande's birthday dinner is an amazing feast. How do the characters react and change through the course of the meal and the evening? How does Caroline change, just by seeing the pleasure and joy that the feast engendered? How is even Vianne made more vulnerable to others through this scene? Compare these scenes with the Count cutting up his wife's dresses and his reaction to the party. Is the Christian faith really opposed to the sensual as depicted in the film?

4. Chapter 19 [1:40:50–1:44:30]—"Don't Worry, Mama." The north wind has been calling to Vianne to leave, and the boat fire is just one more reason to run. Anouk doesn't want to go. In the struggle to pack and leave, something precious is lost, but something is gained—what is it? In the kitchen the little band of friends is happily and busily making chocolate for the festival. When Vianne discovers them, Josephine tenderly reaches out to her. How does this scene function as a healing/redemptive act in Vianne's life? What is the role of community in helping to heal her hurts? What keeps her from leaving?

5. Chapter 21 [1:50:33–1:56:04]—"Freedom from Tranquility." Discuss Pere Henri's Easter sermon. What theological truth and ethic does it raise? What is life-giving about it? Would you change it? If so, how?

Bonus Material

David Brown, one of *Chocolat*'s producers, commented on the film by saying that it is "a fable that tells the truth." Those "truths" as seen by the producers include: acceptance of others and their ways, being open to change in the face of tradition, and not denying yourself the good things in life because of some legalistic fear. These truths represent great currency for a movie in today's postmodern world in which tolerance and personal fulfillment are the gods of our time. However, regardless of its politically correct message, the film is a delightful affirmation of the goodness of life.

The original novel was more simplistic in its attack of tradition, the church, moral duplicity, etc. The novel was a great hit in England, but we felt it was very heavy-handed and shallow in its portrayal of villain and heroine. It felt as though the author had an ax to grind. This is one of those cases in which the screenplay and movie are better than the novel.

Chocolat was filmed in a small town in France, in the west country of England, and at Shepperton studios in London. The town of Flavigny-sur-Ozerain, a tenth-century walled village, was accidentally found by David Gropman, the production designer. He had been scouting villages in France and stopped in the town for a bathroom break. As he walked the square, he knew that he had found the location for the film. Two hundred cast and crew overran the town of 350 people. Many of the extras were townspeople.

Miramax Studios purchased the rights to the novel already having in mind Lasse Hallstrom as director and Juliette Binoche as lead. Being that the film revolves around three strong women, Dame Judi Dench and Lena Olin (well-known Swedish actress and Lasse Hallstrom's wife) were cast next. The other members of the ensemble cast came from the U.S., England, France, and Sweden. Lasse Hallstrom is known for his great ability in working with ensembles and for creating a great community on set, where everyone brings their best and has fun. The actors threw themselves into their parts. Juliette Binoche spent two days training in a chocolate shop to understand the making of chocolate, which she loves. Johnny Depp actually played the guitar in all his scenes (his first time in a film). But unlike Binoche, he hates chocolate, and almost got sick every time he had to eat lots of it for scenes.

The "character" of chocolate was actually played mostly by plastic molds, because when they tried to use real chocolate in the window and counter displays, it melted under the lighting.

But there was enough of the delicious temptation around that some of the cast even got sick from gorging on chocolate during the filming. Lasse Hallstrom felt that the Easter sermon by Pere Henri was key to the film, as he put it, "a simple telling of the Christian message." But he had to argue his point because producers and studio executives were not as keen about the scene, as scripted, being in the film.

Chocolat was nominated for twenty-one awards—five Academy Awards (including Best Picture and Best Adapted Screenplay), eight British Academy Awards (including Best Actress, Best Adapted Screenplay, and Best Cinematography), and four Golden Globes (including Best Actress, Best Score, and Best Picture). It also was nominated for three Screen Actors Guild awards and one Writers Guild of America award. Judi Dench was the only winner, as she walked away with Best Supporting Actress from SAG. Its total box office receipts were over $109 million. Even with all its nominations and box office success, many critics found the film lacking in depth (read "angst and unresolved issues"). Some Christian viewers have been put off by its portrayal of the church. But we feel that the film is a great place to begin a conversation about the renewal of the church and the joy and freedom that come through new life in Christ.

Appendix 1

Movies Listed by Related Biblical Text

Old Testament

Genesis
1:27—*Amistad, Billy Elliot*
1:31a—*Big Night*
2:15—*Spirited Away*
2:18—*About a Boy*
33:4, 10—*The Straight Story*
45:1–3, 14, 28—*The Straight Story, Antwone Fisher*
46:27b—*Antwone Fisher*

Exodus
5:1—*Amistad*
31:1–5, (6)—*Spirited Away, The Rookie*

Leviticus
19:33–34—*X-Men, The Hurricane*

Numbers
15:15–16—*X-Men, The Hurricane*

Deuteronomy
10:17–19—*Amistad*
10:19–20—*Chocolat*

2 Samuel
12:7–9—*The Apostle*

Job
7:11— *Signs, K-PAX, Patch Adams*
7:17–18— *Patch Adams*
11:16—*Smoke Signals*
21:15—*Signs, K-PAX*

Psalms
8:3–5—*Spirited Away*
9:15—*No Man's Land, We Were Soldiers*
30:11–12—*Billy Elliot*
47:1—*Sister Act*
51:1–2—*Tender Mercies*
66:1—*Sister Act*
68:5–6a—*Signs, K-PAX*
103:8,13—*Ulee's Gold*
104:12–17—*Fly Away Home*
107:43—*Signs, K-PAX*
133:1—*The Straight Story*
139:13–14—*Billy Elliot*
145:9—*Tender Mercies*
147:3—*The Spitfire Grill*

Proverbs

3:31—*The Iron Giant*
8:28–31—*Spirited Away*
8:35–36—*Fearless*
10:11—*Big Night*
10:12—*No Man's Land, We Were Soldiers*
13:12—*The Rookie*
13:19—*Crouching Tiger, Hidden Dragon*
13:25—*Big Night*
14:13—*Patch Adams*
15:33—*Crouching Tiger, Hidden Dragon*
17:17—*About a Boy, The Iron Giant*
17:22—*Patch Adams*
18:24—*X-Men, The Hurricane, Italian for Beginners, The Iron Giant*
19:11—*Fly Away Home*
21:21—*Crouching Tiger, Hidden Dragon*
22:6—*Billy Elliot, Remember the Titans, Save the Last Dance*
23:18—*X-Men, The Hurricane*

Ecclesiastes

2:24–25—*Italian for Beginners*
4:9–12—*About a Boy, Italian for Beginners*
4:10—*Antwone Fisher*
5:8—*Amistad*
9:4—*Fearless*
9:7—*Big Night*
9:7–9—*Fearless*
9:9–10—*Signs, K-PAX*
11:7–8—*Signs, K-PAX*

Song of Solomon

2:4—*Life Is Beautiful*
4:7–10—*Life Is Beautiful*

Isaiah

2:4—*No Man's Land, We Were Soldiers*
11:6—*Fly Away Home, Remember the Titans, Save the Last Dance*

Jeremiah

1:5—*Simon Birch*
8:21–22—*The Spitfire Grill*
29:7—*The Year of Living Dangerously*

29:11—*The Rookie*
31:29—*Ulee's Gold*

Ezekiel

34:11–12—*Ulee's Gold*
35:5–6—*No Man's Land, We Were Soldiers*

Joel

3:10—*No Man's Land, We Were Soldiers*

Micah

6:8—*The Year of Living Dangerously*

New Testament

Matthew

3:1–3—*The Apostle*
5:3, 5, 7–8—*The Third Miracle, Signs, K-PAX*
5:23–24—*The Straight Story*
5:39, 43–44—*No Man's Land, We Were Soldiers*
6:1, 5, 7–8—*Chocolat*
6:25, 27, 34—*Fearless*
15:33–37a—*Smoke Signals*
22:37–39—*Sister Act*
25:35–36, 40—*Italian for Beginners, Sister Act*
25:41–43, 45—*X-Men, The Hurricane*
26:26—*Smoke Signals*

Mark

1:29–32, 34—*Patch Adams*
9:24—*The Third Miracle*

Luke

3:7–8, 10–11, 14—*The Year of Living Dangerously*
4:16–19, 21—*The Year of Living Dangerously*
6:37–38—*Antwone Fisher*
11:4a—*Smoke Signals*
15:13, 32—*Ulee's Gold*
15:31–32—*Fly Away Home*

John

8:31–32—*Crouching Tiger, Hidden Dragon*
15:12–13—*The Iron Giant*

Acts
20:24—*Simon Birch*

Romans
1:16–17—*The Apostle*
5:6–8—*The Spitfire Grill*
6:2–4—*Tender Mercies*
8:28—*Simon Birch*
8:38–39—*Signs, K-PAX*
12:14, 17–18, 20–21— *No Man's Land, We Were Soldiers*
12:18—*The Iron Giant*

1 Corinthians
1:26–27—*Simon Birch*
3:18–19a—*Patch Adams*
7:17—*Simon Birch*
9:1–2—*The Apostle*
13:1–3, 13—*Crouching Tiger, Hidden Dragon*
13:7—*Italian for Beginners*
15:9a—*The Apostle*

Galatians
3:28—*Amistad, Remember the Titans, Save the Last Dance, X-Men, The Hurricane*
5:1— *Crouching Tiger, Hidden Dragon; Chocolat*

5:13–15—*Chocolat*
6:2—*About a Boy*

Ephesians
4:1–2—*Simon Birch*
4:22–24—*The Apostle*
4:31–32—*Smoke Signals*
5:25—*Life Is Beautiful*
6:4—*Fly Away Home*

Philippians
2:12–13—*Tender Mercies*

Colossians
3:13, 15a—*Antwone Fisher*

Hebrews
10:23–24—*The Third Miracle*
11:1—*The Third Miracle*
13:7—*Remember the Titans, Save the Last Dance*

1 Peter
4:10—*The Rookie*

1 John
1:9—*The Spitfire Grill*
3:1—*Life Is Beautiful*
3:13–14—*Life Is Beautiful*
3:16— *The Spitfire Grill, The Iron Giant*

Revelation
19:9—*Antwone Fisher*

Appendix 2

Movies Listed by Topic

A boldfaced movie title indicates that the topic is a major theme in the movie, usually with a "Clip Conversation" provided.

Abuse
> *Antwone Fisher*

Affirming the Human Spirit
> **Life Is Beautiful, Amistad, No Man's Land, We Were Soldiers,** *Spirited Away, The Straight Story,* **X-Men, The Hurricane,** *Smoke Signals,* **About a Boy,** *Italian for Beginners, Simon Birch,* **Tender Mercies, The Iron Giant,** *Chocolat*

Anger
> *The Hurricane, Antwone Fisher*

Arguing with God
> **Fearless, The Apostle**

Balance in Life
> *The Straight Story*

Baptism
> **The Apostle, Tender Mercies**

Beauty/Imagination/Creativity
> **Life Is Beautiful; Spirited Away; Crouching Tiger, Hidden Dragon;** *Big Night;* **Billy Elliot;** *Fly Away Home; Save the Last Dance; Patch Adams; The Iron Giant; Chocolat*

Beauty of Creation (*see* **Creation**)

Brokenness/Personal Loss
> *The Apostle, Ulee's Gold, Italian for Beginners, The Spitfire Grill*

Death
> **Crouching Tiger, Hidden Dragon; Fearless; Ulee's Gold; Smoke Signals;** *Simon Birch; Signs; K-PAX*

Grief
> *Fly Away Home, Save the Last Dance, Signs, K-PAX, The Year of Living Dangerously, Patch Adams*

Guilt
> *Save the Last Dance, Signs*

Isolation
> **Fearless,** *Ulee's Gold, About a Boy*

Loneliness
> **Spirited Away,** *Ulee's Gold,* **Italian for Beginners,** *Tender Mercies*

Poverty
> **Billy Elliot, The Year of Living Dangerously**

Suffering
> *Ulee's Gold, Antwone Fisher, Patch Adams*

Celebration
> *Life Is Beautiful, Big Night,* **Antwone Fisher,** *Italian for Beginners, Chocolat*

Children (*see* **Family**)

Choice
> *The Hurricane, The Third Miracle, The Iron Giant*

Choosing Life
> **Life Is Beautiful, Big Night, Fearless**

Church

Baptism
> **The Apostle, Tender Mercies**

Clergy, the Role of
> *The Apostle, The Straight Story, Italian for Beginners, Simon Birch,* **The Third Miracle,** *Chocolat*

Lord's Supper, the
> **Big Night, Smoke Signals**

Negative Images of the
> **Simon Birch,** *The Third Miracle,* **Sister Act, Chocolat**

Nature of the
> **Sister Act**

Worship
> *The Apostle, Sister Act*

Clergy (see **Church**)

Community (*see also* **Community and Friendship**)
> **Remember the Titans, Chocolat**

Community and Friendship (*see also* **Friendship; Community**)
We Were Soldiers, Smoke Signals, About a Boy, Italian for Beginners

Compassion
Ulee's Gold, **The Year of Living Dangerously,** *Patch Adams*

Confession
The Apostle, Smoke Signals, Signs

Courage (*see also* **Living Our Faith**)
Amistad, No Man's Land, Spirited Away, Billy Elliot, **Fly Away Home,** *Remember the Titans, Save the Last Dance, X-Men, The Hurricane*

Creation
Beauty of
The Straight Story, *Ulee's Gold, K-PAX*
Caring for
Spirited Away, Fly Away Home
Goodness of
The Spitfire Grill, The Iron Giant, **Chocolat**

Creativity (*see* **Beauty/Imagination/Creativity**)

Cultures, Clash of
Big Night, *Billy Elliot, The Year of Living Dangerously*

Death
Crouching Tiger, Hidden Dragon, Fearless, Ulee's Gold, *Smoke Signals, Simon Birch, Signs, K-PAX*

Discipleship, Cost of
The Third Miracle

Dreams/Hopes
The Rookie, *Save the Last Dance,* **Antwone Fisher**

Embracing Our Vocation
The Rookie, Billy Elliot, The Apostle, Simon Birch, The Third Miracle, Patch Adams

Evangelism (*see* **Sharing Our Faith**)

Evil
Signs, K-PAX

Faith
Simon Birch, Tender Mercies, The Hurricane, *Italian for Beginners*
Faith and Doubt
The Third Miracle, Signs, K-PAX
Living Our Faith
Amistad, We Were Soldiers, The Year of Living Dangerously, Patch Adams, Sister Act, *Chocolat*
Sharing Our
Amistad, **The Apostle, Simon Birch,** *Tender Mercies, The Third Miracle*

Family

Life Is Beautiful, Spirited Away, *The Rookie, The Straight Story,* Smoke Signals, **Antwone Fisher,** About a Boy, Simon Birch, Signs, K-PAX

Children

The Rookie, Billy Elliot, Ulee's Gold, About a Boy

Parenting/Parents

Fearless, The Rookie, Billy Elliot, Ulee's Gold, **Fly Away Home,** Smoke Signals, Antwone Fisher

Reconciliation within

Big Night, The Rookie, Billy Elliot, The Straight Story, Ulee's Gold, Fly Away Home, Smoke Signals

Food

Big Night, Italian for Beginners, The Spitfire Grill, **Chocolat**

Forgiveness

Smoke Signals, Antwone Fisher, The Spitfire Grill, Chocolat

Freedom

Amistad, Crouching Tiger, Hidden Dragon, Billy Elliot, The Iron Giant, **Chocolat**

Friendship (*see also* Community and Friendship)

No Man's Land, We Were Soldiers, Spirited Away, **Ulee's Gold, Save the Last Dance,** The Hurricane, Antwone Fisher, **Simon Birch,** Signs, K-PAX, The Spitfire Grill

Gluttony

Spirited Away

God

X-Men

Arguing with

Fearless, The Apostle

Nature of

Patch Adams, **Chocolat**

Gospel

Amistad

Grace

Tender Mercies, The Spitfire Grill, Chocolat

Greed

Spirited Away

Grief

Fly Away Home, Save the Last Dance, Signs, K-PAX, The Year of Living Dangerously, Patch Adams

Guilt

Save the Last Dance, Signs

Hate

No Man's Land

Healing
  Ulee's Gold, Smoke Signals, ***Antwone Fisher, K-PAX, Patch Adams, Chocolat***
  Wounded Healer
    The Spitfire Grill

Holy Spirit
    Tender Mercies

Home
    Fly Away Home, ***Patch Adams***

Honor
    Crouching Tiger, Hidden Dragon

Hope
    Amistad, Fearless, ***X-Men, The Hurricane***, *Italian for Beginners*

Humility
    Crouching Tiger, Hidden Dragon

Humor
    Life Is Beautiful, The Straight Story, About a Boy, Patch Adams

Hypocrisy
    Chocolat

Identity
    Spirited Away, X-Men, Smoke Signals, Antwone Fisher

Images of the Savior
    Fearless, ***X-Men, K-PAX, The Year of Living Dangerously, The Spitfire Grill, The Iron Giant***

Imagination (*see* Beauty/Imagination/Creativity)

Inhumanity
    Amistad, *No Man's Land, We Were Soldiers*

Integrity
    Big Night

Interracial Relationships
    Remember the Titans, Save the Last Dance

Intolerance
    X-Men, The Hurricane

Isolation (*see* Brokenness/Personal Loss)

Jesus (*see* Images of the Savior)

Joy
    Billy Elliot, Tender Mercies, Chocolat

Justice
    Amistad, X-Men, The Hurricane, ***The Year of Living Dangerously***

Kindness
    Spirited Away, Crouching Tiger, Hidden Dragon

Lament (*see also* **God, Arguing with**)
Ulee's Gold

Leadership
Amistad, **We Were Soldiers, Crouching Tiger, Hidden Dragon, Remember the Titans**

Life
as Amoral
No Man's Land
as Frenetic
The Straight Story
as a Gift
Fearless, **Tender Mercies**
the Mystery of
Fearless, Signs, K-PAX
a Passion for
Chocolat
the Randomness of
Fearless, Signs
as Sacramental
Big Night
the Sanctity of
Fly Away Home

Living Our Faith
Amistad, **We Were Soldiers, The Year of Living Dangerously, Patch Adams, Sister Act,** *Chocolat*
Discipleship, Cost of
The Third Miracle
Obedience to God
Simon Birch, The Third Miracle

Loneliness (*see* **Brokenness/Personal Loss**)

Lord's Supper (*see* **Church**)

Love
Crouching Tiger, Hidden Dragon, Billy Elliot, Ulee's Gold, Fly Away Home, **The Hurricane,** *Antwone Fisher, Italian for Beginners, Tender Mercies, Chocolat*
Sacrificial
Life Is Beautiful, **Spirited Away,** *X-Men, The Hurricane, Simon Birch, The Year of Living Dangerously, The Spitfire Grill, The Iron Giant*

Materialism
Big Night, *Fearless, Italian for Beginners*

Miracles
The Third Miracle, Signs, K-PAX

Mystery of Life (*see* **Life**)

Nonviolence
The Iron Giant

Obedience to God (*see* Living Our Faith)

Parenting/Parents (*see* Family)

Perseverance
> **The Straight Story**, **Fly Away Home**

Play
> The Rookie, **The Iron Giant**

Pollution
> Spirited Away

Power
> X-Men, The Hurricane

Poverty
> **Billy Elliot**, **The Year of Living Dangerously**

Prayer
> Amistad, **We Were Soldiers**, **Italian for Beginners**, **The Iron Giant**

Promise Keeping
> The Rookie, Fly Away Home

Prophetic, Being
> **The Year of Living Dangerously**

Race (*see* Racism; Reconciliation, Race)

Racism
> **Remember the Titans**, **Save the Last Dance**, X-Men, The Hurricane

Randomness of Life (*see* Life)

Reconciliation
> Family
> > **Big Night**, **The Rookie**, **Billy Elliot**, **The Straight Story**, **Ulee's Gold**, **Fly Away Home**, **Smoke Signals**
> Race
> > **Amistad**, **Remember the Titans**, **Save the Last Dance**, **X-Men**, **The Hurricane**

Redemption
> **Ulee's Gold**, The Hurricane, The Spitfire Grill, Chocolat

Remorse
> **We Were Soldiers**

Renewing the Church
> **The Apostle**, **Italian for Beginners**, **Sister Act**, **Chocolat**

Repentance
> Amistad, **The Apostle**

Sacrifice
> Crouching Tiger, Hidden Dragon

Sacrificial Love (*see* Love)

Saints
> ***The Third Miracle***

Salvation
> *Fearless, The Apostle, Tender Mercies,* ***The Spitfire Grill***

Sanctification
> *The Apostle*

Sanctity of Life (*see* Life)

Second Chances
> *The Rookie,* ***Fly Away Home,*** *Tender Mercies*

Selfishness
> *Crouching Tiger, Hidden Dragon,* ***About a Boy***

Service
> *Life Is Beautiful, The Rookie, The Year of Living Dangerously,* ***Patch Adams,*** *Sister Act*

Sharing Our Faith (*see also* Faith)
> *Amistad,* ***The Apostle, Simon Birch,*** *Tender Mercies, The Third Miracle*

Sin
> *Spirited Away*
>
> Abuse
>> *Antwone Fisher*
>
> Anger
>> *The Hurricane, Antwone Fisher*
>
> Gluttony
>> *Spirited Away*
>
> Greed
>> *Spirited Away*
>
> Hate
>> *No Man's Land*
>
> Hypocrisy
>> *Chocolat*
>
> Inhumanity
>> ***Amistad,*** *No Man's Land, We Were Soldiers*
>
> Intolerance
>> ***X-Men, The Hurricane***
>
> Materialism
>> ***Big Night,*** *Fearless, Italian for Beginners*
>
> Pollution
>> *Spirited Away*
>
> Racism
>> ***Remember the Titans, Save the Last Dance,*** *X-Men, The Hurricane*
>
> Selfishness/Self-Centeredness
>> *Crouching Tiger, Hidden Dragon,* ***About a Boy***

Social Justice
Billy Elliot, The Year of Living Dangerously

Stereotypes
Remember the Titans, Save the Last Dance

Story, the Power of
Smoke Signals

Stranger, the
X-Men, Tender Mercies, The Spitfire Grill, The Iron Giant, Sister Act, Chocolat

Suffering (*see* **Brokenness/Personal Loss**)

Tolerance
X-Men, The Hurricane, Chocolat

Transformation
The Apostle, X-Men, **The Hurricane, Tender Mercies, Chocolat**

Trust
Life Is Beautiful, The Hurricane, Antwone Fisher, The Spitfire Grill

Truth
Smoke Signals

Unity in Diversity
We Were Soldiers, Remember the Titans

Vocation
The Rookie, Billy Elliot, The Apostle, Simon Birch, The Third Miracle, Patch Adams

War
No Man's Land, We Were Soldiers, *The Spitfire Grill, The Iron Giant*

Wisdom
Crouching Tiger, Hidden Dragon, **The Straight Story**

Women
Crouching Tiger, Hidden Dragon

Wonder
Spirited Away, Billy Elliot, Signs, K-PAX, The Spitfire Grill, The Iron Giant

Work
Ulee's Gold, Tender Mercies

Worship
The Apostle, Sister Act

Notes

1. Phyllis A. Tickle, *God-Talk in America* (New York: Crossroad, 1997), 126.

2. Mark Pinsky, *The Gospel According to the Simpsons: The Spiritual Life of the World's Most Animated Family* (Louisville: Westminster John Knox Press, 2001).

3. Robert K. Johnston, *Reel Spirituality: Theology and Film in Dialogue* (Grand Rapids: Baker, 2000).

4. Flannery O'Connor, "The Novelist and the Believer," in *Mystery and Manners* (New York: Farrar, Straus & Giroux, 1969), reprinted in G. B. Tennyson and Edward E. Ericson Jr., *Religion and Modern Literature* (Grand Rapids: Eerdmans, 1975), 69.

5. Johnston, *Reel Spirituality*.

6. C. S. Lewis, *An Experiment in Criticism* (Cambridge, England: University Press, 1961), 19.

7. Jon Boorstin, *Making Movies Work: Thinking Like a Filmmaker* (Los Angeles: Silman-James Press, 1995).

8. Ibid., 162.

9. R. W. B. Lewis, "Hold on Hard to the Huckleberry Bushes," in *Religion and Modern Literature: Essays in Theory and Criticism*, ed. G. B. Tennyson and Edward E. Ericson Jr. (Grand Rapids: Eerdmans, 1975), 55.

10. Gustaf Niebuhr, "Spiritual Values Are In, but Please No Sermonizing," *New York Times*, 1 September 1996, H7.

11. Helen Kromer, *Amistad: The Slave Uprising Aboard the Spanish Schooner*, reprinted by the United Church of Christ. To obtain a copy, call 1-800-325-7061.

Catherine M. Barsotti enjoys weaving the two threads of economics and theology throughout her life. A former real estate appraiser for twenty years, she has worked in diverse ministry contexts within the Anglo and Latino communities. She has been a short-term missionary in Mexico, a youth minister, a part-time associate pastor, and a chaplain at a center for abused women and children. From 1997 to 2002 she served as director of development for Centro Hispano de Estudios Teológicos (CHET)—a Latino ministry training center in southeast Los Angeles. Currently she consults with Christian nonprofit organizations and regularly teaches courses at CHET in theology, ethics, and spirituality. With Robert Johnston, her husband, Barsotti has been writing movie reviews for the last eight years.

Robert K. Johnston is professor of theology and culture at Fuller Theological Seminary. Former president of the American Theological Society and former provost at both North Park University and Fuller, Johnston's latest books include *Reel Spirituality* (Baker, 2000) and *Life Is Not Work/Work Is Not Life: Simple Reminders for Finding Balance in a 24/7 World* (Wildcat Canyon, 2001). His new book, *Useless Beauty: Ecclesiastes through the Lens of Contemporary Film* (Baker), will be released in the fall of 2004. With Catherine Barsotti, Johnston teaches a course each year to all new Young Life staff on how to think theologically about life and faith. They also teach together in the area of film and theology. They have two daughters, Liz and Margi, one a lawyer in Minneapolis and the other studying in Maine to be an elementary school teacher.